# Feminist Social Work

£9.99

i

## Critical Texts in Social Work and the Welfare State

General Editor: *Peter Leonard*

*Pete Alcock and Phil Harris*
Welfare Law and Order

*Ragnhild Banton, Paul Clifford, Stephen Frosh,
Julian Lousada, Joanna Rosenthall*
The Politics of Mental Health

*Paul Corrigan and Peter Leonard*
Social Work Practice Under Capitalism:
A Marxist Approach

*Lena Dominelli and Eileen McLeod*
Feminist Social Work

*Ian Gough*
The Political Economy of the Welfare State

*Chris Jones*
State Social Work and the Working Class

*Paul Joyce, Paul Corrigan, Mike Hayes*
Striking Out: Social Work and Trade Unionism, 1970-1985

*Peter Leonard*
Personality and Ideology: Towards A Materialist
Understanding of the Individual

*Chris Phillipson*
Capitalism and the Construction of Old Age

*Michael Oliver*
The Politics of Disablement

### FORTHCOMING

*Peter Leonard*
A Critical History of Social Work Theory

*Goran Therborn*
Welfare States and Advanced Capitalism

---

Series Standing Order
If you would like to receive future titles in this series as they are published,
you can make use of our standing order facility. To place a standing order please
contact your bookseller or, in case of difficulty, write to us at the
address below with your name and address and the name of the series.
Please state with which title you wish to begin your standing order.
(If you live outside the United Kingdom we may not have the rights for your area, in
which case we will forward your order to the publisher concerned.)

Customer Services Department, Macmillan Distribution Ltd,
Houndmills, Basingstoke, Hampshire, RG21 2XS, England.

# Feminist Social Work

Lena Dominelli and Eileen McLeod

MACMILLAN

First published 1989
Reprinted 1990

Published by
MACMILLAN EDUCATION LTD
Houndmills, Basingstoke, Hampshire RG21 2XS
and London
Companies and representatives
throughout the world

Distributed in the U.S.A. by New York University Press

Printed in Hong Kong

British Library Cataloguing in Publication Data
Dominelli, Lena
Feminist social work. — (Critical texts
in social work and the welfare state).
1. Great Britain. Welfare work. Feminist
theories
I. Title   II. McLeod, Eileen
III. Series
361.3′01
ISBN 0–333–35218–1 (hardcover)
ISBN 0–333–35220–3 (paperback)

*To Maria Guiseppina, Connie, Maria and Rita* (L.D.)

*To Janyce, Nora, Rosemary and Vivien* (E.M.)

# Contents

*Foreword by Peter Leonard*                                              ix
*Acknowledgements*                                                      xiii

**Introduction**                                                          1

**1   The Start of Feminist Social Work Intervention:
     A Feminist Approach to Defining Social Problems**                    21
     Redefining social problems from a feminist
     perspective – 'putting gender on the map'                            22
     Redefining social problems from a feminist
     perspective – an egalitarian process                                32
     The impact of defining and redefining social problems
     from a feminist perspective on professional social
     work practice                                                        34
     The further development of problem definition from a
     feminist perspective in social work and the gains for
     welfare                                                              42

**2   Feminist Community Work: The Nature and
     Contribution of Feminist Campaigns and Networks**                    45
     The identity of feminist campaigns and networks                     46
     The objectives and origins of feminist campaigns and
     networks                                                             51
     Developing egalitarian relations within feminist
     networks and campaigns                                              56
     The impact of feminist campaigns and networks on
     society at large                                                     67
     Consolidating the work of feminist campaigns and
     networks                                                            73

**3   A Feminist Approach to Emotional Welfare: The
     Contribution of Feminist Therapy and Counselling**                  76
     A theory and practice for women's emotional
     well-being                                                          78
     The value of women's relationships                                  88
     'Romantic love' and a loving alternative                            89

A feminist/anti-sexist approach to men's emotional
welfare 95
Emotional liberation for children 97

**4 Creating a Feminist Statutory Social Work 101**
**Introduction 101**
The contribution of radical social work and the
Marxist critique 101
The development of feminist statutory social work 107
Characteristic features of feminist social work practice
in statutory settings 114
Creating a feminist statutory social work 127

**5 Creating Feminist Working Relations In and Through**
**Social Work 131**
Recognition of the problematic nature of women's
material welfare and employment conditions 132
The promotion of women social workers' welfare as
workers 138
The promotion of women social work clients and
client groups' material welfare 144
Fostering awareness of the common material interests
between women social workers and clients 148
The contribution of 'independent' feminist social work
organisations 149
Underwriting the achievement of feminist working
relations in social work 152
The benefits of feminist working relations for
children's and men's welfare 153

**6 Developing Together: a Feminist Political Presence and**
**Feminist Social Work 155**
Underwriting the future of feminist social work 156
The nature of a feminist presence in contemporary
politics 153
The future of a feminist presence in politics and the
contribution of feminist social work 172

*Bibliography* 178

*Index* 194

# Foreword

When the series *Critical Texts in Social Work and the Welfare State* was launched in 1978 it was situated within a particular discourse – that of Marxism. It was argued then that the foundations of a Left politics and practice in welfare must be based upon a Marxist political economy, a Marxist theory of the welfare state and a Marxist theory of interpersonal relations. The aim of the series was seen not as indulging in sectarian dogmatism but contributing to 'the development of the debate on the Left about the nature of the welfare state and the possibilities of socialist practice within it'.[1]

The ten years which have passed since these intellectual objectives were announced have been intensely traumatic years for both socialist practice and Marxist theory. Three factors in this trauma can easily be identified.

First, we have experienced the profound shift in class forces which marks the triumph of the new Right in Western countries. This shift to the Right has had and continues to have a transforming effect upon welfare institutions and practices, and upon the debate within the Left generally. Ten years ago socialist discourse on welfare was situated within a critique of social democracy, its bureaucracies, its elitism, and its alienation from the working class. It took some time for the Left to realise that social democracy as we knew it was dead and buried, and that the radical neo-conservatism of this new era required far-reaching changes in socialist thinking and action.

Second, the politics of existing 'socialist' countries has ranged from disappointing failure to outright oppressive horror. There comes a point when it is increasingly difficult to continue a commitment to the grand project of socialism in the absence of any positive

examples. Within eastern and central European countries, for
example, where the language of Marxism has been pressed into the
service of state dogma, progressive, socialist critiques of welfare
have at this point to look elsewhere than to Marxist analysis
for their frameworks, because Marxist discourse seems hopelessly
debased through its service to oppression.

Third, and most important in relation to the publication of this
particular volume in the series, are the deeply significant critiques
of Marxism which have been articulated within wider progressive
political forces and their organic intellectuals. Of these various
critiques, it must be acknowledged that the most profound and far-
reaching have emerged from the women's movement and from
feminist scholarship directed at the analysis of gender relations in
every field of human activity. Although debates within feminism
between the various tendencies that are represented within the
broad movement have been politically divisive, all feminists agree
on the centrality of gender relations to any analysis of the social
order, its institutions and ideologies. Furthermore, feminist analysis
claims to provide a more complete understanding of the politics of
welfare than a Marxist interpretation is capable of, and most
importantly, a more complete guide to practice within the welfare
field.

Lena Dominelli and Eileen Mcleod's *Feminist Social Work* stands
firmly and impressively in this growing tradition of critiques of
Marxist theory and practice as part of its development of a feminist
politics within every level of welfare. Although it is thoroughly
critical of previous writing in the area of radical, socialist, social
work practice, including all the relevant volumes in this series, it
is most importantly practical, empirical and prescriptive in its
approach. It demonstrates convincingly the outstanding virtue of
the best feminist writing, a determination to give priority to political
practice rather than abstract theorising

The authors of *Feminist Social Work* approach practice through
an examination first of the definition of social problems and how
a feminist perspective illuminates our understanding of the significance of gender in their construction. They then give an account of
a range of feminist work in campaigns and in therapy before
exploring the possibility of a feminist practice in the most recalcitr-
ant of settings – that of statutory social work. They then turn to
the working relationships which might be established among social

workers on the basis of feminist principles. Finally, Lena Dominelli and Eileen McLeod write optimistically about the wider political presence of feminism as the context for the effective development of feminist social work.

Given its highly critical stance in relation to 'socialist' practice, where is this book located within the series? It has become increasingly evident in recent years that any simple pairing of feminism with socialism is exceptionally problematic and at this juncture impossible.[2] When feminism enters into a dialogue with Marxism, it is bound to be sharply critical, unmasking and challenging in the most profound way possible, namely not only about *what* we see in the world (and what we fail to see) but also *how* we attempt to understand it. Feminists are right to argue that classical Marxism, at least, is inadequate as a basis for understanding the social world and our internalisations of it. Marxism, if it is to remain a dynamic and reflective theory and method has to be *feminised*, and undergo the thorough changes that this process implies. Certainly, no socialism is now conceivable which fails to address the issue of gender as central to any development of egalitarian and non-exploitative social relations. On its side, feminism also benefits from its discourse with Marxism; it must confront the core theory and practice of the socialist tradition if it is to pursue its own politics. This book makes its own valuable contribution to this discourse.

In a review of Linda Gordon's study of family violence in Boston 1880-1960,[3] Kenneth Keniston raises the most important issue which confronts the dialogue between feminists and Marxists:

For Marx, the social relations of production were the Rosetta stone that unlocked the languages of ideology, consciousness, the state, economics, religion and historical change. Contemporary feminist scholarship suggests that even if gender is not the Rosetta stone, it is more than just another variable. Gender is the first, most unchanging and deepest of all the meanings attached to human beings. The achievement of scholars like Linda Gordon is to give gender a role in explanation equal to the role it plays in life.[4]

Whilst some feminists seem to see gender precisely as the Rosetta stone, those who interact closely with socialist thinking, as do

Dominelli and McLeod, refrain from this final step, one which would subordinate all other social divisions, including class and race to the dominant imperative of gender. This book engages with this question of the relation of gender to other divisions and finds, unsurprisingly, the feminist analysis of this relation to be the most satisfactory. Their answers are likely to be subject to some debate among social workers; what will be welcomed by all readers are the careful spelling out of the implications of the feminist perspective for day-to-day practice in social work at every level of intervention.

*McGill University*                              PETER LEONARD
Montreal

*Notes*

1. Corrigan, P. and Leonard, P. (1978) *Social Work Practice Under Capitalism* (London: Macmillan) Editor's Introduction.
2. Wilson, E. with Weir, A. (1978) *Hidden Agenda* (London: Tavistock Publications).
3. Gordon, L. (1988) *Heroes of their Own Lives* (New York: Viking).
4. Keniston, K. (1988) 'Wife Beating and the Rule of Thumb', *New York Times Review of Books*, 8 May.

# Acknowledgements

We warmly thank the women, children and men, too many to mention individually, who shared their experiences and opinions with us and continually provided us with fresh insights into our work as we were writing. We also want to express our deep gratitude for the practical support offered to us by our families, and close personal and academic friends. In particular, we wish to thank our readers – Sally Cherry, Mary Langan, and David Howe, for their helpful comments and constructive suggestions through the draft stage; Chris Woods for her efficient and speedy typing of the rough manuscript; David Whiteley whose willingness to do childminding, offer computer advice and endless loving support has been invaluable through the whole process of seeing this book through; and Anna McLeod for her understanding, encouragement, and shrewd advice. Finally we thank our friend and former colleague, Peter Leonard, for his support, advice and commitment to seeing *Feminist Social Work* in print.

LENA DOMINELLI
EILEEN MCLEOD

# Introduction

Feminist social work is in the process of formation. Its principles have come from a whole range of activities within the broader women's movement and are still being refined through further action, discussion and controversy. Its practice emanates from the same source, but is gaining a specific set of characteristics as feminists engage with the task of creating a feminist social work. This pattern of development follows the lines adopted by a host of other feminist initiatives in fields as diverse as publishing, geography, health work, and management. Feminist social work is also informed by feminist analysis of social problems. At the same time, it is beginning to make its own contribution to taking such analysis further, as for example in the conclusion coming out repeatedly from feminist group work that any attempt by women at organising must take care of the emotional burdens accompanying gender subordination if their potential for activism is to be realised (Donnelly, 1986; Curno *et al.*, 1982; McLeod, 1982).

We argue that feminist social work as it stands is already of value, but that it has the capacity, if work aimed at underwriting and sustaining its development is carried out, to make a profound contribution to the welfare of women, children and men.

*Principles informing feminist social work*

At the heart of feminism is a very simple idea: that there are not two sorts of people in the world, the superior and the inferior, or in terms of power relations, the dominant and the subordinate. We are all equal irrespective of our gender. Social relations that obliterate this fact must therefore be transformed and recreated in ways that reflect equality in terms of gender. In keeping with

1

this, a feminist stance endorses egalitarianism across all social dimensions. Therefore, feminists are also against other social divisions which reflect dominance and subordination such as race, class, heterosexism, ageism and 'ablebodiedism'.

The preceding description in fact encapsulates the outcome of work on identifying and refining convictions at the heart of the contemporary women's movement during the past twenty years. Feminist scholarship has by now documented the way in which struggles to secure gender equality have been proceeding across the centuries and taken a variety of forms (Banks, 1981). The resurgence of the contemporary Women's Movement in the 1960s was marked by women highlighting the emptiness of their existence as beings whose boundaries were contained within and by their domesticity (Friedan, 1974). Thousands of women discovered for themselves the message made public by Betty Friedan, became aware of how sexuality, maternity and domesticity were acting against their interests and contributing to their unhappiness, and came together, determined to do something about it (Dreifus, 1973). The reasons why women undertook or renewed this sustained and public questioning of the injustice of their role at this particular historical juncture remain controversial. The three most commonly advanced theories are that it represented a revolt against post-war domesticating norms; that there was an emergence of a young educated female élite facing the contradiction of a powerless future framed by the demands of marriage and the family; there was a further wave of revolt in the wake of student and black power initiatives, but these theories only partially answer the question of why *women* became motivated to take a critical stance on their own circumstances and why *at this time*. What is clear is that gradually in and through private thoughts, informal conversations, writings, early consciousness-raising groups, social events, campaigns, mass meetings and lobbies, the conviction of the injustice of women's inequality became articulate (Coote and Campbell, 1982; Oakley, 1972). In the process, the welfare of women became established as a significant social problem across every continent (Jayawardna, 1986).

But to return to Britain and to the process through which feminist principles have been refined here, which is paralleled by similar initiatives worldwide. This has taken the form of a continuing drive to test what feminist principles should mean through constant criticism and renewal. In the course of this, the specifics of such principles have been consistently revised and extended. The development of the women's movement has been characterised by a series of running controversies where a seemingly more powerful group has been shown to be reinforcing particular forms of inequality. For example, working-class women have brought home to their middle-class sisters that the dimension of class cannot be ignored as a profound determinant of social circumstances (Curno *et al.*, 1982). This has meant that middle-class feminists have come to appreciate the significance of working-class women's involvement in issues such as play facilities, child-care provisions, employment and housing through community action and workplace struggles. Black women have found that they cannot afford to let go of either the class struggle or the gender one and must take on board the anti-racist struggle as well. They have upbraided their white sisters for falling into the trap of racism by omission in assuming that sisterhood encompassed the interests of black and white women alike. They have gone on to organise as black women and to assert that white feminists must be anti-racist if their egalitarianism is to be worthy of meaning. Besides drawing away from their white sisters because of the effects of racism, black feminists have distanced themselves to some extent from their black brothers because of their sexism in order to dwell on the specificity of their own situation (Bryan *et al.*, 1985). Lesbians have challenged 'straight' women's heterosexism and have established lesbians as an entirely legitimate mode of emotional and sexual expression. This has resulted in the broader women's movement acknowledging that lesbianism can transcend other forms of sexual experience for women. Controversy around whether women's espousal of men as sexual love objects runs counter to feminist aims of not yielding superiority to men has raged and continues to do so. But whatever the outcome of this debate and without assuming that heterosexism has withered away for women who would regard themselves as feminists, the principle that feminists are acting in a contradictory way if they fail to oppose heterosexism has been established.

A further twist to the debate relating to lesbianism within the women's movement, but one which illustrates the continuing commitment to examining what genuinely represents egalitarian principles, has been the attention recently paid to lesbian sado-masochism. At the nub of the argument has been the dilemma of whether respecting the principle of self-defined sexuality in terms of the form sexual expression takes means feminists endorse lesbian sado-masochism or reject it as inconsistent with feminist aspirations because relations of domination-subordination appear to be a dominant motif in lesbian sado-masochist relationships. (Ardill and O'Sullivan, 1986). Once again, the central issue is how to resolve what emerge as contradictions in feminist behaviour in terms of feminist egalitarian aims.

Meanwhile, struggles in several other areas are insuring that feminists take sufficient account of social divisions other than gender that affect women's welfare. For example, there are continuing efforts to bring about a situation where more than merely token gestures are made towards the defeat of 'ablebodiedism' (Campling, 1981), and the way in which ageism maps not only the treatment of older women by younger women but also corrodes all women's self-identity is now on the agenda for discussion and action (Warren, 1985).

The process we have been describing is not complete and, as products of a hierarchical society, feminists are not immune from reproducing hierarchy through their own social relations. Thus, social divisions yet to be lodged in feminist awareness remain to be unearthed. The form or intensity that feminist concern will assume in taking these on board is also unknown. Yet we would suggest that feminist responses to criticism of their theory and practice is sufficiently advanced to demonstrate that incorporated as a central feature of a feminist stance on social inequality is the rejection of all social divisions and not simply those based on gender.

Meanwhile, the question of where the origins of subordination in terms of gender are appropriately located has itself been under constant scrutiny among feminists. To date three main tendencies seem to have characterised attempts to explicate this. Radical separatist feminists have identified men, the architects of patriarchal social relations that impose powerlessness on women, as the enemy. As a consequence, radical separatist feminists posit that the only effective solution to provide for women's welfare is for women's existence to be as independent of men as possible, sexually, emotionally and materially. This position has resulted in such practices as forbidding the entry of male children to feminist crèches and women's centres, and in its extreme form in America, in the formation of the Society for Cutting Up Men (SCUM) by Valerie Solanas (Solanas, 1974).

In general terms, the actions of radical separatist feminists have been characterised by developing autonomous spaces, resources and networks for women only, such as the early initiatives of Women Against Violence Against Women. But whilst we accept the importance of having a women-centered approach to gender oppression, we would argue that the extermination of men in theory or practice as human beings runs directly counter to feminist egalitarian concerns. Moreover, its feasibility as a genetic enterprise in the foreseeable future is questionable. Such an approach also ignores the way in which in the medium-term women's behaviour reproduces patriarchal assumptions (Wilkinson, 1986) and is itself an appropriate target for change. We do, however, agree that for us as women to remain true to feminist practice, it is essential for us to have autonomous women-only groups and amenities. These enable women to develop feminist theories and ways of working further without having to contend with the full weight of sexist pressures and processes at the same time. Thus, we stand against feminist separatism as it is commonly understood, but we favour the establishment of groups and resources for women only.

A further tendency amongst feminist writing and action has been to locate gender oppression in patriarchal social relations, and to see these social relations rather than *men* as the prime target for change (Oakley, 1981). Admittedly, it can sometimes seem difficult to separate the two! But, in this analysis, while patriarchal social relations secure male domination and power over women, two possibilities emerge. One is that men's interests as human beings are not fundamentally served by this set of social relations. For example, men's capacity for emotional engagement with other men, women and children is stunted and distorted through their socialisation into the norms of the dominant male role. The significance of this for feminists is that if this is true, it may be possible for negotiations to begin with men, on the grounds that patriarchy is not totally in their interests, and thereby enlist their energies in its overthrow. There is some evidence that this is happening with the development of men's consciousness-raising groups (Tolson, 1977), in male anti-sexist discussions about their involvement in child-care (Hearn, 1983), and in men theorising on masculinity (Festau, 1975).

The second possibility opened up by such an analysis is that of securing change in male behaviour if and when dominant patriarchal forms of social relations can be and are changed. In this analysis men are not 'naturally' bad and do not therefore require to be written out of future history elaborated through a feminist perspective. On the contrary, as women's welfare is secured, and the patriarchal relations which stunt and distort man's lives are dissolved, the welfare of men benefits in the longer term.

The tendency in feminist thought we have been referring to here does not itself engage with the problem of the relationship between social divisions based on gender and other social divisions such as class. The analysis of class as the other critical determinant of social disadvantage has frequently been linked with an analysis of patriarchy undertaken by socialist and marxist feminists (Adamson *et al.*, 1976; Barrett and McIntosh, 1982). The upshot of their work has been to elucidate the way in which women's disadvantaged position as long-term members of the reserve army of labour has profound drawbacks for women's material, physical and emotional welfare, while also being in the interests of male dominance and capital. They have also clarified the way in which the family as a social institution underpins the interests of male dominance and capital while mediating women's labour. This means that on the one hand women rarely lose their prime burden of domestic labour (and if they do are stigmatised for it) and consequently enter the realms of waged labour with a built-in handicap. The problem with this analytical tendency has lain in attempts at resolving the question of whether class or patriarchy appropriately takes precedence in determining women's oppression. Where class oppression has been given priority over gender oppression it has failed to take account of the specificity of women's experience within a class framework (Magas, 1971; Coulson *et al.*, 1975). In practice, attempts at eradicating class oppression in China and the Soviet Union have not automatically led to the elimination of gender oppression (Molyneux, 1985). Where patriarchy has been given precedence over class this has begged awkward questions about whether the subordination of women can cease without the reorganisation of the labour market, and at what point men and women can or do get together on a truly egalitarian basis (Hartmann, 1981). Faced with such a theoretical impasse it is not surprising that seasoned feminist activists and analysts are currently seeking refuge in a separate state approach (see, for example Wilson, 1986). The argument here is that there is both a class struggle and a feminist struggle to be fought, but for the time being, because the appropriate interconnections between them are so unclear, perhaps it is best to pursue both separately.

While viewing patriarchal relations rather than men as the prime target for change, and acknowledging the importance of a class dimension to women's oppression, our position moves beyond concentrating on the issue of whether or not to prioritise one over the other, or which that should be. We also see where we stand as reflecting the viewpoint of many women currently engaged in tackling problems of women's welfare. We consider that it is difficult for even feminists to decondition themselves from patriarchal forms of thought, imbued with notions of hierarchy, and in this case there must be a primary cause of oppression. Moreover, our processes of constant self-criticism as described earlier may provide us with the feminist mechanisms through which we can extricate ourselves, albeit slowly, from such monocausal hierarchical assumptions. Whilst we would not want to foreclose the debate on the ultimate origins of oppression, we wonder at the usefulness of such an approach. We feel that because we can never have the total evidence which would be required to establish the historical origins of oppression and its concomitant social relations based on hierarchical forms of domination and subordination, we should not expend our energies on the matter. We also see attempts to do so as having ended in simplified caricatures of past historical events, for example, Engels (1972); Firestone (1971); and Minford (1984).

Furthermore, from our point of view, searching for one cause is an inadequate way of conceptualising the problem of oppression. There are so many forms of oppression, all of which are interconnected and interacting with one another, we can never be sure that we have found them all and we cannot expect one single factor to explain their diversity. Thinking of oppression in this way also forces us into thinking of one form as being more important than another. In other words, the very formulation of the problem becomes hierarchical. If the feminist principle of establishing egalitarian practice in our theoretical work is correct, then we must conceptualise the problem itself in egalitarian terms. That means that we do not impose a hierarchy of order on the different forms of oppression. None can be prioritised over the others because doing so would be at someone else's expense. Thus we arrive at the position that there are an indeterminate number of forms of oppression. Work to eliminate those of which we are aware must be undertaken at one and the same time to offer the chance for people's well-being to flower fully. Unless we approach the problem in this way, we may jeopardise the establishment of egalitarian social relations as it comes to taking action by simply aiming to remove one form of hierarchy, ignoring certain other aspects and forms of oppression for the time being, and promising people relief from them in the distant future. For example, the prioritising of economically based oppression over all others, we would argue, has resulted in the failure of Eastern Europe's 'socialist' countries to eradicate hierarchical social relations in general or gender (Scott, 1976) and/or racial oppression in particular.

We have reached this realisation through our commitment to feminist principles and practice and our reflections upon these. Our involvement with other women has revealed that whilst we share a commonality in being oppressed as a gender, our experiences of it are very different. The experiences of white women differs from that of black women, that of working-class women from middle-class women, that of lesbian women from heterosexual women, that of young women from old women, that of ablebodied women from that of women with disabilities. These differences have to be taken on board in a way which does not belie the importance of those experiences as they are actually perceived by those suffering from them, and which at the same time does not polarise women into dualistic opposition amongst themselves. In addition a feminist reading of a women's experience demonstrates how oppression may operate on a number of different dimensions simultaneously affecting the individual. So, for example, a black working-class lesbian woman could be experiencing the impact of prejudice and discrimination resulting from her gender status, her class status, her racial status and her sexual orientation at any one point in time and all the time.

## The nature of feminist practice and its engagement with social work

Complementing and indissolubly fused with feminism's egalitarian stance on welfare is its concern to engage in egalitarian practice to realise its aims. We would argue that this has been a hallmark of feminist action in whatever sphere since the emergence of the contemporary women's movement. Again the idea at the heart of it is a simple one. If feminists aim to create egalitarian social relations then these must be reflected in their practice, otherwise it contradicts feminist aims and whatever social relations are being created, they are not feminist ones. Consequently, as will be discussed in detail in Chapter 2 – women active in the women's movement have paid a lot of attention to the processes of feminist action. It has been seen as a legitimate task to work at establishing non-hierarchical organisational structures legitimating the value of everyone's contribution and the empowering outcome of cooperative work (Collins *et al.*, 1978; Curno *et al.*, 1982). At the same time the attempt to do this has brought home to the women concerned, admittedly often retrospectively, just how steeped we all are in the assumptions and practices of hierarchical social relations (see Chapter 2). Accounts stemming from feminist work on a wide range of issues indicate how interpersonal rivalry and competitiveness, class, sexism, discrimination along racist, ageist, heterosexual and ablebodist lines all mark feminist initiatives (Mayo, 1977; Curno *et al.*, 1982; McLeod, 1982) irrespective of their strong egalitarian intentions. We would argue that ironically such critical accounts of the realities of sisterhood are the best testimony to the principle of egalitarian practice being applied. It is only as work is undertaken with this in mind that the full depth and reach of the inequalities marking our social relations is uncovered. What is involved is well illustrated by the following account of the minutiae of practice:

I can recall one incident at a local day workshop on women's health. Several women from outside the area came and spoke about their experiences on a variety of women's health projects; this included one especially inspiring and thought-provoking talk by two women who had helped start a women's therapy group. A small group of working class women responded enthusiastically to the talk and said they wanted to start their own therapy group. They asked the two speakers (who came from fairly nearby) to come and help them start off. One of the two women replied, 'But you don't really need us, you can do it on your own; we did.' In her desire to minimize differences between herself and the women who were asking for help, she fell into the 'false-equality trap' and ignored the fact for example, that for those women, focused group discussions were likely to be a novelty, whereas she, as a former student, had been quite used to them when she helped start her group. She therefore withheld support which the women asking for it may have badly needed. (Barker, 1986, p.87)

Embodying the feminist principles we have described, albeit in a fractured, unfinished form, we argue that feminist practice has already made a significant contribution to welfare in the sphere of social work. It has done so in respect of the four main activities that comprise social work: the definition of social problems for intervention, community work, counselling and statutory social work. In the body of this book, we go on to discuss the detail of this work so far, how it needs to be developed further and how this might be brought about. But here we want to indicate what we see as distinctive about the impact of feminist action on social work and the stage this has reached.

Before carrying our discussion further we want to make clear that though the forms may vary, we regard all social work in Britain as coming under state control in some way and therefore being viewed appropriately as state social work. Social work's espoused primary aim is to promote people's welfare but the way in which this is carried out varies by agency and the legal constraints imposed upon it. The main bureaucratic division in social work is between the community action and voluntary sector and statutory social work. Statutory work is directly funded by the central and local state and is empowered by the law to protect people's personal welfare when that is endangered by themselves or others, and to provide them with the necessary means for becoming 'good citizens'. Both these functions are defined in terms that are consistent within prevailing ideology. Community action and voluntary sector work on the other hand are not necessarily directly dependent on state funding. Whilst their brief may be to compensate for gaps in existing statutory welfare provisions, the hallmark of their activities is organising with the people concerned to pursue the development of their own definitions of welfare. However, we would argue that ultimately these forms of social work should also be seen as being encompassed by state social work. Our argument for this is that when it comes to challenging the existing distribution of power and resources even community action and voluntary sector work can come up against the reality of state control as expressed through the sanctions of funding, the law and the appeal to dominant ideology (Bridges, 1968; (CDP) Community Development Projects 1977).

Returning to the first of the main activities comprising social work: the definition of welfare problems for intervention, feminist action through the contemporary women's movement has put gender oppression on the map of social problems, exposing its detrimental effect on women's welfare. In doing so, it has unearthed the innumerable ways in which patriarchal social relations undermine the whole of women's well-being. These include women's right to emotional and physical health, access to material resources, political power, freedom from fear, and enjoyment and definition of their own sexuality and talents. Arising from their work with women, feminists have also discovered that patriarchal social relations adversely affect the welfare of children and men. For example, child sexual abuse has been revealed as being both widespread and an expression of male dominance (Ward, 1984). Similarly, it has been recognised that men experience emotional deprivation as a result of the pressure to conform to stereotypes of masculinity (Cartledge and Ryan, 1983).

While thereby making a significant contribution to the issue of the substantive nature of social problems that require intervention, feminist action has produced a critical shift in the nature of the power relations surrounding work on the definition of social problems. In feminist activity, the women immediately affected by certain specific gender-based problems, and other women working with them from a feminist perspective, have located the social origins of those problems, not in individual women's defective psyche or emotional make-up, but in patriarchal social relations. Thereby, as each extensive social problem has been unearthed from a feminist perspective, so it has represented a move away from psychopathologising the person and/or the area in question towards a concern with the defective state of our relations generally. Some idea of the scale of what is involved is conveyed by mentioning domestic violence, rape, incest and sexual harassment, where such a shift has ocurred. Psychopathologising tendencies persist in scholarly and popular debate as the literature on all those areas indicates (Lederer, 1982) but a feminist approach has retained a powerful presence in framing the debate (Mitchell and Oakley, 1986) in terms of the power relations that exist between men and women and their ascribed social roles.

Accompanying this approach to the definition, or redefinition, of social problems within the areas mapped out by feminist work, has been a move away from social problem definition as being the prerogative of the social science 'expert'. Instead, informed by the direct experience of gender oppression, women in all corners of society have been credited by themselves and other women with the ability not merely to produce narratives of pain for the 'experts' to analyse, but also to pinpoint the social origins of that pain themselves and thereby discharge the role of analyst. The circular outcome of this process is that because it legitimates such work on the part of women, it facilitates the confirmation that the problems experienced are universal social phenomena and not individual peculiarities – thereby strengthening the evidence for the analysis that this is so. To take one example, legitimation of incest as reflective of social relations dominated by male power, as opposed to being an indication of personal or family pathology, has encouraged women on a widespread basis to share the fact of their experience of it. As a result, the extensive nature of incest and its social origins have both been exposed (Nelson, 1982; Ward, 1984; Dominelli, 1986).

Moving from the definition of problems for intervention to modes of intervention themselves, feminist action has already had a substantial impact on community work through the development of feminist networks and campaigns. Community work had emerged as a distinctive form of social work just prior to the early development of the women's movement in Britain. The 1960s had been marked by an interest in community development as a way of responding to poverty. This focused on organising local communities and improving co-ordination between welfare agencies. The main methods used were individual welfare rights advice, advocacy, and campaigning. Such an approach represented an advance on psychodynamic casework in that it did not hold individuals responsible for the material disadvantage they experienced. However, its promise of marked improvement for the welfare of individuals and communities was not fulfilled. Despite their intentions to the contrary, community workers reinforced notions of community pathology as the source of the problem. Increased uptake in welfare benefits and better communication between different departments within the local authority did not substantially alter the position of poverty-stricken communities (Bennington, 1973). Further work on the issue revealed that economic decline and the conflict of interests between capital and local communities were responsible for their plight. Such analyses were the hallmark of what came to be known as community action. Community workers who styled themselves as community activists dissociated themselves completely from 'social work' and what they saw as its emphasis on individual pathology. Placing themselves outside social work, they organised themselves as a distinct professional discipline orientated towards working in egalitarian ways with community groups (Wood, 1976). But community action as a social movement unfortunately remained locked within sexist parameters, for women's contribution to community work, particularly in action at the grassroots level, and their specific needs as women, were virtually ignored (Mayo, 1977; Dominelli, 1982).

Whilst meshing with and drawing on community action's structural analysis and collectivist approach to material problems, feminist networks and campaigns since the earliest days of the women's movement in Britain have pinpointed its following weaknesses, and as we discuss in Chapter 2 provided the means of rectifying them. Feminist criticism of community action has focused on the following issues in relation to its analysis and practice – how it has paid insufficient attention to the emotional component of people's problems; how it has failed to engage with the importance of gender in its theory; or to make it explicit in its programmes of action (see, for example, Loney, 1983) and employment practices (Hopkins, 1982); how it has forged only temporary links between the labour movement and those involved in grassroots community action (for example, Curno et al., 1982); and how it has posited the notion of assuming state power through community action as an independent force, without any clearly discernible forms of mass support or material or political resources at its disposal. But although feminist initiatives have had a constructive impact on community action, their potential for transforming it has only been partially realised.

Similarly, we would argue that feminist therapy has not as yet transformed the field of counselling with its varied schools of thought. Nevertheless, we do maintain that already it has placed both the specific psychological and emotional injuries of gender on the agenda. It has also demonstrated the power of attempts at creating more egalitarian relations between women within feminist therapy to explicate women's psychology in a non-stigmatising way, and to offer effective support to women to engage more actively in constructing personal relations that meet their emotional needs. Such work is gradually moving across class barriers and beginning to mesh with statutory and community work practice. As it does so, traditional counsellor/worker – client relationships are dissolved, in the realisation that the problems under consideration are common to all women, albeit varying in degree. Therefore it is in the interests of all concerned to tackle them on the basis of solidarity between women when confronting the demands of constructing anti-sexist personal relations, rather than on the basis that the counsellors, however non-judgmentally so, are removed from the onslaught. The presence of feminist therapy and the lessons emerging from it have also legitimated throughout feminist practice the need for attention to women's particularly heavy emotional load if their potential for action is to be fostered to best effect.

In terms of assessing the nature and extent of the impact of feminist action on statutory social work to date, we must begin by acknowledging the contribution radical and Marxist critics have made in revealing its social control function. They have demonstrated that it has continued to play a diversionary role in respect of eradicating social deprivation. Statutory social work's function and ideology still endorse the idea that those who suffer relative poverty and associated problems of the management of human material resources have only their own inadequacy to blame, rather than attributing it to profound inequalities in the distribution of material wealth and power. Meanwhile, contact with social workers has been shown to have a stigmatising effect upon clients, and on balance, statutory social work is not viewed by them as their preferred welfare resource. More positively, Marxist critiques have gone on to indicate that social workers are ideally placed to gain knowledge of the devastating effects of our current social divisions through contact with clients and can share their understandings of the social origin of problems facing clients in an attempt to lesson the stigmatising effect of their intervention (Corrigan and Leonard, 1978). However, this approach underplays the significance of clients themselves having already divined where the origins of their problems lie. Moreover, as we discuss in greater detail later, the impact of a Marxist and radical approach on practice has been limited in various ways. First, in failing to render a gender-specific account of dependency and caring, it has not even begun to broach the question of how to develop a practice addressing the suffering of women, who form the majority as clients, carers and social workers. Second, it has not elaborated the form to be taken by an egalitarian model for practice which is capable of connecting up in its intervention a sensitive response to intra-psychic suffering, addressing personal experience and wider social problems while drawing on the resources of local and central government bureaucracies and grassroots networks.

Explicit feminist discussion of statutory social work, for example Wilson (1977), begins however, with a critique of its social control role which incorporates a gender specific account of this. Thus it has clarified the way in which the social control function of statutory social work, as represented by current policy and practice, above all prejudices women's interests by perpetuating the status quo. Social workers' efforts on balance are seen as instrumental in reinforcing women's roles as carers in situations inimical to their own welfare and at times threatening to the well-being of their charges. More symbolically, statutory social work as an institution functions to underwrite the idea that women's primary value is correctly seen as being that of domestic labourers reproducing a labour force fit to meet the demands of capital. Where women's own happiness and safety is at odds with the maintenance of male dominance and keeping the family intact, then social workers tend to encourage women to submit and comply. When women despair in the face of such pressures, the main thrust of practice is to steer them through what is treated as their individual inadequacy in coping to a point where they can resume 'control' (Wilson, 1977). Meanwhile, social work as a profession reproduces the common patriarchal pattern of women making up the base of the pyramid of management with men occupying the summit.

While early feminist analysis of statutory social work thus began to set out the need for action to change the situation, authors such as Wilson did not go on to elaborate the form this could take. Feminist writers and practitioners such as Brook and Davis (1985), and Wise (1985) have developed the discussion to the stage of arguing that a truly feminist social work can be established within state social work pretty much as it stands. However, the examples of practice the authors use, reveal the shortcomings of this approach. These are that while work consistent with feminist aims can be carried out, it remains a minority activity set alongside the dominant routines of practice constantly reinforcing the sexist nature and social control role of statutory social work. Moreover, beneficial as it may be for the women concerned, we could argue that the impact of feminist practice, if carried out along these lines, becomes truncated and diluted without a feminist presence at local and central state levels underwriting it. Such situations leave the individual feminist social worker feeling isolated and vulnerable as well. Feminist statutory social work also requires the creation of social conditions more generally reflective of feminist aims as the context in which it occurs.

Our discussions move beyond the two most developed feminist positions in relation to statutory social work to date. We argue that the transformation of statutory social work along feminist lines needs to take the form described below. Our starting point is that the most developed forms of feminist social work have taken place outside statutory social work, in feminist work on redefining social problems, developing feminist campaigns and networks, and work on feminist therapy. For statutory social work to become truly feminist it needs to embody such egalitarian initiatives within its practice. But for this to happen both these initiatives and a feminist statutory social work in turn need to be underwritten by egalitarian relations in the workplace, to ensure that women have adequate material resources for participating powerfully in the public arena and by a feminist political presence at local and central state level. Without change along these dimensions, feminist statutory social work can only develop to a very limited degree and become easily incorporated by existing structures.

*The development of feminist social work*

Our account of feminist engagement with the four main spheres of social work indicates that the feminist social work that emerges in these respects has a valuable contribution to make to welfare. Therefore it is important to develop this further. We discuss the areas of problem definition (Chapter 1); feminist networks and campaigns (Chapter 2); feminist therapy (Chapter 3); and feminist statutory work (Chapter 4) in their own right, to facilitate exchange of information about this. An intrinsic feature of their development as discussed in relation to statutory social work is that as one area builds up so it fosters development in another and, in fact, each area needs to be underpinned by the development of the others to maximise its potential. We aim to bring out the importance of the interconnected nature of this relationship in our discussion of what we identify as the constituent parts of feminist social work. Further, as we have done in relation to feminist statutory social work we want to bring out how, in relation to the development of feminist social work as a whole, two areas of action which are not usually considered central to the development of social work practice must be considered so if feminist social work is to have any substantial future. These are feminist initiatives in workplace relations (Chapter 5); and a feminist presence in the local and central state (Chapter 6). The former is to ensure that the material and emotional welfare of women as workers and as clients is promoted to redress persistent serious inequality. Any form of social work practice that does not take account of labour relations at work in this respect is demonstrating a very superficial reading of what promoting material welfare demands. Also, as the work of local authorities endorsing feminist issues and the by now widespread networks of women's committees in local authorities indicates, feminist social workers are not necessarily on a collision course with the local state. It depends on its political complexion. Therefore the development of a feminist presence in the local state emerges as a *sine qua non* of the establishment of a secure power base for feminist social work. The forms of practice leading to this and the interrelationships between a feminist presence in the local state and other spheres of feminist social work therefore requires serious study on the part of feminist social workers and those interested in promoting feminist social work.

As the history of the demise of the Greater London Council (GLC) following clashes with the central government on its anti-racist and anti-sexist initiatives has demonstrated (Campbell and Jacques, 1986), the power of the local state rests ultimately on the political complexion of central government. For a fuller discussion of the tenor of the significance of the policies of the GLC, see Chapters 5 and 6. Unless and until central government reflects a feminist political presence, the gains of feminist social work as undertaken by the local state remain precarious. Reviewing the record of support for and achievement with regards to feminist initiatives of any major political party in Britain is not encouraging. However, this lack of progress does not alter the hard fact that the establishment of a strong feminist political presence in central government is a requirement for the fullest development of feminist social work. The scale of work required and the interrelationship between it and other aspects of feminist social work again therefore require serious consideration if one is to achieve any realistic understanding of the nature of the task of developing feminist social work. Throughout our discussion of all the areas of feminist social work under consideration we want to emphasise the dialectical nature of the relationship between them. So we see the development of feminist material and political equality as dependent in turn on feminist work on redefining social problems, developing campaigns and networks and creating egalitarian personal relations. The fullest development of feminist social work is therefore possible only as it forms an integral part of a feminist transformation of social relations generally. And as a feminist social worker develops, so it contributes to such a transformation.

We have been writing this book throughout a period when the thrust of the feminist action we have been discussing has been embedded in a counter-political thrust emanating from central government and underwritten by the dictates of international capital. The emergence of new right monetarist policies and ideologies have weakened women's position in the labour market and intensified internal and ideological pressure for them to regress to accepting direct responsibility as carers in the home against their own interests. The trends are quite clear. Women are being forced to assume responsibilities for those welfare provisions which the state is abandoning, for example care for the elderly, the sick and the handicapped. As leading monetarists have stated:

> Society rightly feels that elderly parents and relatives, for example ... are the responsibility of next of kin to help. The same is true for handicapped children. (Minford, 1984)

However, though the radical right chooses in certain circumstances to ignore this fact, 'the next of kin' as Janet Finch's work (1984) has shown are women.

Our argument is that such a situation makes it essential for a feminist social work practice to be worked at if the ground previously gained by feminists themselves is to be held and if engagement with the problem of avoiding further deterioration in the social conditions that women, children and men experience is to be carried out. The conjunction of women as the majority of social workers at field level and of women as their clients, both likely to swell in numbers for the reasons described above as economic conditions deteriorate, may also provide the context for the development of a feminist social work practice. Meanwhile, other social divisions based on class, race, dependency and a more strident conservative morality are likely to sharpen, rendering feminist consciousness of the importance of developing a feminist practice which is sensitive to social divisions other than those based on gender even more relevant to promoting welfare.

At the time of writing the women's movement is also undergoing a period of reflection, reassessment and seeming fragmentation. This, together with the sobering economic and ideological scene described above, has suggested to some (Delmar, 1986) that feminism as a force for social change is in decline. We would argue differently. Feminist activists from the early days of women's movement now entering middle age may be particularly conscious of the passing of a relatively smaller and tighter network which originally constituted 'the movement'. But even in those days the point was made (Collins *et al.*, 1987) that such a decentralised, self-directing, diverse series of initiatives could not be confined within conventional membership rituals but would constantly be regenerating itself beyond existing boundaries. Even more to the point, feminist analysis from early days on has made it clear that patriarchal social relations are so deeply and universally entrenched that they are likely to take the work of more than one set of lifetimes to transform. Feminists would be going against the lessons of their own analysis if they thought that the fact that patriarchal social relations had not been eliminated by twenty years worth of work by a readily identifiable movement indicated that feminism had failed. Along with feminists such as Christine Delphy we take the view that what is currently happening is that feminists are 'digging in' in more specialised but ever more widespread and varied spheres to undertake the long-term work of irreversibly changing gender oppression. In this context, explicitly feminist engagement with social work is of its time, not a symbol of retreatism but a further demonstration of the capacity of feminist action to advance in the interests of promoting welfare.

# 1
# The Start of Feminist Social Work Intervention: a Feminist Approach to Defining Social Problems

A key feature of the women's movement has been the way in which work on defining and redefining social problems has led to the development of a whole range of initiatives which have focused on the specific welfare needs of women, for example the Women's Aid Network, rape crisis centres, well-women clinics, and so on. Such work resulted in putting gender oppression on the map of social problems, exposing its detrimental effect on the welfare of women, children and men and equalising some of the power relations embedded in work on defining what constitutes a social problem. In this way a feminist approach to defining social problems forms a crucial element of a feminist social work. Most of this work to date has occurred predominantly outside professional social work, that is salaried community work or statutory social work undertaken primarily in social services and probation departments. Instead, it has originated in self-help initiatives which have subsequently attracted funding and paid workers. However, their work may have proved influential in terms of reorienting professional social work (see McLeod, 1982). And the boundaries between voluntary or self-help feminist initiatives and paid community work or feminist therapy may have been blurred as feminist projects have acquired paid workers or women have gained experience in feminist projects before moving into paid work. But it is only across the past few years that professional social work practice in the form of statutory practice has been viewed in any detail as a site of gender oppression and a potential site for the development of feminist intervention (see, for example, Warwick Feminist Social Work Practice Conference Group, 1979; Brook and Davis, 1985; Donnelly, 1986; Wise, 1985; Hale, 1984; Marchant and Wearing, 1986). This follows work on the problematisation of statutory social work as a social institution reinforcing women's subordinate position (Wilson, 1977).

In keeping with the sequence of these developments, in this chapter we will be examining the nature of problem definition as an integral part of a feminist social work and the consequences for the welfare of women, children and men, in the following order. First, drawing mainly on voluntary self-help initiatives, we shall examine the lessons to be drawn from problem definition from a feminist perspective and discuss the positive outcomes of such work. Then we shall discuss the inroads that feminist initiatives in respect of problem definition have made on professional social work and the consequences of this. Finally we shall consider the conditions that are necessary for such work to be taken further.

We shall be arguing that feminist activity in redefining social problems in social work embodies the feature common to all truly feminist social action: that is, that the significance of the work lies not in simply how good a *description* of social conditions is produced, but in how effective this is in bringing about social change. For at the heart of feminism is a commitment to identifying and challenging social relations based on gender oppression with the intention of *transforming* them into social relations promoting equality.

## REDEFINING SOCIAL PROBLEMS FROM A FEMINIST PERSPECTIVE – 'PUTTING GENDER ON THE MAP'

Redefining social problems from a feminist perspective means in the first place considering all problems in terms of their specific impact on women's welfare. This requires an examination of problems in ways which take as their starting point women's experience of them. Thus, feminist work on redefining social problems has focused on: identifying the specific ways in which women experience their existence; drawing people's attention to the lack of resources, power and emotional fulfillment which hold women down; exposing the social relations and social forces responsible for creating this state of affairs; and placing the plight of women firmly on the agenda for social change. The process through which this occurs carries within it an acknowledgment that women are in a subordinate and powerless social position. Moreover, this process aims to expose the dynamics through which the subordination of women is reinforced and perpetuated by society's failure to take seriously their welfare needs.

In the second place, redefining social problems from a feminist perspective means attempting to carry out such work in an egalitarian way. Thus, in this section, drawing out the lessons of a feminist perspective on problem definition as an integral part of a feminist social work, we shall first consider the substantive issues and then examine questions of process.

## The extent of the problem

First, feminist action aimed at ensuring women's welfare has by now unearthed a vast array of substantive issues for public attention as social problems. These have included, amongst other things, equal pay, health, housing, domestic violence, reproduction rights, sexuality and child-care provisions.

The indications from feminist work to date are also that no corner of women's existence is free from gender oppression in one form or another. Therefore, any issue or interaction may appropriately become the subject of attention from a feminist perspective. It is not the case that some subjects are feminist issues and others are not, even though some may have received more attention from feminists than others. So, issues around women's health have been the subject of considerable and long-standing feminist activity. Others, such as incest abuse, have received feminist attention only in the past few years. Even more recently, interest has developed in the exploited nature of women as carers in terms of the elderly and infirm. Feminists have become engaged in redefining a range of social problems, from those affecting large numbers of women, for example equal pay, to those involving particular groups of women, for example, women with disabilities. Equally, feminists have ventured into fields where few women have been found, and have organised groups in them, for example, areas of new technology, management and engineering. Moreover, as the number of women committed to feminism increases and those already engaged in it get older, new areas of interest and concern will come to the fore. This process is particularly evident in feminist activity revolving around the way in which the problems of older women, particularly those concerning the ageing process and menopause are now becoming areas of major significance in feminist discussion and action (Kyle, 1981; Reitz, 1983). In addition, feminists have not eschewed controversy in pursuing the elimination of gender oppression. Engaging in controversial matters around their redefinition of the problem away from women and towards the way in which society has defined women's roles has particularly characterised feminist action in relation to meeting the needs of women suffering from domestic violence. The messages that patriarchal relations are responsible for endorsing male violence against women (Dobash and Dobash, 1980), and that sexuality has been defined in terms consistent with the needs of men (Lederer, 1982), have been unpalatable ones for society to accept.

## Women aren't the problem

In taking on individual issues and considering them in terms of their implications for gender oppression, feminist action has challenged the popular notion, also still current in mainstream social work, that it is women who are the problem and who must be helped to fulfill their socially ascribed roles more effectively (Dominelli, 1984: Brook and Davis, 1985). Instead, feminists have demonstrated that it is the patriarchal construction of social relations and not the women enmeshed in them which constitute the social problems which need addressing (Nelson, 1982). So, for example, through the equal pay campaign, feminists have challenged the view that women lack the potential required to meet the demands of high-powered jobs and that it is their lack of acumen and skill which prevents their rising to the higher echelons of the labour hierarchy. Instead feminists have revealed that women are locked into a segregated job market because certain low-paid, part-time occupations such as cleaning, typing and nursing are defined as being appropriate only for women. This is the case not only because such jobs replicate labour women undertake freely in the home, but also because they are structured around employers' assumptions that women's availability for work is tempered by their familial obligations. Women are expected to be mothers, wives and carers first, and waged employees second (Aldred, 1981; Armstrong, 1984). So, in redefining the problem from one which focuses on women's inability to carry out certain types of work, to one which highlights women's socially circumscribed position, feminists have been able to demonstrate that the problem which needs tackling is not women, but the social relations which mediate the opportunities available to them in life.

## Making connections

As feminist work has developed, so it has revealed the *interconnected* ways in which patriarchal social relations operate to oppress women. Thus feminists have found that for one particular problem to be addressed adequately, a range of initiatives/changes are required at other levels of social interaction. For example, feminist work on domestic violence has revealed that blaming the woman and holding her responsible for her plight is wholly inappropriate. The work of the National Women's Aid Federation (NWAF) has revealed that women not only need a place of safety which a refuge can provide, but they also need emotional and psychological support in order to gain their confidence as women and accept the legitimacy of having their needs, particularly those concerning their emotional and material security, met. Moreover, NWAF's work has demonstrated that all those traditionally involved in helping battered women, whether they are social workers, doctors, or the police, have not necessarily given equal attention to the needs of the women themselves compared with those of the children and the men involved. Thus, social workers have put pressure on women to maintain the stability of their families, the police have refused to take their assaults seriously because it was seen as a matter between husband and wife, doctors have failed to pick up on the danger to women's personal safety because this has been masked by their unsatisfactory personal relationships, and have prescribed tranquillisers to help women cope better with their situation (Pahl, 1985). Feminists who initially tried to respond to battered women's needs found themselves hamstrung both by the legal bureaucracy in social services and in housing, and by the police acting as enforcers of a system endorsing male supremacy. It was these feminists who defined the real problem to be tackled, not simply as one of getting men to behave themselves, but as one addressing the subordinate status of women in intimate family relationships which accorded men the right to control and chastise women (Dobash and Dobash, 1980). But for this redefinition of the problem to be effectively taken on board, action had to be undertaken simultaneously on a number of 'domestic' fronts. For example, the police's definition of 'domestics' as matters of private concern and of little significance for their intervention had to be challenged, and their recognition of domestic violence as a public issue endorsed (SWAF, 1980). Changes had to be initiated in housing legislations, for example, the Housing (Homeless Persons) Act of 1977; in legislation concerning divorce (Matrimonial and Domestic Proceedings Act of 1978); in training facilities made available for women's right to an independent income (LWLC, London Womens Liberation Campaign of 1979). All these initiatives have had to be undertaken in addition to making provision for women to have places such as refuges which can provide them with both immediate safety and the support necessary for them to develop their sense of self-esteem and confidence.

Moreover, in delving into the emotional and physical damage endured by women and in exploring its interconnections with different aspects of their lives, feminists have also unearthed ways in which patriarchial social relations adversely affect the welfare of children and men. For example, feminist concern to reveal the lack of safety in the family for women has facilitated their discovery of its dangers for children. Thus, feminists have been able to highlight the fact that rather than being protected by known adults, children are often sexually abused within the family framework primarily by adult men whom they trust (Nelson, 1982; Ward, 1984). This has underscored men's failure to develop non-exploitative relationships with children as long as they think of them as possessions in the way endorsed through patriarchal ideology. Feminist work on child-care has also picked up on the inadequacy of current definitions of fathering and shown that the exclusion of men from the child-care arena has caused emotional deprivation amongst men who do not have close contact with their children. Drawing on feminist analysis, male writers themselves have begun to indicate that men suffer emotional deprivation from having to live up to their sex-role stereotype in this way (Tolson, 1977; Hearn, 1983).

*Analysis of origins*

Feminist attempts to explicate the effects of gender oppression and its manifold manifestations have led them to consider how gender oppression came into being, so that the central forces underpinning its development and existence might be dismantled. Such considerations have resulted in feminists producing an elaborate body of work theorising the social origins of gender oppression and this work has had a profound influence on the way in which different groups of feminists define and redefine social problems. It remains controversial, and reflects power struggles within feminism between different schools of academic and political thought and the differing social situation of feminists themselves. Radical feminists have identified women's reproductive capacity as the source of their oppression. Shulasmith Firestone has argued that it is men's control of this which has denied women their rightful place in history as initiators of action. This is identified as patriarchy – a system whereby men control women's lives to their advantage. Moreover, radical feminists claim that as a system, patriarchy has been a common thread running throughout previous history.

Socialist feminists find this response to the origins of gender oppression extremely problematic. For them, it ignores oppression stemming from other sources, for example capitalism, and felt no less keenly by women. Class is of particular concern to them. It is clear to socialist feminists that middle-class women have resources, particularly material ones, which are not available to working-class women. They also feel uneasy about the separation of men and women into two hostile camps because their analysis of class has pinpointed the significance of capitalism in oppressing both men and women. Hence, socialist feminists believe that there are points at which the interests of men and women converge as well as others in which they diverge (Rowbotham *et al.*, 1979).

Black feminists are concerned that both radical and socialist feminists have neglected the impact of race in their analyses of the origins of gender oppression, and that these distort their experiences by trying to make them fit into a white mould (Carby, 1982; Davis, 1981; Bryan *et al.*, 1985). Whilst accepting that relations between black men and black women are problematic, black feminists do not believe that at this point in time focusing on gender oppression at the expense of racial oppression in the manner suggested by

white women really safeguards their interests (Bryan *et al.*, 1985).
Since white women have a role in oppressing black women as well
as black men, the tendency has been for black feminists to decide
they prefer to spend their energies eliminating racial oppression
first, and subsequently tackling gender oppression in their own
ranks (Bryan *et al.*, 1985).

Feminists of our persuasion, recognising both the multiple dimensions on which oppression operates and their simultaneous impact
on individuals, agree that socialist feminists have been quite right
to point to class as a source of division amongst women and as a
basis of specific interaction with men. We also agree that black
feminists have justifiably highlighted a different position in the
constellation of social relations affecting black women from those
involving white women. But we feel uneasy about the exclusion of
other dimensions of oppression, the prioritisation of some forms of
oppression over others, and the hierarchical ordering of these in
the analyses of both black feminists, radical feminists and socialist
feminists. Moreover, we feel that although there are already an
indeterminate number of sources of oppression, including heterosexism, ablebodiedism, ageism and racism, new ones will undoubtedly
be brought to light as our understanding of social processes and
their effect on oppression increases. We feel that these too must be
incorporated more centrally into feminist analysis.

The nature and outcome of the struggles over the different types
of feminist analysis are significant in terms of feminist action
because they affect what problems feminists seek to address and
how. Radical feminists, for example, maintain that the best means
of dealing a body blow to social relationships constructed on
the basis that women are responsible for caring for others and
reproducing them on both generational and daily levels is to develop
a separate society for women which parallels the existing one, and
excludes men. This, they believe, would put the control of resources
and the definition of what constitutes appropriate social behaviour
in the hands of women. Thus, they have created women-centered
organisations such as Women Against Violence Against Women
and have concentrated their energies on initiatives which involve
only women, for example the Greenham Common Women's Peace
Camp.

Socialist feminists believe that dealing effectively with gender oppression requires them not to exclude men from their analysis. In fact, since men are primarily responsible for creating both the capitalist and patriarchal conditions under which gender oppression occurs and the means whereby there are reproduced, it is considered important for socialist feminists to enter into a dialogue with men on the nature of oppression. In other words, for socialist feminists, patriarchy is something that is shaped by capitalism and vice versa. Thus, for them, the question is not that men control society, but that society is organised in a way which is detrimental to the interests of both men and women.

Black feminists feel that they would be evading their responsibilities in struggling against racism if they focused their energies on gender oppression and allowed black men alone to take up those issues dealing with the burdens racism imposed on the quality of life for all black people. Moreover, black feminists do not wish to see the specificity of their condition submerged under the cloak of a common sisterhood in the way suggested by white women. For these reasons, black feminists have preferred to address sexism within their own communities through their own autonomous organisations whilst white feminists tackle that prevailing within white society (Bryan et al., 1985). They have also pointed out the necessity for white feminism to respond appropriately to their critique because their experience of the white feminist movement has been that by prioritising gender, it has been racist (Lorde, 1984). We are at one with black women in so far as in our view it is necessary not to prioritise the different dimensions along which oppression occurs because this pits one form of oppression against another. Moreover, there is strength in the continuing tradition within feminism, albeit imperfect, faltering and slow, of feminists being subjected to criticism on egalitarian grounds from other women. In this way existing feminist thought and conduct may become more genuinely egalitarian.

This process, we would argue, is well illustrated in terms of black women's interaction with feminism. Whilst the slowness of the response of white feminists to the black feminist critique has infuriated black women, it has facilitated the formation of autonomous black feminist groups. The development of such groups and the achievement of an understanding of the significance of applying the relevance of their different life experiences to their particular struggles has meant that white feminists can no longer act as such a drag on the development of black feminism and their right to take up issues on their own behalf. In responding to the criticisms made by black women, white women have begun to develop a healthy respect for the contributions and achievements black women have made in the struggle against gender oppression (Barrett, 1986). This acknowledgement of differences has also led to changes in the definition of the social problems initially posited by white feminists. In terms of abortion, for example, the black feminist critique revealed that, for black women, the problem tended to be not one of getting access to abortion, but stopping medical practitioners from forcing it upon them (Bryan *et al.*, 1985). Similarly, black feminists have expressed the concern that by highlighting gender and marching through black neighbourhoods, the 'Reclaim the Night' Marches organised by radical feminists were used by the popular media to link attacks on white women with the hysteria around black criminality (Carby, 1982). Though issues around white women's handling of racism are far from being completely resolved, black feminists have made white feminists more sensitive to their differing experiences, and the question of the differential impact of issues on their lives has become more directly addressed in consequence. Thus, respect for one another's autonomy has enabled feminists to acknowledge openly the fact that although they have considerable differences to contend with between them, black and white women are also grappling with common causes, and that therefore the principle of sisterhood need not be lost (Barrett, 1986).

*Changing conditions*

At the time of writing we have also entered a new era in terms of problematising gender since the early days of the contemporary women's movement in the 1960s and early 1970s. In general terms, problem definition from a feminist perspective is no longer geared exclusively to establishing gender oppression as a public issue rendered invisible by being embedded in layers of patriarchy. The public at large has accepted certain elements in the feminist message, particularly those highlighting society's failure to recognise women's contribution to its growth and development; to include large numbers of women in parliament; to promote women to top jobs in public corporations and private enterprise; and to acknowledge the male bias in much of our language, for example the use of 'he' to describe most situations where names and gender are not specifically given. So, although the explanations regarding women's oppression remains controversial, the message that women are oppressed has got through. Even the media and popular culture, including that depicted through soap operas, have adopted vulgarised forms of the feminist message (Wolffe, 1983).

Yet, it cannot be assumed that having established the significance of eliminating gender oppression as a social issue, the clock will not be turned back. So, for example, the safeguarding and enlargement of women's rights at work, particularly with regard to pregnancy and maternity pay achieved in the 1970s are being rolled back as a result of change in legislation during the 1980s (Claimants' Union, 1984). Women are now finding that the time period in which they can decide whether or not to return to work following the birth of a child has been decreased. Maternity grants have been made available only to those on low incomes, whereas they used to be available to all women who had either paid for their own national insurance contributions or who had acquired such rights through their husband's contributions. The guarantee that women can return to work no longer means that they will not have to accept a different, usually inferior, position to that held prior to taking maternity leave (LSSC, 1986). We are now having to meet the anti-feminist onslaught of monetarists and New Right ideologies and policies which, if successful, will bury feminist work again. Rightist ideologies and policies, particularly in their attacks on women's right to work, their right to control their own fertility, and their access to public child-care facilities, represent powerful efforts to deproblematise the nature of women's social situation and convince them of the 'naturalness' of their position as carers (Loney, 1986). If these attacks are not countered by feminist initiatives in terms of social-problem definition they will contribute to dismantling social resources such as waged labour opportunities, health care and day-care which have both underwritten the possibility of alternative definitions of women's existence coming into being and provided concrete demonstrations, which could be pointed to, of the feasibility and desirability of this.

## REDEFINING SOCIAL PROBLEMS FROM A FEMINIST PERSPECTIVE – AN EGALITARIAN PROCESS

Feminist work to date has recognised that to promote egalitarian social relations it is not enough simply to define or redefine problems that need to be addressed. It has also acknowledged that the processes whereby problem definition itself occurs need to be carried out in an egalitarian way in order to foster the egalitarian relations that are being sought. This has brought about a critical shift in the nature of the power relations surrounding such work, a shift away from both 'psychopathologising' the origins of 'individual' problems and accepting the appropriateness of placing the analysis of social origins of individual misery and the right of the oppressed to speak for themselves. In reducing the control experts exercise over the definition of the problem and asserting that which they developed themselves, women have acquired a public voice which speaks specifically of their oppression (Dreifus, 1973). Thus, feminist work has demonstrated that substantial, though otherwise inaccessible, evidence as to the nature of social problems and the suffering this entailed is opened up by legitimising the analytical standing of the accounts of those immediately affected. Feminist work on incest can be used to illustrate this point. In their work on this issue, incest survivors have used their accounts collectively to challenge their treatment as if in some way they were the offenders rather than those who were abused, and demand changes in the way that the police, courts and social workers handled their situations (Nelson, 1982). This has, in turn, led to a highlighting of the centrality of men's socially-sanctioned right to subordinate women's and children's needs to their own in incest abuse; a questioning of the way in which the abused have been treated as the culprits; and the inappropriateness of placing the responsibility for the abuse taking place on the shoulders of women (Dominelli, 1986).

The two critical processes underpinning work on problems definition from a feminist perspective, making it possible to put the focus of feminist social action on social relationships, have been the method of consciousness-raising and the *realisation* that 'personal is political'. The latter has been reduced almost to a slogan, but its significance lies in representing the achievement of the women's movement in breaching the corrupted 'liberal' division of the personal sphere of 'freedom', from the public domain subject to governmental regulation. Women have shown over and over again that, under patriarchy the private 'deregulated' sphere of domestic, intimate or family relations has offered men the licence to behave in a most brutal way towards women and children. In raising 'the personal' in public discussion, feminist action has in this way both questioned and begun to challenge some of the most extreme manifestations of male power and has, therefore, great political significance.

Consciousness-raising, or the demystification of social relations through the collective sharing of individual experiences, was a technique which originally drew on the Chinese socialist feminist tradition of 'speak bitterness meetings' which centered around women publicly exposing men's violence against them in the home (Dreifus, 1975). But American feminists adapted it heavily to suit circumstances prevailing in the West (Dreifus, 1973). Feminist consciousness-raising groups in Britain have in turn provided the means whereby women coming together as a group have aimed to achieve equality amongst themselves by providing each woman with the space to put her point of view and have it treated with as much importance as anyone else's contribution, thereby sharing their individual experiences and developing a collective identity which empowers them in several ways. This includes realising that their individual experience is mirrored in the lives of large numbers of other women. Through the process of becoming aware of the shared similarity of experience and the causes of their misery, women's individual problems become defined as social issues (Longres and McLeod, 1980). Consequently, the solutions to these problems are sought in the public rather than in the private domain.

The consciousness-raising process has given women strength by ending their feelings of isolation. Participation in a wider collective has provided women with a sense of solidarity and of being at one with others in a common cause (Coote and Gill, 1974). It also means that they are able to redefine their situation and turn their private griefs into issues of social concern with implications for the well-being of humankind (Pizzey, 1974; Longres and McLeod, 1980). Women are further empowered by the redefinition of their problems on a social level in that their collective organisation validates their subjective feelings, giving them the status of social facts with a legitimacy of their own, which can be used to challenge the facts trotted out by 'experts' (for example, Homans, 1985;

Cartledge and Ryan, 1983; Holland, 1984). In other words, the relationships between women in the consciousness-raising groups have provided women with the confidence necessary to challenge the professionals' understanding of their situation, including the definition of the women themselves as the passive victims of their own inadequacies, and the disparity in power between themselves as service users and the professionals as service providers.

The following extract illustrates these processes of consciousness-raising at work through the experience of women involved in a community television project which started as an adult education project:

> We are six in the group: three of us are mothers of children under five. We are all of differing religions (Protestant, Agnostic, Catholic) and of varying political affiliations ... We could write three chapters of your book, telling the story of bloody housing schemes, the isolation, the widespread depression, and so on, and the parallel story of how we each became involved in our project and how our attitude progressed from 'What the hell' to 'Christ! we must do something about this'.

> Our main objective at the moment is to have our films shown to as many people as possible, to men, women and teenagers, both to individuals and to members of organisations ... The benefits to each individual member of our group during the programme have been immeasurable and these we hope to be able to pass on to each and every housewife/mum, worker who sees our films. We hope they'll make people think deeply and not in a despairingly shallow way. (Collins *et al.*, 1978, p. 97)

## THE IMPACT OF DEFINING AND REDEFINING SOCIAL PROBLEMS FROM A FEMINIST PERSPECTIVE ON PROFESSIONAL SOCIAL WORK PRACTICE

Feminist initiatives on problem definition have now begun to have an impact on professional social work in terms of the ways in which it is theorised and taught and the ways in which it is practised. To start with, the gender-blind nature of the dominant forms of social work theory has been revealed. For example, Mayo (1977) has problematised the male-orientated basis of community work. McLeod and Dominelli (1982) and Marchant and Wearing (1986) have attacked systems theory for ignoring the implications of gender in its theory and practice of social work. The lack of a penetrating analysis of gender in radical social work and psycho-analytic theory has been exposed by Marchant and Wearing (1986). Although these authors highlight one exception to the general trend, Leonard (1984), which tries to take the gender dimension seriously, they indicate that even this work is flawed by having class as the main determinant of oppression. We would go further and maintain that when considered in terms of a perspective on problem definition, Leonard (1984) remains firmly within the Marxist tradition of prioritising different forms of oppression and putting them and their abolition in a hierarchical ranking order which makes progress in the elimination of what it sees as the major form of oppression – class – the precondition for movement in getting rid of other types of oppression. In other words, it continues to be bounded by the limitations of the conditional road to women's liberation, that is, women's freedom being conditional upon the elimination of capitalism. Or in feminist terms, women waiting for their liberation to occur after men have sorted out theirs, as has happened in countries which have attempted to initiate the socialist revolution, for example, China and Russia, where, in practice, women's liberation has yet to be realised (Croll, 1983; Johnson,1983).

The critique of contemporary social work theory has been developed by feminist social work teachers (Marchant and Wearing, 1986) who together with other anti-sexist colleagues have implemented it in their teaching. This has result in the growth of courses on feminist social work practice as a subsidiary but integral part of social work training. These both now span the country and exist around the world (IASSW, 1984; Marchant and Wearing, 1986). They have also fostered the production of published papers by students both highlighting issues of sexism encountered in practice and explicating forms of intervention from a feminist perspective, (for example, Warren, 1985; Evans, 1985; Donnelly, 1986). There is also some evidence that in their attempt to hold true to feminist principles of working in a more egalitarian way, they provide within their teaching, experience in approaching feminist social work as an issue in a co-operative, non-competitive manner (for example, Smith, 1986). The indications are that these consolidate and encourage an interest in gender as a problematic issue in social work and one to be addressed as students become practitioners (Smith, 1986;

McLeod, 1987). In addition, they can serve as resource and support groups to practitioners (for example, 1979 Warwick Feminist Social Work Practice Conference Group; Brook and Davis's (1985) account of a women in social work group).

Meanwhile, feminists have also demonstrated that practice and employment conditions in the field of community work (Cockburn, 1977), mental health (Howell and Bayes, 1981) and statutory social work (Brook and Davis, 1985) have in the main ignored or subverted interests of women as clients and workers. In community work 'women's issues' such as child-care and play facilities had been relegated as secondary or 'soft' issues compared with those to do with the 'hard' issue of employment and housing (Dixon, *et al.*, 1982). The work of women activists had been unsung until the advent of feminist analysis of community work (see Mayo, 1977; Curno *et al.*, 1982; Dominelli, 1982).

A succession of feminist writers have by now shown that the dominant motif in statutory practice has been that of reinforcing women in their role as carers in the domestic setting – irrespective of its effects on their welfare – and pathologising or stigmatising them as individuals when they 'fail' (see the work of Wilson, 1977; Dale and Foster, 1986; Pascall, 1986; Brook and Davis, 1985; Dominelli, 1986; Marchant and Wearing, 1986). Moreover, a feminist critique of 'community care' policies, which conservative and monetarist tendencies have increasingly prompted, has decoded such moves as placing increasing demands on women's capacity as carers of the young, the old and the infirm (Finch, 1984). In terms of employment conditions, feminist writers have explicated how social work as a field is characterised by hierarchical employment ladders in which men are located primarily in the top managerial rungs whilst women occupy the lower ones with the direct contact with clients (Skinner and Robinson, forthcoming). Thus men are responsible for managing the enterprise and making decisions about resource allocation in its broadest sense, whilst women undertake the caring roles. This has been well documented with regards to statutory social work (*Community Care*, 1986; Skinner and Robinson, forthcoming). According to Skinner and Robinson, 'By 1986 the picture "at the top" has changed little; there were 95 male Directors of Social Services and 10 women in such posts.' Even in their work with clients, the increasing use of corporate management techniques and managerialism in mainstream social work has lead to a diminution of control available to basic grade social workers as autonomous professionals whether in planning their intervention or managing their specific workload. Consequently, women are being constrained in their freedom to define their caring role and their relationships with the people they are working with in the terms they deem most appropriate (Skinner and Robinson, forthcoming).

Although progress in tackling 'managerialism' has been limited in statutory social work, gender as an issue has been taken up in a widespread way through union activity, in relation to issues, like equal pay and campaigns against sexual harassment at work. The National Association of Probation Officers (NAPO), The National Association of Local Government Officers (NALGO) and The National Union of Public Employees (NUPE), the major public sector unions concerned with organising social workers in the statutory sector, have come out in favour of examining the specific needs of women workers and have embarked on campaigns to remove sexual harrassment from the workplace and to provide measures aimed at increasing women's participation in their organisations, for example, by providing crêches for meetings, being wary of using sexist language, and establishing training facilities aimed specifically at women (Benn, 1983; Coote, 1980). These changes in union attitudes towards women have been the direct outcome of feminist work on problem redefinition whereby feminists have put pressure on trade unionists to stop women being treated as 'honorary men' and to examine their specific needs, and have gone on to develop women's caucuses.

Although smaller management 'pyramids' exist in community work organisations, feminist writers have produced commentaries which demonstrate that the same pattern holds (Batley Community Development Project (BCDP), 1975). Moreover, the shape of the working day is constructed in such a way that it gives great importance to workers being available at all hours. This definition of the situation disregards women workers' domestic responsibilities and places them at a disadvantage against male workers in career terms (Dixon et al., 1982).

As well as devoting some of their energies to improving their position as workers, feminists have allocated a great deal of their time to taking up gender as an issue in their practice. This has led to their establishing gender as an important issue for practitioners, though the attention given to this has not been uniform throughout the field of professional social work and, as our account will demonstrate, there is no professional social work agency where work on problem definition is as yet highly developed.

In community action, gender has been established as a central issue for practitioners as a result of feminist initiatives through community based campaigns and networks concentrating notably on housing provisions (Mayo, 1977), domestic violence (Binney *et al.*, 1981), health issues (Ruzek, 1978), community nurseries (David and New, 1985) and play facilities (*Community Action*, 1977). However the long-term impact of such work is frequently limited by the precarious nature of the sources of funding. Initiatives often rely on urban aid grants and the willingness of local authorities or charitable trusts to award them limited sums of money from time to time. This in itself reflects the relative insignificance the state attaches to providing in a securely resourced way provisions geared specifically to meeting women's needs, particularly if those provisions endorse a political commitment to challenging patriarchal relations – an inevitable outcome of the feminist process concerning problem definition.

In the counselling field, a new school of therapy in the form of feminist therapy has also been established. This takes women's social position as subordinate beings as the starting point of its intervention and relates it to the specific predicament of the individual women seeking help (Ernst and Goodison, 1981). It aims to develop women's self-confidence and strength so that they can make real choices concerning the direction they personally wish their lives to take and in doing so enable the woman concerned and those with whom they relate to lead more rewarding lives (Eichenbaum and Orbach, 1985). But the resources available for feminist therapy remain puny compared with those available in psychiatry as a whole, the counselling 'element' in general practice, and in social work generally.

Within statutory social work, feminist activities on problem redefinition have become directly concerned with the nature of the services provided to women as clients and have highlighted the importance both of looking at women's needs as women, and of establishing non-hierarchical relationships between the social worker and the woman/women she is working with. In the process, feminist work has also highlighted the social origins of individual problems, more publicly raised the question of the power relations embedded in the personal interactions involved, and increased the status of women's own accounts of their situations.

To begin with, the work of such feminists highlighted the specific nature of women's experience of statutory social work, the lack of resources, respect and dignity allocated specifically to them, and the absence of recognition of women's contribution both to society and to their individual family's well-being, often made at the expense of their own. Such revelations make poignant reading. For example, Warren's (1985) work with older women reveals the suffering endured by women in their old age and how by and large traditional social work practice ignores their physical needs, aspirations and emotional well-being.

Feminist practitioners have given accounts of how working from a feminist perspective has made it possible to reframe the nature of individual problems away from individual pathology and towards meeting the interests of the woman concerned. For example, this is evident in the following comments from students endeavouring to work from a feminist perspective:

> I think (hope) that I have come to appreciate the struggles of women more – a woman client may not on the surface appear to be particularly successful but her life *in context* may show quite astonishing ability to cope against considerable odds . . . It has helped me to begin to form a basis for looking at and reflecting on 'problems' in a non-pathologising way – to being confident that women's life experience counts and is relevant in practice, i.e., both the worker's and women's experience. (McLeod, 1987)

The possibility of achieving such a depathologising approach through group work carried out from a feminist perspective within a statutory agency has also been described, as in the following account by Harris (1987). Here, she is talking about working from a feminist perspective with a small group of women suffering from depression:

> When I joined the group I wanted to become another group member and minimise any differences in power between myself and the other women, to attempt equality of participation. It was made very clear to me early in my involvement by the other

women that they saw me as having a particular role to play. I was the woman with access to knowledge. I was responsible for the weekly organisation of the group, keeping the discussion going within it and making sure certain members were not intimidated. I realised that coming to the group with particular ideas of how I should fit into it had been patronising and elitist in its own way. (Harris, 1987, pp. 43 – 4)

Evidence also exists of two further types of approach benefiting women's welfare being developed in a statutory setting as a result of redefining problems from a feminist perspective. First, the establishment of counselling resources acknowledging that specific emotional problems are experienced by women generally and can be catered for on that basis. This is as opposed to assuming that the problems do not exist, or that if they do, they reflect an individual's inability to cope. It is on the basis that women have emotional problems in common that a number of social workers working from a feminist perspective, in a hospital setting, for example, have established stillbirth and miscarriage counselling facilities to deal with the emotional trauma of such events. These emotional needs had not been fully addressed by the medical practitioners concerned and therefore women suffered in isolation and tended to feel that they were either individually 'weak' or unbalanced. But the feminist approach has been able to reassure them that this is not the case and reaffirm that their emotional welfare as individuals irrespective of whether or not they have entered motherhood is important (McAndrew, 1986).

Campaigning action on the part of statutory workers to secure social justice for clients has also proceeded from the redefinition of social problems from a perspective. This has been clearly demonstrated in the formation of the Programme for the Reform of the Law on Soliciting (PROS) (McLeod, 1982). In, PROS, probation officers and lawyers formed alliances with working-class street prostitutes to end the blatant legal discrimination against them which they saw as enforcing the tendency to scapegoat prostitutes as the psychopathological originators of the problems of prostitution. In the course of the campaign not only was direct imprisonment for street offences ended, but a shift brought about in serious public debate of the subject towards an emphasis on the roots of prostitution as lying instead in women's comparative poverty and the dominance of male sexuality and its stereotypes (McLeod, 1982). Moreover, through their campaigning activities, working-class street prostitutes themselves were able to challenge definitions of their powerlessness and passivity held by both the public at large and professional social workers (McLeod, 1982; Dominelli, 1986c).

The redefinition of problems from a feminist perspective within statutory social work has also had an impact on the position of men as workers and as clients. Confronted by the presence of feminist work on gender oppression, and its demand that men take an active role in dismantling patriarchal relations, statutory social work is one male professional corner where men are taking seriously the issue of anti-sexism. Men's response to it has been so fragmentary as to be barely discernible, but that such a trend does exist is evidenced by examples of practice and some writings. Ric Bowl's work on masculinity, for example endorses the feminist insistence that male social workers start addressing the emotional issues relating to the men they encounter in their work. His work (Bowl 1985) marks an advance on traditional practice which tended to focus on intervention with women and children whilst the emotional state of men was ignored, by calling on male social workers to undertake specific work with men. Such work relies heavily on earlier feminist work on problem definition, feminist scholarship and feminist demands that men take responsibility for the social organisation which they created. For example, Leonard and McLeod (1980) exposed the significance of male sex-role stereotyping in contributing to domestic violence, and suggested that this was an important issue for social workers to address when dealing with such violence. Dominelli (1979) argued for the establishment of consciousness-raising groups for men who had battered women, as a way of helping them to come to terms with their behaviour. This is now being undertaken as a serious proposition in one social services department, in Bristol, where anti-sexist men have set up such groups (Calder, 1987).

Our conclusions based on our reading of secondary sources and contacts with practitioners across the country indicate that the impact of the redefinition of problems from a feminist perspective on statutory social work so far is that such activities have been fragmented and restricted. Gender issues are still not a central preoccupation in statutory practice. Moreover, the question of their being taken on board relies heavily on the resources of either individual women, small women's groups, feminist support groups (Evans, 1985) or specific single issue campaigns, for example PROS. In addition, attempts to fuse concern over gender with that focusing on other forms of social division such as racism, heterosexism, ablebodiedism, and so on, are at a rudimentary stage. Work on these is currently being carried out almost as a series of discrete specialisations. So, for example, much of 'ethnically sensitive, multi-racial' practice ignores the issue of gender (see Cheetham, 1972, 1982; Ely and Denney, 1987). Furthermore, feminists themselves have highlighted the isolation women endure as workers in the statutory setting. Wise (1985) became disillusioned with mainstream social work's propensity to remain relatively untouched by the activities of individual feminists beavering away at the creation of non-oppressive forms of practice in relation to women clients. She has also indicated the difficulties social workers in a hierarchical institution such as social services encounter in attempting to initiate egalitarian ways of working with their clients in the one-to-one relationship.

## THE FURTHER DEVELOPMENT OF PROBLEM DEFINITION FROM A FEMINIST PERSPECTIVE IN SOCIAL WORK AND THE GAINS FOR WELFARE

Our discussion so far has indicated that professional social work is amenable to work problematising gender. Thus we can conclude that there is nothing inherent in professional social work that prevents this from happening. However, our discussion has also reflected that its development is circumscribed at present by; (i) the lack of commitment by both local and central state to feminist aims and objectives; (ii) policies and practices which are infused with dominant ideologies subordinating women; (iii) the lack of numerical strength of feminist/anti-sexist workers in professional social work settings; and (iv) feminist commitment to working from independent grass-roots bases as one way of avoiding the dangers of incorporation. Nevertheless, we would maintain that changes in all these conditions are possible and as such hold the promise of gender becoming an extensive and well-established issue in social work.

Our grounds for arguing in this way are: first, it is not necessarily the case that feminist action in professional social work, whether in a statutory setting or a community work one, is on a collision course with local state policies. It depends on the extent to which feminist presence exists in both the local and the central state: Second, changes in professional social work are brought about by changes in other spheres which both develop and underwrite initiatives taken by feminist social work practitioners. So we would argue, for example, that Sue Wise's disillusionment and failure to extend her feminist practice within her agency was a result of her attempting to work as an isolated individual without the support of either like-minded individuals in her workplace or her trade union, and managerial support at the higher level of the management hierarchy including political support through the social services committee and the authority. In other words, we would argue that for feminist social work practice in statutory settings to be meaningfully sustained at the individual level, it must encompass organisational change too. Beyond this, such work also depends on the development of a feminist stamp on working conditions, the ideologies and ethics permeating personal relations, and on the continuing development of feminist organisations and networks at a grass roots level. Third, feminist social workers are by now located in professional social work and the indications from training are that their numbers are likely to increase. From the literature on feminist support groups in practice, we also get the impression that the numbers of feminist practitioners are going up (Falk, 1986). Meanwhile, feminist workers are generally more interested in establishing themselves within bureaucracies, including taking up managerial positions. Moreover, there is now a greater ideological commitment amongst feminists to work within the state bureaucracies, for example in teaching, medicine and social work. Fourth, professional social work will be affected by feminist activities and changes occurring in other fields of work. As feminist social work develops it also becomes clearer that most 'social work problems' are in fact a complex of interacting social processes that interconnect with one another and therefore need to be addressed simultaneously by feminists working in different disciplines and settings such as education and the media as well as social work, for thorough going changes in promoting welfare to be made.

Fifth, meanwhile, as we hope to demonstrate in greater detail in the rest of the book, as feminist practice develops, so in turn it fosters further work on the definition of problems both within social work agencies and beyond in feminist practice more generally. For example, women working from a feminist perspective in probation have not only taken up sexist employment practices in terms of their own working conditions, but have also initiated the provision of housing resources for single homeless women (Cherry, 1984). Finally, a general demand for women's emotional fulfilment which will not go away without being met. Evidence is starting to come through on an extensive scale in feminist writing on organising through community action, group work, and family and individual work that women's emotional experience is a repository of such profound injury as a consequence of patriarchal power that when women are organising, our emotional welfare requires constant attention if we are to have any chance of achieving our potential in asserting our individual and collective rights and needs. Such evidence is by now so powerful and consistent that it should rank as a 'discovery' of feminist social work available to all women, and be seen as a result of feminist work on problem definition in social work which has refused to accept that women's emotional turmoil is something to be borne in silence. Thus we believe that within social work, problem definition from a feminist perspective embodies a range of dynamic processes which will make it extremely difficult for practitioners to ignore their responsibility in promoting women's welfare.

# 2
# Feminist Community Work: the Nature and Contribution of Feminist Campaigns and Networks

Feminist campaigns and networks form the basis of feminist community work and as such are an integral part of feminist social work. They have contributed substantially to identifying the gender implications of social problems in the way described in the previous chapter. We will turn to analysing them as a form of practice and draw out their significance for feminist social work as a whole. In doing so, we will examine the significance of the forms feminist campaigns and networks take, how they promote welfare, and how their efforts in this respect need to be underwritten by other feminist initiatives in order to reach their full potential and have an enduring effect. The material involved in our account comes from our experience of organisation, contact and discussion with women in a range of groups, and a reading of secondary sources. We examine the fine detail of the experiences and interactions involved, in the hope that such an exercise will be useful to other feminist activists 'caught' in equally demanding situations.

As our account will show, the history of feminist campaigns and networks is not primarily a matter of women already formally employed as community workers turning to feminism, although a number of women community workers have developed feminist practice (see for example, Dixon *et al.*, 1982). In terms of the myriads of initiatives that have developed, some have been far removed from any contact with professional community work. Nevertheless, feminist action has gradually suffused the existing discipline of community work with feminist concerns, principles

and practices, while also retaining an identity not totally incorporated within professional community work (Dominelli, 1982). In a
similar way, although perhaps not to such an advanced degree,
feminist campaigns and networks have begun to be influential in
counselling and statutory practice. Their impact in these arenas
will be discussed in greater detail in Chapters 3 and 4.

We are working to a definition of feminist campaigns and
networks as initiatives that emerge when a group or groups of
women organise collectively around issues aimed specifically at
tackling gender oppression. Such groups are tackling the way in
which structural constraints affect women's individual experience
of emotional misery and material deprivation and are aiming to
work together on an egalitarian basis. Although egalitarian relations
to a certain extent have been successfully created in feminist
organisations, these have also been marred by continuing to be
permeated by the forces which they are seeking to challenge, for
example, sexism, racism, class and hierarchy. Whilst feminist
campaigns and networks have been created with the intention of
making an immediate impact on women's existence, they have
gradually begun to have an effect on the lives of men and children
too.

## THE IDENTITY OF FEMINIST CAMPAIGNS AND NETWORKS

Although feminist campaigns and networks may hold egalitarian
aims and objectives in common, they are very diverse in form.
They can incorporate mass movements and demonstrations, as in
the National Abortion Campaign (Banks, 1981) and the Women's
Peace Movement (Thompson, 1983). Alternatively, they can be
very localised, as in the case of Women in Social Work groups,
involving a dozen or so women and aiming to provide mutual
support as they try to establish feminist practice in particular towns
and cities (Brook and Davis, 1985). Feminist networks can also be
ad hoc, a matter of two or three women offering each other help
within an institution or in relation to a particular issue in the
interests of furthering feminist aims. The identity of campaigns can
also be indissoluble from their existence as networks ministering
to individual women. For example, the Women's Aid Federation
has undertaken collective action to challenge and change the status

quo; but from the outset, through its refuges, it has also provided relief for individual women in acute distress. On the other hand, members of feminist networks may not set out to campaign but their practice may embody a direct challenge to existing social conditions which necessitates campaigning activities. For example, Women as Carers groups initially got together women who were looking after elderly and/or sick relatives, to provide one another with mutual support. But in the course of doing so, they realised that appropriating the resources women needed to fulfil their responsibilities with respect to this caring work necessitated the establishment of a national network capable of undertaking a campaign aimed at changing public opinion on the value of the work they were undertaking, and shifting government policies towards them (Bonny, 1984; NCCED, 1984; Toynbee, 1984). On the other hand, feminist action concentrating primarily on one-to-one and small group work can represent an activist challenge to the way in which society is currently organised. Women in feminist therapy groups and centres, for example, are primarily concentrating on strengthening women's control over their own emotional and mental life, on an individual or small group basis (Ernst and Goodison, 1981). Nevertheless, if and as the idea that it is appropriate for women to be free to determine the quality of their intra-psychic processes catches on, it promises to have a revolutionary impact on current social relations. It would mean that women were no longer primarily dependent on male approbation for feelings of self-worth. It would also mean that women were not prepared to subordinate their emotional needs to those of men (Eichenbaum and Orbach, 1985). Both these developments carry revolutionary implications because they would initiate a critical shift in the balance of power in existing relations between the sexes.

Feminist networks and campaigns also come into being in a very fluid way as women get together in groups, withdraw, regroup and establish themselves in innumerable settings, addressing a host of different issues (Coote and Campbell, 1982). Tracing which ideas, elements of organisation and material resources have been incorporated into subsequent groups whilst also giving due credit to the original but now defunct group is no easy matter. In considering the scale of different groups' achievements, attention must be given both to the contribution made through the intersection of different feminist activities and to what is achieved through separate initiatives. To take one example: at this moment the range of feminist campaigns logging the preponderance of male violence in different settings – in the home, in the streets, at the workplace, in the media, in national and international politics, and their complementary nature, make it hard to deny any longer that such violence is an integral and inevitable feature of male dominance.

In fact, it may be a misnomer to talk of feminist campaigns and networks as having a distinct identity, such is the wealth of resources exchanged between them. The variety of support offered in this way was brought home to one of us whilst she was campaigning to change the law on prostitution. Across a number of years, apart from coming forward as members, feminist sympathisers offered supportive coverage in the press, produced film, television and radio documentaries, canvassed within unions and political parties, wrote articles and plays furthering the campaigns' aims, organised workshops and raised funds (McLeod, 1982).

A further advantage of the extensive and varied support offered through the existence of a pool of feminist activists is that of enhancing the chances of specific groups and networks surviving during an epoch when funding of community initiatives is scarce and likely to decline even more (Mayo, 1980). It also makes it more feasible for groups and networks to survive the withdrawal of funds if they espouse political positions considered unacceptable by the central or local state administration of the day. For example, The Women's Right to Income group in Coventry formed to counter the actions of the Special Claims Group of the Department of Health and Social Security in their attempts to reduce 'welfare fraud' amongst single parent women (Mayall, 1981) has survived despite its failure to attract public funds by operating on a shoestring budget and relying on the unstinted support and resources which women have provided amongst themselves as part of a wider grouping of feminists and their sympathisers (Gray, 1986).

The continued development on a wide scale of feminist activism is not only important in terms of underwriting the existence of separate groups as regards material resources, but also in terms of work on broad ideological issues which highlights women's social powerlessness. The objectives such work exemplifies and the processes entailed in carrying it out are described in Binney's account of the position of Women's Aid:

Ideologically, the specific battle is to combat the containment of battering within a psychiatric interpretation and to insist upon the very real powerlessness of women within the family. In this, Women's Aid cannot survive alone; its fate is inextricably bound up with the successes and failures of the women's movement as a whole. To the extent that the women's movement makes a lasting impact, the attempt to contain battering at 'acceptable levels' will be weakened. (Binney *et al.*, 1981, p. 125)

By now, the enormity of the task feminists have set themselves in seeking to eradicate gender oppression through feminist campaigns and networks, the seemingly slow progress made in terms of the realisation of this objective, the attack of the New Right on previous feminist achievements, and the changing nature of the feminist movement itself have shaken the confidence of feminists. Recently, a number of feminists prominent in the earlier days of the women's movement have initiated a debate about whether the movement as such is passing away (Delmar, 1986; Orbach, 1986). Others are questioning those elements which now constitute the actual identity of feminism and are asking to what extent they are truly feminist (for example, Mitchell and Oakley, 1986). At times, feminist writers sound as though they are mourning for a past creation, for example Sheila Rowbotham interviewing Jean McCrindle on the miners' strike:

Jean: 'There was also the anarchy of the women's meetings . . .'
Sheila: 'We had this problem in the women's movement didn't we?'
Sheila again: 'People now assume that people like us who are veterans of women's liberation are somehow or other these individuals who could always do these things, but we were just thrown up because of a movement . . . And we found our voices because there was a context collectively that we could express ourselves in. That was seventeen, eighteen years ago and we still haven't forgotten – even if our enthusiasm has been knocked about a bit.' (Rowbotham, 1986, p. 123)

Our view in relation to feminist networks and campaigns is not that feminist activism has died or is dying out. Rather, the earlier forms of the women's movement have peeled away as energies have been directed into a somewhat different range of initiatives. The readily identifiable movement in terms of a national gathering which could be assembled, a reckonable number of central campaigns, and a number of well-known feminist figures which characterised the women's movement during the days of the Women's Charter, for example, has passed (Coote and Campbell, 1982). But even at that stage any attempt to assemble an index of feminist activism revealed a series of diverse, fragmented, fluid grass-roots initiatives, responded to by a spectrum of involvement and engagement, and running beyond the reach of those documenting it (see, for example, Collins, *et al.*, 1978). As Walsgrove (1986) has argued, perhaps the current state of mourning for the lost movement on the part of seasoned, well-known feminists contains an element of unfeminist 'ownership' of the cause which was always more apparent than real. Thus, our response to the question of 'What is feminism?' has to proceed on the premise that by now feminist initiatives and the principles on which they are based are so diverse and have passed through so many revisions and changes that the answer lies in both identifying and explicating a number of influential 'feminisms'. As we see it, the main developments that have occurred are in respect of feminist campaigns and networks. The issues now being addressed through feminist action have become ever more diverse. One illustration of this is provided by work on women's health issues which has moved from a preoccupation with initiatives challenging male professional control of measures relating to women's health, to addressing a variety of issues relating to women's physiology, experience of conception and childbearing, mental and physical health, diet and preventative medicine (Ruzek, 1986). Meanwhile, feminist networks and campaigns have obtained institutional resources on a greater scale, as exemplified by the spread of women's centres, and established a presence in a range of social institutions such as the media, education, local government, social work and commercial enterprises. The gains and drawbacks of more formal or entryist forms of activism therefore require evaluation (see Chapters 4 and 5). Direct action through specific campaigns has been and remains necessary to launch consciousness of certain issues and work on them. However, increasingly a more sophisticated understanding has developed on the depth and reach of social change necessary to amount to the creation of gender equality (Delphy, 1984). This is the lesson that earlier campaigns and networks signalled. In so doing, they were pointing to the need to move beyond direct grass-roots action to achieve the aims of that action. The test now of feminist progress is the extent to which this larger political enterprise is being addressed and how feminist initiatives are faring in doing that. This is the context in which we shall be carrying out this analysis of feminist networks and campaigns' contribution to developing a feminist social work practice. The ways in which a more generalised feminist political presence can be achieved will be considered in greater depth in Chapter 6.

THE OBJECTIVES AND ORIGINS OF FEMINIST CAMPAIGNS AND NETWORKS

Despite the varied, fluid and changing nature of feminist activism referred to here, collectively it has certain distinctive features. Its central aim remains that of challenging the social determinants of women's inequality. In this respect, its popular origins have been in keeping with its egalitarian objectives. The tendency has been for women (and sometimes sympathetic men), not necessarily seasoned campaigners or holding a highly developed feminist philosophy, to initiate or participate in groups in the following way. They have encountered problems which confront women in their everyday work and lives and have located the origins of these problems in social relations at large, taking a moral stand on the injustice concerned and attempting to work collectively to eradicate it. This process reflects the way in which the analysis of social problems and preparedness to act on them exists beyond the ranks of the media, professional community work or formal political activity and is accessible to people from all walks of life. The following examples of action on a diverse range of issues illustrate what is involved:

In 1985 the staff and a parent embarked on a project to work at sex stereotypes in children's books at a nursery. This decision was taken as a result of discussion between the staff and some parents. We were concerned about the influence of sex-stereotyping in books and television on children's behaviour. In observing children's play we particularly noticed the preoccupations with aggressive games in boys and language that expressed the stereo-

types that they identified with e.g., 'He-man, Spiderman', etc . . .
We have distributed our project research to all our parents. We
have also informed the local library that we are vetting the
books before handing them out in the nursery. We have become
members of the Letterbox Library Non-Sexist, Non-Racist Children's Book Club. We deliberately display in our book corners,
books which positively represent the insights we have gained.
(Barrett, 1986)

In another sphere, Carpenter (1982) outlines the early stages of the
current feminist women youth worker groups as follows:

Many a meeting was spent with the women youth worker's group
devoting part or most of its time to considering the problems of
an individual member. Invariably the individual problems were
common to most or all of us and were the result of negative and
completely anti-women attitudes and policies. After a few months
of meeting it became apparent to the group that we were going
to have to start campaigning on behalf of other women workers
and of girl's work. (Carpenter, 1982)

The following account comes from a woman married to a miner,
who became active in the local women's co-ordinating group during
the miners' strike 1984 – 85:

though there were some women keen and enthusiastic, it was
hard to get other women to come and involve themselves. Especially when not many of the men seemed to be encouraging the
women's action groups at all. For whatever reason, they had the
attitude that women were alright helping in the strike, as long
as it was 'in the kitchen' work and that sort of thing. But apart
from that attitude, they didn't see what the women could achieve.
I think we proved during the strike that we have been able to
do other things, and we have won a lot of men over to thinking
the same way as we do. But it was a hard struggle and in every
different area the women have been received with a different
response. (Seddon, 1986, p.32)

The proliferation of feminist groups and activities also means
that it is now possible for women to have gained organising

experience in one area of the women's movement before concentrating their efforts on another. But even in these circumstances women do not tend to approach new issue as 'experts'. While they may take a stand on a new issue on the basis of existing experience, they are likely to refine their analysis and strategies in relation to that issue as they work on it. This is illustrated in Caroline Crawford's interviews with women involved in establishing rape crisis centres across the country:

> Rape was identified as a feminist issue within the Women's Liberation Movement . . . detailed understanding of the feminist analysis was acquired by many subjects after they joined the groups . . . As one subject put it, 'yes, I was aware of articles in *Spare Rib* etc and had been involved with the Women's Liberation Movement for a number of years, but I did most of my reading on rape after I joined the centre. (Crawford, 1981, section II, 3)

The objectives embedded in feminist activism which we have been illustrating are also different in one crucial respect from those found in non-feminist women's self-help groups. These groups do not embark on challenging the social determinants of women's inequality. Instead they concentrate on helping women cope with the status quo. A comparison between a non-feminist self-help group and a group embodying feminist objectives working in a similar field illustrates the difference. Parents Anonymous Lifeline is principally run by women volunteers and contacted by women. It exists to offer a voluntary 'first aid' telephone counselling service to parents who feel they might be tempted to batter their children, or who have done so (Muss and McLeod, 1980). Unlike the feminist National Childcare Campaign (NCC) it does not seek to challenge existing assumptions and practices in child-care which consign the bulk of the responsibility to women in isolated under-resourced circumstances. (NCC, 1985). Other comparisons can be made by considering the ways in which incest is being handled by feminists and non-feminists. Feminists have organised primarily around Incest Survivors Groups. The women involved in these groups have usually been abused themselves and can speak to others from their direct experience. They use the skills derived from their experience of sexual abuse to create the space for acquiring confidence and strength, developing their own support networks and securing the freedom to express their needs and requirements in their own terms. In contrast, *Childline*, the campaign set up with the help of TV personality Esther Rantzen to offer abused children a 24-hour telephone counselling service, has created a hierarchy of concerned experts who hear the voices of those who have been abused. In other words, the helper's main concern is to provide their callers with a sympathetic ear. Although a minimal referral service has been incorporated into its activities, *Childline* does not try to organise the abused in any way (BBC, 1986).

As women organise on specific issues the question of what should constitute feminist objectives has been subject to a continuing process of debate and refinement within the woman's movement as discussed in the Introduction (see pp. 2–8). This process is a dialectical one whereby particular issues are brought to the notice of feminists more generally through meetings, workshops, publications and a variety of media. At the same time, efforts are made to clarify the way in which such issues relate to women's position as a whole (McLeod, 1982). The process is characterised by controversy, there being no finally agreed feminist position. Its strength is that the nature of each initiative can be examined in terms of its specific contribution to women's welfare, what it offers to promoting women's welfare more generally, what can be gained from placing it in the context of a feminist perspective, and what a feminist perspective gains from such work. An example of what is involved concerns women experiencing various disabilities. Some of their number have prevailed upon other feminists to acknowledge the insensitivity of feminists to their particular requirements and the importance of meeting them if discrimination on the grounds of disability, in itself antithetical to feminist principles, is not to occur. This issue has begun to be taken up by feminists more generally. Meanwhile, disabled women have also started to articulate the way in which they feel especially vulnerable to the forms of assault that women generally are subject to (Cross, 1984).

Even though the objectives of feminist groups may be set on achieving greater equality for women there are many ways in which pressures to deviate from this can arise. For example, campaigns can face powerful influences moving them towards ameliorating welfare problems on an individual basis rather than continuing with the aim of tackling their root causes. If campaigns succumb to this process they can miss their chance to make their most profound contribution to women's welfare. One way in which such pressure can come about is through the demands of obtaining funding. The experience of one of us in PROS (Programme of the Reform of the Law on Soliciting) was that organisations were prepared to consider offering PROS funds if it transformed itself into a welfare rights cum rescue service for prostitutes. Otherwise it was hard to get money to underwrite our main aims of ending the scapegoating of prostitutes through the current law, securing fairer treatment for women working as prostitutes and encouraging public appreciation of the social origins of prostitution (McLeod, 1982). The desire to meet the establishment halfway in order to get some gains can also threaten to compromise objectives. This situation can result from feelings of powerlessness and fatalism on the part of group members (Selma James quoted in McLeod, 1982).

A further complication involved in maintaining long-term objectives is that problems confronting women immediately on an individual basis are worthy of relief. Therefore one must be deeply convinced of the merits of the contribution of one's long-term objectives to hold to these. This can be particularly difficult when one is a fledgling group with few discernible achievements to one's credit.

Despite their best intentions, feminist networks can also be forced into positions at odds with their main objectives because massive social change is not theirs to command. Through state inaction they can become involved in compensating for deficiencies in state provisions as opposed to obtaining good facilities for women from the state. For example, alongside their positive attributes, refuges for battered women also provide emergency housing very cheaply and for considerable periods of time and thereby lessen pressure on local authority housing departments (Binney *et al.*, 1981). Networks and campaigns can also be reduced to concentrating on defensive strategies because the more profound social changes which will make these irrelevant are such long term propositions. So, for example, the task of challenging male violence with a view to eradicating it may be under way but in the meantime campaigns and networks are still confronted by the need to offer women protection from male violence.

For feminist initiatives to make progress, however, it is not necessary for all the women involved to be committed to common objectives in the same way. In the authors' experience, it is quite usual for women to occupy a range of positions while organising together. Typically, these vary from concentrating on shorter-terms, more instrumental goals, such as bringing about a particular change in the law or establishing a day nursery, to a more general concern with social change in relation to which specific projects are viewed very much as constituent elements. Action which is not self-consciously feminist may also be compatible with feminist objectives in terms of seeking a shift in the distribution of power and resources more in women's favour, as in Wendy Savage's stand as a consultant against the unquestioning employment of medical intervention in childbirth by the medical profession (Jewell, 1986).

### DEVELOPING EGALITARIAN RELATIONS WITHIN FEMINIST NETWORKS AND CAMPAIGNS

In keeping with their egalitarian stance, feminist networks and campaigns have provided women with opportunities for self-fulfil-ment, previously denied them as a result of their subordinate status. There are many testimonies to just how much women have gained from participation, in terms of fun, feelings of well-being and the release and use of previously undeveloped talents (see for example, Mayo, 1977; Curno et al., 1982). Moreover, through feminist campaigns and networks constructed around their specific needs, women have demonstrated that although they may lead isolated lives they need not be confined by the walls of domesticity. The Homeworkers' Campaign, for example, is indicative of feminists' ability to organise fragmented groups of women and give individuals an identity as part of a larger constellation of women (Hopkins, 1982).

While such gains accrue, participation in a feminist group has been at the cost of considerable personal risk and suffering for a large number of women. One common feature of this is that a male partner resents a woman according priority to the demands of her group as opposed to meeting what he sees as his needs or interests (Mayo, 1977; Curno et al., 1982; McLeod 1982). The upshot can be a very difficult dilemma for the woman concerned. Does she put what may be her principal source of emotional and material support at risk? Or does she compromise her own integrity by yielding to such demands and in so doing contribute to perpetuating similarly difficult situations for herself and for other women? This dilemma confronting women is a harsh reminder of the way in which social relations generally are not yet in tune with feminism. Making this point is not to deny that many men are supportive. However, an element of risk or tension may be added to a woman's involvement with a group because she cannot assume her male partner will support her or that she will gain respect from him for standing her ground. The dicey nature of what is at stake is revealed in one woman's account to her Housing Action Group after she had been away from home on a demonstration:

> She grabbed hold of Mike and said, Guess what? he made me a cup of tea when I got home. We did not understand what she was trying to say. Her husband had made her a cup of tea and asked her if she wanted to lie down, when she had thought he was going to beat her up! She was so excited – he had seen her on the News on the TV and had suddenly felt really proud of her (SWAT, 1982, pp. 24 – 5)

Their feminism may also lead women to 'come out' in ways that still attract considerable stigma. Accounts by lesbian women demonstrate some of the personal consequences of this. Two youth workers describe their experiences as follows:

> There are internal conflicts and tensions about coming out to young people and being prepared to talk openly about ourselves. These tensions are about realising the degree to which we as youth workers can be viewed as corrupt, deviant, immoral and even insane ... For one of us, some of the management is supportive of the way she works, but some of our employers would rather we kept these personal details to ourselves. Co-workers can and have been supportive on a personal level, but some are afraid to take that further. Women youth workers in general, whilst respectful, find us threatening and too hard-line. Some youth workers have even made attempts to threaten our jobs because of being open about our lesbianism. (Green, 1982)

The evidence is not systematically available that feminist groups invariably take account of such strains. However, written material on women organising at least displays an awareness of such demands on individuals (Mayo, 1977; Holland, 1984). Documented accounts of feminist groups also indicate that in any event, there is an appreciation of the importance of caring for the welfare of individual members, to guard against undue suffering or unnecessary disadvantage. Descriptions of group members' treatment of each other reflect undertaking understanding of the fact that ordinary life is hard, that we all need help to get through it and that anyone may experience problems that require special attention (McLeod, 1982). This shared understanding makes it possible for feminists to acknowledge that women's prime responsibility for child care and domestic labour demands especially careful attention to arrangements to ensure their freedom to participate in groups. Where women community workers have been working in male-dominated groups they have commented on what a struggle gaining recognition for this still is (Dixon *et al.*, 1982; McLeod and Dominelli, 1982). The need for compensatory training or support is recognised on the basis that this may be required before women engage in activities such as public speaking, which have tended to be a male preserve.

Feminist groups have also sought to foster a co-operative approach within their organisation and there are many examples of this being achieved (Collins *et al.*, 1978). While no administrative measures can guarantee egalitarian practice (see Dixon *et al.*, 1982), this approach centres on treating the responsibility for handling information, tasks and offices as being shared rather than vested in particular individuals or cliques. The most important outcome of this is that groups can come to embody the sort of egalitarian social relations they are seeking to establish more generally and that their members gain experience of these. An example of what this can mean when it is working well is provided in the following account of the Tyneside Rape Crisis Centre:

We are non-hierarchial that is we do not have an executive committee or elect offices, as these functions are shared amongst the members. We also try to pay as much attention to the form and process of our meeting and interactions as we do to the content, trying all the time to be aware of each others feelings, ensuring that all women are involved in decision-making and the tasks of the group. Often those more used to formal structure and hierarchial organisations will query whether feminist principles are compatible with getting things done – but we can say to them that we managed to set up rape crisis service after only a few months of work. (SWAT, 1982, p. 176)

There has been some discussion in the literature on community action about whether women are more inclined towards co-operative efforts than men. The argument runs that this is the case because traditionally women have concentrated on subjugating their immediate needs and desires in the interests of helping others to cope, as opposed to espousing the male model of competitive individualism (Mayo, 1977). Also women as a subject group have needed to combine for self-protection against dominant male power. This line of reasoning is problematic in a number of ways. It runs the risk of positing an almost metaphysical transmission of co-operative skills from woman to woman as a result of their collective past history. It overlooks the fact that men too can work co-operatively and that women do not uniformly behave in this way. Moreover, it disregards the amount of effort required to maintain co-operation in women's groups.

For while co-operation exists, in the context of competitive social relations generally, and women's lack of experience in working collectively with other women, it is only created and maintained by a considerable struggle (Dominelli and Jonsdottir, 1988). Feminist groups are fraught with the practice and notions of hierarchy, class and racism of society at large. Taking these in turn, hierarchy is insidious because it can seem so natural – individually and collectively it can be perpetuated without a thought. Jenny Finch, a community worker active in organising a women's health group describes this occurring as she and other members endeavoured to work along non-hierarchical lines:

One example concerned the agenda which I had started in order that the group could share in full awareness of what we needed to be doing. It was not until a visitor to the group pointed it out that I realised that I was continuing to exercise power through looking after the agenda while we could have been moving to rotating it. (Finch, 1982, p. 133)

Personality clashes which may seem inevitable can also represent or mask hierarchial struggles on the basis of an individual's determination 'not to be dictated to' or alternatively to wield the sort of power that is appropriately 'theirs'.

A further problem is posed when a campaign or network started and previously run by volunteers acquires funds for the post of paid organiser or co-ordinator. This is a fairly common pattern among feminist groups. There may be gains in terms of the impact the campaign makes. However, information, expertise and the role of representative tend to be concentrated in the hands of the paid worker and thereby cause power to be concentrated in her hands. There is then the danger that other participants can assume that someone is doing the work on their behalf when this should not be the case; alternatively, suspicions arise that collective interests are not being represented. As a result, unpaid volunteers can feel distanced, and if their involvement declines the paid worker can feel unsupported. The sad irony of such circumstances is that these struggles can weaken a campaign at a point when it has finally achieved considerable support. This particular dilemma has not received a lot of attention in print but there is now some work being done on it. For example, the Tyneside Rape Crisis Centre Collective referred to earlier has argued that it is important to recognise this problem when trying to work as a group and that there is a need to experiment with ways of better integrating the efforts of paid and unpaid workers. They have tried in turn a worker's support group composed of members of the collective and a pairing arrangement whereby the worker may choose one member of the collective to offer them support (Tyneside Rape Crisis Centre Collective, 1982).

Within feminist groups even a 'feminist' stance can be adopted in such a way that it alienates women by making them feel rejected as inferior. The situation is complicated by the stereotyped view, purveyed through the media, of feminists as strident and dismissive (Coote and Campbell, 1982). This may make some women wary, or they overreact to unintended insults. Even if this does not keep them out of feminist groups it may cause them to withdraw very readily when faced with a quite minor rebuff. It is difficult to know the number of women lost to feminist action through feelings of rejection but it is important to guard against this process occurring because it is hurtful and antithetical to ideas of equality. A cameo from our own experience illustrates what it can mean. In 1976, one of us was involved in developing the Birmingham Equal

Opportunities Action Group to publicise rights opened to women through the recent equal pay and sex discrimination legislation and to encourage women locally to take action to assert those rights. At an early meeting the subject of fundraising had to be dealt with. One member, a housewife, suggested that women could run coffee mornings for us. This was treated with derision. Angry and hurt, she retorted, 'You don't know what the world is like', and didn't come to the group again.

If hierarchy is present in feminist groups, so is class. Middle-class women have tended to initiate the most extensive feminist campaigns and networks such as National Women's Aid Federation, National Abortion Campaign, women's health groups, rape crisis centres, and women's therapy groups (Coote and Campbell, 1982). They also constitute the majority of women concerned with organising within them. Most paid community workers engaged in building feminist groups are middle-class. Where groups offer services it tends to be middle-class women rather than working-class women who are ministering to others (Hanmer, 1977). On top of this, some working-class women have argued that it has been middle-class women's ability to define what activities are encompassed by the women's movement through their greater access to the media and publishing enterprises that has downplayed the contribution of working-class women that does exist. They maintain that working-class women have been organising around women's interests and in large numbers, but they have done so through industrial action and other activities related to workplace and housing issues because these concerns rather than those of more immediate interest to middle-class women, for example control over their fertility and sexuality, are more significant in their day-to-day lives (Packwood, 1983). Therefore, it is possible to argue that in these respects the women's movement, if not necessarily *reinforcing* existing class/power divisions, is at least *replicating* them.

However, while class discrimination does operate within feminist networks and campaigns (Barker, 1986) this is being equalised in several ways. In the main, the model upon which middle-class women are basing their actions is one of shared experience and knowledge. The idea is that the women involved in a feminist group or initiative will have experienced, in some form or degree, being oppressed as a woman in a patriarchal society. Therefore, they will all have some understanding of problems confronting other women but can also learn from them, be in sympathy with them and in helping them will help to ease the yoke on all women (Donnelly, 1986). Such an approach is far removed ideologically from the one which has dominated women's activities in conventional social work's approach to women. Here, the traditional relationship between the helper and the helped is based on the hierarchical assumption that women clients need help because they are in some way inferior and that women workers can offer help because of their superior qualities – be they knowledge, understanding, well-integrated personalities or a combination of all three (Wilson, 1977). As most social workers are middle-class and most clients working-class this working assumption tends to reinforce ideas of class superiority.

Of course not all middle-class women at all times act in an egalitarian way in feminist groups: the true test of such an approach is not middle-class intentions either but working-class women's experience and perception of what is happening (Barker, 1986). Unfortunately, working-class women's reactions to what is on offer is sparsely documented. But, even when it is on record that working-class women have experienced some dissolution of class divisions, an awareness of them though fading into the background remains. The following account of working-class women's experience in a battered women's refuge indicates the complexities of the issues under discussion:

> Anne said, 'I don't think you need a warden, someone doling out pills, to me that is a warden. It's got to be a person they class as a friend, like Hilary, they'll sit in the front room and they'll have a laugh and a talk with her, and they are stunned when they find out she is a social worker. That puts a barrier. If they don't know about that barrier until they have made a relationship, O.K., then she's not a social worker. She's Hilary. (Pahl, 1978, pp. 54 – 5)

Although the relationship between working-class women and middle-class women is problematic in the ways outlined above, what is also clear is that middle-class women are putting their resources at the disposal of feminist groups in a way that enhances the organising potential of working-class women, thereby equalising power within the group (Mayo, 1977; Curno et al., 1982). Claire

Torkington's account of the efforts of a community work student in Coventry's Women's Right to Income group, to secure a better deal for women claimants, provides an example of this process:

> I was able to draw on support from other students for the group, e.g., in the staffing of the crèche. Transport was another area of help I was able to offer as a means of keeping the group together. Women on supplementary benefit cannot afford to have a telephone nor can they afford bus fares. Access to transport was useful in informing members of the group of last minute plans or transporting the women and display materials etc to conferences ... One area where myself and the welfare rights worker attached to the group had to take a prominent role was in situations where it was dangerous for the women to be acknowledged as members of the group ... My address and telephone number was used for contact purposes in order to decrease these risks. (Torkington, 1981, pp. 54 – 5).

In small ways such work counterbalances the inequitable distribution of resources in society more generally. Therefore it needs to be maintained not only on ideological grounds, but also on practical ones. Telephones, cars, cash, contracts, greater leisure and access to office facilities are not suddenly going to flower among working-class women participants. Therefore middle-class women may need to continue to underwrite campaigns or networks for lengthy periods of time if these are not to falter or collapse for lack of such resources.

Feminist networks and campaigns also offer working-class women the opportunity to represent the interests of other women in a way that is customarily the preserve of the middle-class. As this happens it seems to reflect women's belief in the value of 'the cause' and faith in the strength of the group. The following account concerns the connection between working-class women's participation in a local women's group and an Anti-Road Campaign:

> Perhaps most significantly on the estate itself, the Womens's Group has provided the impetus and organisation behind the Braunstone Anti-Road Campaign: although the campaign was conceived of separately, it went through the Women's Group to become a stronger force. The first form of direct action to protest against the proposed construction through Braunstone of the final

stage of the Western District Distributor Road was undertaken by a small group of women who visited County Hall to make an unannounced entrance into, and brief occupation of the office of the Director of Planning and Transportation . . . (Cathy) '. . . we decided we wanted to speak to the man at the top so we literally forced our way into his office – and it was so exciting. It really gave everybody a real buzz because everyone felt they were in control, they were actually doing everything and they were standing up to this faceless authority'. (Donnelly, 1986, p. 32.)

We would argue that feminist networks have also become a medium for establishing recognition of working-class women's efforts in grassroots organising to further women's equality, whether or not such efforts style themselves feminist. Only through complete disregard for recorded material could working class women's activ-ism in a whole range of settings ranging from tenants' campaigns to workers' co-operatives to trade union disputes to the arts now be overlooked (Packwood, 1983; Curno et al., 1982). This develop-ment is important in two ways. First, it should encourage middle-class women to approach organising with their working-class sisters on the assumption that both have a capacity for organising which demands respect. Second, as means are found of transmitting this knowledge back to working-class women it may increase their confidence in their own abilities to organise and not to let the terrain be defined by middle-class women and their activities.

As feminists have come to pay increasing attention to class divisions as they organise, gradually more attention is being paid to racism as an issue in its own right rather than one submerged within other forms of oppression. Until recently, white feminists have paid little attention either to the way in which sexism and racism interact to compound women's disadvantage, or to the possibility that racism may present a heavier burden than sexism. It is as though the invisibility of women as a group experiencing distinct social problems which characterised social analysis prior to the advent of the women's movement has been paralleled within that movement by the invisibility of black women. This situation is changing as white feminists have begun to acknowledge that black women have been organising collectively to cater for their specific interests, and have begun to recognise that black women have been organising around workplace issues for some time. In

Britain, this has included taking industrial action in a number of disputes which have questioned the stereotypes that white trade unionists have about black women and their docility at the workplace, for example, Imperial Typewriters, Mansfield Hosiery, Chix, Kigass, and so on. This also indicates the significance of class as it affects black women. But the acknowledgement of black women's specific position has come about as a result of black feminists highlighting the racism located within the feminist movement (Carby, 1982). Although now defunct, the Organisation of Women of African and Asian Descent (OWAAD) represented black women's attempts to overcome racial divisions perpetuated through racism by enabling black women to challenge racist stereotypes and divisions in their midst and come together collectively to improve their position both within the black community and the white society in which they live (Bryan *et al.*, 1985). Whilst black women occupy a contradictory position in relation to white women because they have to find ways of fighting gender oppression within their own community at the same time as they have to maintain their ties with black men rather than with white women to fight racial oppression, OWAAD has had a significant impact on white feminists who have wished to fight their own racism. OWAAD's work has challenged racist assumptions held by well-meaning white feminists as well as those dear to the racist right wing fringe in the National Front. Foremost amongst these are the assumed passivity of Asian women; the pathologising of the black family; white arrogance in assuming they know which changes are appropriate for the black community; and the sexual abuse of black women by white men.

Black women's writings have also highlighted racist interpretations of historical events which have ignored black people's contributions to major social events. By making their struggles visible, black women have sought to keep their liberty and dignity, and to prevent the exploitation of their labour power by white men and women (Davis, 1981; Hooks, 1981). Black women authors have also exposed the specific nature of the quadruple oppression of race, gender, class and sexual orientation which affects black lesbian women (Parmar, 1982).

Black women's efforts are being logged within the women's movement (Curno *et al.*, 1982; Carby, 1982; Mama, 1984; Parmar, 1982). Moreover, the importance of race as an issue is being reflected in the policy of a number of campaigns and networks. The National Child Care Campaign (NCC) for example is specifically setting out to combat racism as an integral part of their campaign platform and appointing black workers to facilitate this (NCC, 1983).

Feminist youth workers are also making racism awareness training an inherent part of their work (Carpenter, 1982). An additional feature of fighting their own racism entails highlighting the lack of youth facilities for Asian girls, and ensuring that resources are specifically set aside for their use.

Although these activities indicate that white feminists are beginning to take seriously black women's criticisms of their racism, the matter remains problematic. Feminists have still to work out the point at which black and white women come together to organise collectively on an equal basis for their mutual benefit. An appreciation of the international nature of women's struggles in terms of common problems experienced by women, and differences in kind and degree, has not been prominent within the women's movement in Britain (Jayawardna, 1986; El Saadawi, 1979). Nevertheless, there have been notable exceptions, such as campaigns developed by feminists which have published gross abuse of the welfare of women and children in the Third World and sought to bring pressure to bear on this, for example, by work on the dangers to infant life and health of the promotion and sale of dried milk for babies (Doyal, 1983). Support for black feminists' work on the agonies inflicted by the practice of female circumcision (McLean, 1980) has brought these problems to the notice of the general public, not merely to other feminists. In addition, the advent of the Women's Peace Movement has brought a greater understanding of the international scale of social problems and their interconnecting nature. Women active in it have come to appreciate and emphasise that relinquishing an insular approach to social problems is essential to grasping the issues involved. Bel Mooney, one of the contributors to a collection of articles emanating from the Women's Peace Movement, comments on how many women react with numbness to how the use of nuclear weapons has affected Japan and what nuclear war would mean in the future:

I would walk from house to house and tell Mrs Smith and Mrs Jones that unless they learn to be angered for the sake of Mrs

Yamasaki and Mrs Tomoyasu, and to weep for those who still weep, then there is more and more likelihood that it will happen and to their own daughters, their own sons. (Mooney in Thompson, 1983, p 7)

Women involved in the Greenham Women's Peace Movement have also supported women in other parts of the world in establishing Women's Peace Camps, for example at Comiso in Italy and Keflavik in Iceland. In doing so, they have offered each other psychological support through personal interaction and financial aid, often through the use of imaginative schemes. For example, articles in the feminist press urged women from all parts of the world to each buy one square metre of land for the women protesting around the American army base in Comiso so that they could oppose the transport of nuclear arms to and from the base. Women using their joint resources in this way enabled the Comiso Peace Camp to be established. Thus in some respects sisterhood has been able to cross international boundaries and offer a more sustained challenge to the status quo regarding arms agreements and military alliances (Dominelli, 1986a).

THE IMPACT OF FEMINIST CAMPAIGNS AND NETWORKS ON SOCIETY AT LARGE

In addition to the extent to which they have been the locations and incubators for egalitarian relations, feminist networks and campaigns have produced a range of distinct achievements for women's welfare generally. Besides the benefits accruing from the identification of social problems described in Chapter 1, in terms of Britain alone, they have created material and personal resources which by now have contributed to the well being of at least hundreds of thousands of women. These include refuges, rape crisis centres, facilities for health care, publishing, broadcasting, job diversification and childcare (for example, Collins *et al.*, 1978; Coote and Campbell, 1982; Oakley, 1981; Curno *et al.*, 1982; Eichenbaum and Orbach, 1984; Webster, 1984; Dale and Foster 1986; David and New, 1985). They have also secured or resisted changes in the law, whatever their shortcomings, which have brought relief to thousands of women, for example, through the Domestic Violence

Act 1976 and Housing (Homeless Persons) Act 1977, the abolition
of imprisonment under the Street Offences Act 1959 in the Criminal
Justice Act of 1982, and blocking further dismemberment of the
1967 Abortion Act.

As campaigns and networks have grown, so women who have
become involved but not necessarily remained active within them
have gained a sense of encouragement, purposefulness, confidence
and freedom from subordination from each other that it is impossible to quantify, but which radiates through accounts as discussed
earlier (see pp. 46-50, 64). Hard evidence is difficult to obtain, but
we would also suggest that an equally large number of women have
gained encouragement in combating their individual subordination
as a result of personal contact from women themselves, encouraged
by their own participation in feminist activism. The booming sales
of feminist books – frequently derived from campaigning initiatives
or the work of feminist networks and one of the few growth areas
in publishing – also testifies to the extent to which women's interest
in securing a more egalitarian existence has been aroused.

Through feminist networks and campaigns women have become
their own representatives concerning their interests in an important
range of issues dealt with by powerful state institutions. This does
not necessarily make a revolutionary impact on the treatment
women receive in relation to the issues in question, but it makes it
less easy for action or inaction to be legitimated on the basis of
distorted accounts. It also offers encouragement to other women to
get their point of view across to make sure it is listened to, and also
for something to be done about it. In this way, the point of view
of battered women and prostitutes has been put to Parliament; the
views of raped women to the police; of women workers to unions;
and women residents to local authorities.

Feminist campaigns and networks are also still interacting with
each other to extend their strategic range. Until the advent of the
feminist Women's Peace Movement, the women's movement had
managed to problematise male violence against women but that
still begged several questions relating to male violence more generally: How problematic was male violence against men? What was
the relationship of male violence against women and men to
patriarchal social relations? Should violence be met with violence?
The logic of the women's peace camps has engaged with all these
questions and set out a possible way forward. Their insistence that

women should protest on their own against nuclear weapons because otherwise the involvement of men would inevitably lead to violence has the following implications: that no form of violence is legitimate, that is, that violence should be met by non-violence and that patriarchical relations, that is men determining events, inevitably gives rise to violence against men and children as well as women and on these grounds should be eradicated (Feminism and Non-Violence Study Group, 1983; Cook and Kirk, 1983; Dominelli, 1986a). It remains to be seen whether other feminists accept the idea of patriarchy as the fountainhead of violence to men, women and children; that male violence to men and children should be their concern and that feminists should be pacifists (Feminism and Non-Violence Study Group, 1983).

The question remains of the impact to date of feminist campaigns and networks on the welfare of men and children. As indicated in the Introduction, we have great sympathy with autonomous women-only forms of organising, whilst not adopting a radical feminist perspective on separatism. We are both of the opinion that at specific historical junctures and in relation to particular issues it is right for women to organise unilaterally and to withdraw from men. As a grander, all inclusive strategy, however, we consider that separatism holds the danger of seeking to subordinate concern for the welfare of men and male children. This is anathema to feminism, whose origins lie in the refusal to acquiesce to any form of subordination. We also suggest that the bogey is patriarchal social relations and not necessarily men themselves, though it may be very difficult to separate the two at times. Along these lines, therefore, we regard it as appropriate to assess the contribution feminist networks and campaigns have made to men's welfare.

Inasmuch as women have equalised their position with men's as discussed in this and other sections of the book, we would see that as a gain for men's welfare. It means that men do not have so great an opportunity to dominate – a dehumanising activity at best for all concerned (Freire, 1976). Beyond this, feminist networks and campaigns have produced subtle improvements in men's welfare, though it is hard to deduce their extent. The women's movement as a whole has encouraged man to reflect on the way and degree to which they too are trapped and oppressed by gender relations. Accordingly, men have met together in consciousness-raising groups and examined the ways in which male dominance in society leads them to oppress women and in turn to experience distorting and inhibiting social relations (Achilles Heel, 1983; Tolson 1977; Bowl, 1985). In Men Against Sexism groups, small groups of men have tried to redress the exploitation of women in society by undertaking supportive activities usually expected of women, for example, by undertaking child-care. Accordingly, they have run crêches to offer support to women who are holding workshops, conferences, day schools and public meetings (Men Against Sexism Group in Birmingham, 1983). Such activities are not dramatic and the impression is that they involve perhaps hundreds of men at the most across Britain. Nevertheless, our experience is that as a side-product they are supportive to the development of feminism as they demonstrate that there is goodwill and practical assistance available from men to help feminists to realise their aims, and that even to a limited degree, the feminist message is getting across.

It is very difficult to detect whether men have learnt to treat each other better, that is less hierarchically, as a result of feminist networks and campaigns, although there is some evidence that certain groups of men have been trying to do so (Tolson, 1977; Festau, 1975; Achilles Heel, 1983). It feels like a rather strange question to pose. This reveals in turn the strength of the idea that men's way of doing things is superior. How could men in dealing with each other have anything to learn from women? Nevertheless, whether out of positive choice or painful necessity created by women's changing roles, men are beginning to question seriously the price of being thought superior (see for example, Festau, 1975). It is not a change often recognised by the popular media. Women as sex objects and the culturally masculine concern with violence and confrontation still make better copy. But this development is vital. We would argue that the goals of feminism cannot be achieved without a humanisation of *both* gender roles.

It is impossible to calculate how many men who never feature in public life or in a named group have made a distinct effort to support feminist activities either directly or through assisting women who are involved. It is also difficult to know their motives – love for a particular women, general humanitarianism, a desire to atone for what men have done, modishness, or the conviction that feminist objectives are correct? Reviewing our experience in non-separatist campaigns suggest that men offer considerable 'back room' support, for example, making facilities available, helping to raise funds, babysitting, and so on. Meanwhile it is quite possible for them to lead sexist lives in many other respects, for example by ignoring the impact of sexism in their personal lives and relationships, by treating women as sex objects, or by expecting women to provide them with services. They may also not be active in their own sphere of influence in ending general features of women's disadvantage such as comparatively low pay.

As women have spoken out about various issues, so it becomes easier to identify the degree of oppression that men experience in various ways, and easier for men to speak out about it. Also, men are beginning to voice the opinion that not only is the current sexist division of labour in child-care unfair to women and children, it also deprives men of contact with their children and brings in its wake emotional stultification and anguish for them (Hearn, 1973). The understanding that has gained ground during the life of the women's movement – that existing conventional gender relations are corrosive of male sexuality as well as female sexuality – has led some men to register the importance to them of alternatives to stereotyped 'macho' forms of sexual relations (McLeod, 1982; Reynaud, 1983). Enforced cuts in working hours as well as in jobs themselves have accelerated as a result of the current recession. But apart from this, feminist groups organising for more flexible working arrangements to enable women to participate in the labour market but not to the exclusion of unwaged activities that are important to them, have encouraged some men to seek similar flexibility on a voluntary basis for themselves as a departure from careerist norms (Bell, 1983).

Children have gained various benefits as a result of feminist networks and campaigns. Already, together with their mothers, they are offered an escape route from domestic violence, through the existence of refuges, although the conditions are usually not very comfortable (Binney *et al.*, 1981). They are also offered the experience of less sexist upbringing, care and education in numerous family, group and institutional settings, although this could not be called universal or widespread as yet (Coote and Campbell, 1982; David and New, 1985). Their mothers are in many cases less traumatised, less depressed, slightly better-off and more self-fulfilled as a result of feminist initiatives on rape, women's therapy, women's income and the arts. They are therefore likely to have a less negative impact on their children. As discussed earlier some slight gains have been made in developing less sexist paternal care and involvement in child-rearing.

In the longer term, girls will not have to start where their mothers did in terms of establishing the need for feminism and elaborating its concerns and strategies – if the positions reached to date alone are held. Nor will boys have to learn all that their fathers have had to in appreciating women's inequality. Work on bringing up male children in a non-sexist way in terms of immediate parental involvement remains very undeveloped, however (Arcana, 1983).

As yet neither feminist campaigns nor networks have grappled with one blind spot in women's treatment of children (Gordon, 1986); that is their routine use of violence towards them in the course of everyday child-care (Newson and Newson, 1976). The possible reasons for this and the desirability of developing such work on the part of feminists are analysed in detail in Chapter 3. Through rape crisis centres, incest survivors' groups and feminist networks more generally, attention has, however, been paid to the high incidence and universal nature of child sexual abuse. Its origins have been located as lying in the way in which social relations have been constructed and emphasis has been placed on the primacy accorded to the satisfaction of men's sexual urges, as a reflection of patriarchal domination (Ward, 1984; Dominelli, 1986). At present, however, public debate and response to incest is dominated by the 'child protection' school of thought. While publicising the extent of the problem, it lays the emphasis on 'victim self-protection' through such ventures as *Childline* and *Say No* campaigns (see, for example, Elliott, 1985; and see Jones (1986) for a critique). It proceeds from the premise that it is still possible to reintegrate the child into the family and safeguard its welfare, while sidestepping the conflict of interests between children and fathers which is rooted in patriarchy (Jones, 1986).

While feminist initiatives may be bringing both short-term and longer-term benefits to children, at the same time women's participation in feminist action has made demands on their children. They may experience the weight of stigma attaching to their mother 'coming out' as a feminist, as in the following description of local reactions to a child being brought up by her mother while living with a group of other women:

'We live in a fairly respectable area, so most of the other children come from very conventional families. Sarah had a birthday party and when we invited one little boy, whom she really likes, his mother said, 'Oh! she must come to Edward's party next week'. But when they came here I noticed the parents looking round, they were obviously aware that something was afoot. And Sarah never got invited to Edward's party. I felt really sorry for her. (Collins *et al.*, 1978 p. 176)

The additional load or overload of activism on top of a full-time job, on top of motherhood, at the very least may make for less attention: for example, attending crêches on top of a full week at school or nursery may be quite demanding on a child, but putting children in them may be only the way in which women can be freed to attend meetings.

## CONSOLIDATING THE WORK OF FEMINIST CAMPAIGNS AND NETWORKS

Feminist campaigns and networks may have made an important impact on society at large, as we have shown. However, as they have done so, the campaigns have also demonstrated that their work needs to be amplified by other forms of social change if an enduring contribution to welfare is to be made. These forms of social change include changes in attitudes and personal behaviour, in central and local state policy, and in party political and union activity. Detailed discussion of what is entailed follows in subsequent chapters. However, the specific point can be illustrated here by taking in turn examples of the interrelation of feminist campaigns and networks with these different spheres of action.

Perhaps the clearest example of the scale of work that remains to be done in terms of changes in attitude and personal behaviour is provided by the issue of domestic violence. Women now have a sanctuary in the face of domestic violence and greater help with re-establishing themselves independently, and National Women's Aid Federation has been instrumental in creating both. Nevertheless, the phenomenon of domestic violence is still rife and there remains plenty of evidence that not only is such violence still regarded as legitimate by large numbers of men who beat their wives (Dobash and Dobash, 1980), but also that it is condoned by large numbers of the population working in such institutions as the police, medicine, the law and welfare agencies, who are charged with protecting or enhancing the personal welfare of women as well as men (Pahl 1985). In these circumstances it is hard to imagine the practice of domestic violence disappearing, until it becomes generally unthinkable to engage in it.

The extent to which local and central government policy needs to complement feminist campaigns' and networks' efforts in order to establish their objectives is well demonstrated in the case of the National Childcare Campaign. This has managed to establish and maintain a network of groups around the country, to attract government funding, to place its stamp on Labour Party policy for day care, and to sustain coverage nationally in the media for the sort of day care it would like to see established (NCC, 1985). The sort of child-care the NCC envisages as a right is provision for children aged 0 to 5 flexible in terms of availability and times of opening, but compatible with working hours, combining education and care provided by the state with parental involvement and management. This would not necessarily be based on nurseries but would have decent physical conditions and resources for children and staff as a prerequisite. The regimes involved should aim to eradicate sexism and racism.

This approach would mean the following major changes in the current situation: local authorities would need to accept responsibility for universal day care provisions as opposed to catering for a tiny percentage of children as 'priority' cases maintaining the low cost exploitative options of childminders and that responsibility would extend to children after school hours and during school holidays. At a national level it might require a merger of responsibility for child-care into one Ministry. It would without question require a substantial increase in the budget made available and the acknowledgement of a state of affairs previously managed only by the government in wartime – that the need for state-funded day care provisions for working parents is axiomatic (Riley, 1983).

Political parties of any persuasion still occupy a concessionary position in relation to the women's movement, its campaigns and networks. Whereas the Labour Party, for example, has a programme in relation to women's situation which is in tune with feminist demands (Labour Party, 1984) no party is fully committed to implementing policies that will unambiguously underwrite equality for women. The current situation relating to provisions for abortion illustrated the unremitting struggle this entails. All main parties currently acquiesce in the maintenance of provisions for abortion but none have legitimated abortion as a woman's right. Therefore it remains ground to be fought over repeatedly by feminists and their supporters, rather than ground that can be counted as securely won through parliament. Amongst the other forms of social change required to underwrite the gains of feminist campaigns and networks is therefore a powerful feminist presence in party politics.

Campaigns to equalise women's income and employment opportunities have demonstrated, (LWLC, London Women's Liberation Campaign, 1979) that union support is essential to achieve better conditions, but also that although progress has been made in putting women's achievements on the agenda, trade union activity remains sufficiently unreflective of woman's welfare for it to be regarded as a zone still to be won over (Coote, 1980).

Feminist campaigns and networks should therefore be regarded as an important means of intervention to promote women's, children's and men's welfare. They both originated and sustained valuable initiatives and the egalitarian intent of their objectives and organisational forms have been an integral part of this. Nevertheless, as they have emerged as a cornerstone of feminist social work practice, so their own work has demonstrated that it requires the establishment of a feminist presence in a range of social spheres to make it irreversible.

# 3
# A Feminist Approach to Emotional Welfare: The Contribution of Feminist Therapy and Counselling

As the rest of this book demonstrates, and as will be reflected in this chapter, feminists see no divide between material and political considerations and women's emotional welfare. The quality of child-care, educational, health, workplace, financial and housing provisions for women have all been documented as having a critical bearing on their emotional health and self-esteem (see, respectively, David and New, 1985; Stanworth, 1983; Oakley, 1981; Marshall, 1984; Barrett and McIntosh, 1982; Binney *et al.*, 1981). At the same time, as discussed in Chapter 2, feminist initiatives not primarily addressing emotional concerns have both engendered positive emotional experiences and encouraged women to expect and seek greater emotional fulfillment. In addition, through the growth of feminist therapy and feminist writings on psychology and emotional experience, a theory and practice *specifically* addressing the issue of women's emotional welfare has been developed with beneficial consequences for women's well-being and significant implications for the well-being of children and men too. The main features of this work are that the social origins of women's emotional suffering have begun to be delineated, thus reducing the labelling of women individually, by themselves and others, as inadequate. The pivotal point of women's psychology has been relocated, thereby endorsing their capacity for emotional fulfilment. Feminist practitioners have also engaged with those they are counselling on a more egalitarian basis by explicitly endorsing the commonality of the problems women are experiencing, thus lessening the stigma of being coun-

76

selled. The indications are that the influence of such work has already begun to spread beyond feminist therapy centres themselves into statutory and community work practice (see, for example, Hale, 1984; Donnelly, 1986) and to a degree into the work of women counsellors more generally (Ernst and Maguire, 1987). It has also excited popular interest directly through the media of print and television (Orbach, 1982).

Feminist therapy and feminist writings on psychology and emotional experience have led to and encouraged other forms of action catering for women's emotional welfare; these we also discuss below. Feminist work in this field has given recognition to what women can gain emotionally from relationships with other women, as opposed to treating these as necessarily inferior experiences when compared to emotional relationships with men. Feminists have exposed how the institution of romantic love as it currently exists is problematic to women's emotional well-being and begun the exploration of alternative forms of love more conducive to women's welfare. They have also encouraged men to begin to explore for themselves the ways in which their emotional experiences have been overlaid and distorted by gender stereotypes, to their emotional detriment as well as that of women and children. And finally, feminists have begun to map out how children are the emotional victims of gender inequality and how this may be countered.

We are aware of the fact that our account focuses primarily on white women and their experiences in both the therapeutic relationship and in their lives more generally. While we feel it is not appropriate for us as white women to speak on behalf of or for black women, it is imperative that we comment on the 'anglocentric perspective' evident in much of the theory and practice of feminist therapy at this point. (The term 'anglocentric perspective' was coined by the White Collective for Anti-Racist Social Work which was founded by one of the authors. A discussion of the term is contained in *Anti-Racist Social Work* by Dominelli (1988, Macmillan).) We are quite clear that whilst the life experiences of both black and white women may have some common threads, they are rooted in *differences* (Carby, 1982; Lorde, 1984) and that this holds different implications for the ways in which, and the terms on which, the personal and emotional development of black women and white women takes place. In the remainder of the chapter we shall seek to offer some account of this.

## A THEORY AND PRACTICE FOR WOMEN'S EMOTIONAL WELL-BEING

The central characteristic of feminist therapy is to relocate what has previously been seen as personal, emotional failure into the realms of experience common to other women and to explore the degree to which this is socially determined. Through the lessons derived from feminist therapy, feminists have demonstrated the unacceptability of the subordination of women's emotional well-being. Moreover, they have revealed that it can and should be resisted and that women both legitimately seek their own happiness and support each other while they do so. This then becomes the focus of their attention and as a result women's preoccupation with self-denigration and self-hatred is lessened. Instead, it becomes more appropriate to ask why and how women generally have come to have low self-esteem in various respects and what help they can offer each other with this. To illustrate what is involved, the end of the matter is no longer, 'It's my face', 'my figure', 'my lack of confidence', 'my inability to cope', 'my jealousy' that is so wrong. The question becomes *why* it is that women are so preoccupied with their physical appearance, their feelings of inferiority and 'possessing' and 'being possessed' by men, and what they can do about it (Eichenbaum and Orbach, 1982, 1984).

As the work of feminist therapists and women's therapy centres has developed, so the central focus of women's psychological development has been redefined away from hinging on men's and towards having an importance and capacity for self-fulfilment in its own right. This has happened through women sharing with therapists and other women their *actual* experience of parental love, the feelings they have towards themselves, and the reality of their experience of central adult relationships (Baker-Miller, 1978; Eichenbaum and Orbach, 1982, 1984; Ernst and Maguire, 1987). What has become apparent through this activity is that women's sexual and emotional development is far from being inevitably subordinate to that of others, as the Freudian paradigm which still dominates psycho-sexual psychology suggests:

Quite different are the effects of the castration complex in the female. She acknowledges the fact of her castration and with it, too, the superiority of the male and her own inferiority; but she rebels against this unwelcome state of affairs. From this divided attitude three lines of development open up. The first leads to a general revulsion from sexuality. The little girl, frightened by the comparison with boys, grows dissatisfied with her clitoris, and gives up her phallic activity and with it her sexuality in general as well as a good part of her masculinity in other fields. The second line leads her to cling with defiant self-assertiveness to her threatened masculinity. To an incredibly late age she clings to the hope of getting a penis some time. That hope becomes her life's aim; and the fantasy of being a man in spite of everything often persists as a formative factor over long periods. This 'masculinity complex' in women can also result in a manifest homosexual choice of object. Only if her development follows the third, very circuitous, path does she reach the final normal female attitude, in which she takes her father as her object and so finds her way to the feminine form of the Oedipus complex. (Freud, 1977, p. 376)

Women's accounts in feminist therapy indicate that the situation of having their experience denigrated and measured according to the male yardstick is not an inalienable feature of womanhood but that it has been forced on women through the social construction of their role. Their personal development has been wrenched out of true at the price of their personal happiness. This has been and is still being done in the name of maintaining male dominance and as the outcome of dominance and subordination characterising interpersonal as much as public relations. Drawing on the accounts of the experience of women coming to a women's therapy centre. Louise Eichenbaum and Susie Orbach write:

The first psychological demand that follows from a woman's social role is that she must defer to others, follow their lead, articulate her needs only in relation to theirs . . . As a result of this social requirement, women come to believe that they are not important in themselves. Women come to feel that they are unworthy, undeserving and unentitled. Women are frequently self-deprecating and hesitant about their own initiatives. They feel reluctant to speak for themselves, to voice their own thoughts and ideas, to act on their own behalf. Being pushed to defer to others means that they come to undervalue and feel insecure about themselves, their wants and their opinions. (Eichenbaum and Orbach, 1982 p. 29)

In addition to such evidence, the lie to this state of deference being the appropriate or natural state for women is given in several ways. Once the possibility of such emotional servility being incongruous with women's emotional well-being was legitimated through the development of the women's movement and in particular through the establishment of women's therapy, increasing numbers of women have pinpointed this incongruity as a prime source of personal unhappiness, have struggled against it and broken through to a new emotional serenity. There is testimony to this in text after text emanating from the contemporary women's movement since its earliest days (see Collins *et al.*, 1978; Brittan and Maynard, 1984; Curno *et al.*, 1982; Cartledge and Ryan, 1983; Ernst and Goodison, 1981). This is not to imply that women's lives are problem-free once the issue of their emotional subordination is broached, nor that the work entailed is easy or swiftly carried out (Lorde, 1984). Evidence from writings addressing the processes involved indicate that it is painstaking, the gains are vulnerable and that is tackling but one dimension of women's subordination (Eichenbaum and Orbach, 1984; Ernst and Goodison, 1981).

The argument that many are happy with lives devoted to the care of others despite the detrimental effect on their emotional needs is also ever-present (Howell and Bayes, 1981). By implication it suggests that those seeking the insights of feminist therapy are simply a modish, selfish or neurotic fringe. But the case against this position now amounts to the burden of proof falling on the opponents of feminist therapy. It can no longer be assumed that the characteristic subordinate role women occupy in their personal lives is a happy one or benign in its impact on their emotional well-being. If one adds together the emotional burden being carried by women represented by the numbers of women who have 'come out' emotionally since the early days of the women's movement and those who are contacting women's therapy centres in a steady stream, we have the factual evidence challenging this claim. What their version life experiences has revealed is the misery women endure, and the pathetic responses society has made towards meeting their psychological needs. The unacknowledged nature of their plight and its extensive nature is further reflected in the far higher incidence of clinical depression amongst women than among men (Nairne and Smith, 1984) and the plague of tranquilliser dependency among women (Howell and Bayes, 1981). Central features of their predicament have been the by now well-documented emotional cost to women of enduring violence in marriage (Binney *et al.*, 1981; Andrews, 1982) and the impact of carrying the prime responsibility for the care of the young and of dependent elders (David and New, 1985; Finch and Groves, 1983). Where women are content with deferring to the needs and wants of others as a central feature of their role, the revelations referred to above raise the question of whether this constitutes an unnecessarily limited existence. The parallel lies with other forms of servitude where there is a prior acceptance that these individuals can only hope to achieve a certain sort of predetermined existence. Therefore, if they succeed in that, be it life in a ghetto of waiting at a master's table, they at least have the fulfilment of knowing that they achieved the 'possible'. In being content with this, they also know that they do not have to deal with the extra demands made by struggling to achieve more. Second, the revelations from feminist work question whether the contentment of an unknown number of women is being bought at a morally unacceptable price in terms of reinforcing a set of social relations that are fundamentally detrimental to women's emotional welfare. Ignoring the possibility of such a dilemma may also be part of the price of that contentment (Friedan book originally published in 1963).

The preceding arguments are not aimed at disregarding the phenomenon of the woman who is emotionally dominating in her relations with women, children or men. Systematic evidence is not available to enable us to be categorical about this, but we suggest that the woman occupying an emotionally dominant position in all spheres of her life is an extreme rarity. Ironically, the stereotyped presentation of where this is supposed to exist tends to give the game away: the successful working women of women's magazines still have to function as sexual and love objects for men and hold prime responsibility for the maintenance of domestic standards of care (Winship, 1978). Thus we would suggest that where a woman is emotionally dominating this represents her incorporation into the gender-derived dominance-subordination mode of emotional interaction. Therefore women in this position depict the maintenance of the status quo which feminists are struggling against, rather than their entry into a more liberated state. (See Judy Marshall's discussion of the role options open to women in management (Marshall, 1984) ). Whilst it reads almost as a caricature of what is entailed, the following extract from a local newspaper on women 'getting on' in the world of business and commerce illustrates what is afoot:

A group of high flying businesswomen divulged a few tips on how to make it to the top at a 'Careering Ahead' Seminar in Birmingham ... Janet says, 'I had to check my husband out before marriage to ensure he did not want children. There comes a time when you have to be a nice person or get what you want. An important rule is not to be too trusting ... Birmingham-born computer expert Sue ... According to her, being thick skinned and determined are the prerequisites of success. She said, 'I just did not see myself as a wife and mother. I wanted to succeed.' (*Birmingham Daily News* (1986) p. 2)

Feminist therapy, consciousness-raising groups and writings on the subject should not be either as projecting the assumption that women are bound to be 'in the right' or that their emotional needs should dominate to the exclusion of others. On the contrary, the work carried out along feminist lines is based on the principle that one person's feelings of self-worth should not be built on the denial or denigration of another's (Baker-Miller, 1978). And if women depart from this they are ceasing to hold true to the spirit and the practice of feminist therapy. For example, if a woman engaged in feminist therapy uses the concentration on her emotional experience to justify disregarding the feelings of, say, her friends, her male partner or her children, she is slipping into a dominant – subordinate mode which feminist therapy is set to challenge and counteract.

Within feminist writing, criticism has been raised of women's therapy proving to be a cul-de-sac. Raymond (1986) has argued that concentrated and at times prolonged analysis by women of their 'feelings' and the emotional suffering arising from male-dominated personal relations can become an end in itself. As a result, she argues, over-preoccupation with the state of one's relationships or 'relationism' can seduce women away from taking action to tackle the social conditions which give rise to the relationship problems. Instead, women continue in a state of retreat from the world. Moreover, she sees women's relations with each other becoming debased through 'therapism' into a perpetual round of emotional victim-support work, rather than women actively trying to work together to create relationships and social conditions truly expressive of women's needs and talents. It may be the case that what Raymond (1986) describes is true for some women's experience of feminist therapy, although she herself does not supply specific evidence of its occurrence. But even if this were the case, for some women this may represent an advance on a demoralised and uncomforted existence. However, and more to the point, the evidence coming through from women having experienced feminist therapy is that their ability to exert some purchase on the circumstances they are in is enhanced as opposed to their feeling driven by events in a passive way (McLeod, 1987b).

This is illustrated by the evaluation of the outcome of therapy by the women attending a provincial women's therapy centre in Britain in its first year (BWTC Birmingham Women's Therapy Centre 1986). One of the authors was allowed access to the total number of returns (84 per cent of the total number of women contacted). All commented on the positive nature of the therapeutic experience and all indicated that the women were more actively engaged in directing their own lives as a result of therapy. This endorsed the picture provided in the report in question, where women commented as follows:

'I feel less self-hatred, less hopeless. I feel sharing my highs and lows had made the lows especially less – I guess dangerous.' (BWTC, 1986, p. 13)

'I think that – it is still the case the problems remain very powerful. The time – 6 months – is short really to be building trust. But yes, I don't want to die anymore. That's a change because of what it means. If I choose to live then it means I have some good feelings about myself too . . . Here my problems aren't viewed as 'sickness' that changes how I perceive them. I don't feel sick anymore but going through a period of growth. I get a lot of support whilst doing that but I'm not treated as being helpless. (BWTC, 1986, p. 14)

We would go on to argue that the perspective provided by feminist therapy that equal importance should be given to women's emotional needs – needs to be incorporated more centrally into women's day-to-day existence. It is not enough for the present situation to continue where the insights and support provided by feminist therapy are still seen as something of a psychological ante-room to everyday life or campaigning or organising, as though occasional contact with it is all that is required before returning to the fray. This ignores the way in which accounts of women's experience in groups and one-to-one contact indicate how all-pervasive and crippling are the problems of emotional inferiority that women are grappling with (Collins *et al.*, 1978).

In our view the cumulative loss of personal happiness and of the application of talents which results from the inhibitions feminist therapy is uncovering and endeavouring to tackle is terrifying. To appreciate something of the scale involved, women readers could spend a few minutes thinking of themselves and any two other women friends, and consider what each of you has failed to do and how much each of you has suffered as a result your emotional subordination to men.

While making a contribution to women's welfare that is important in its own right and potentially very significant, feminist therapy has its weaknesses. A contradiction persists at the heart of its theoretical work. On the one hand, through its practice, feminist therapy has demonstrated that in terms of their psychological development, emotional fulfilment is both women's birthright and within their capacity to promote. Nevertheless, writers such as Eichenbaum and Orbach still turn to Sigmund Freud's work as an important theoretical underpinning. This is despite the fact that, as referred to earlier, Freud's theoretical constructs of how our personalities develop and our cognition of this emphasise the inevitability of women relating their psychic development to that of men, and women's consciousness of their own inferiority from their earliest days:

In turning to psychoanalysis, we as feminist psychotherapists

recognised the importance of Freud's discovery of the unconscious and the existence of a psychic life that was a powerful
determinant in the politics of everyday experience. At the same
time we rejected a view of a 'self' conceived outside culture and
began to see how individual reality and personality is shaped by
the material world. We see the unconscious as the intra-psychic
reflection of our present childrearing and gender relations.
(Eichenbaum and Orbach, 1982, p. 15)

Superficially, this idea of the unconscious as an empty bottle to be
filled by Freudian or feminist notions of psychically influential
forces, sounds all right. However, there are two theoretical problems
with it. First, at a deeper level there is a misfit between the feminist
and the Freudian approach. In Freud's work, quoted earlier, the
construction of the unconscious in women is seen to depend on a
perceived inferiority to men. Therefore to weld feminist insights
into psychic development on to such a view of the formation of the
unconscious is to be forced into accepting a theoretical inconsistency
– that women's psychic development in terms of their subordination
is at root biologically determined, whilst feminist analysis holds
that it is socially determined. Second, retaining the notion of the
unconscious but seeing its function as essentially the internalisation
of patriarchal relations (see Mitchell, 1975) still begs the question
of how women's capacity for emotional fulfillment originates. Janet
Sayer's work has focused attention on this issue (Sayers, 1986) but
still takes the matter only as far as examining how women's
resistance to subordination arises, as opposed to postulating that the
problem may turn around now the original capacity for emotional
fulfillment may have become undermined. Ironically, the conceptual
leap embedded in feminist therapists' practice – that the bedrock
of young women's and girl psyches is a belief in themselves which
then gets overlaid to various degrees, may hold the key to this
problem. In order to make use of it, feminist therapy theorists may
need to trust more to their reading of the past in the way that they
are encouraging the women they work with to do. As this happens
the lessons from the social construction of women's psychology
which their own work points to may through more consistently;
that unless those surrounding young girls influence them to do so,
they may not be particularly preoccupied with men and boys as
their emotional lode stars. Also, they might not start lugging a sense

of their inferior worth around with them. If writers on feminist therapy approached their work more confidently in this way they would be building on an existing tradition in feminist scholarship and consigning Freud's work to what might then more clearly emerge as its appropriate sexist and historically specific place. As Mary Wollstonecraft suggested two centuries ago:

> I have probably had an opportunity of observing more girls in their infancy than J. J. Rousseau. I can recollect my own feelings, and I looked steadily around me . . . I will venture to affirm that a girl, whose spirits have not been dampened by inactivity, or innocence tainted by false shame, will always be a romp. (Mary Wollstonecraft, quoted in Stacey and Price, 1981, p, 50).

If Mary Wollstonecraft's analysis and feminist therapists in their practice are on the right lines, another important possibility emerges. It may be far easier for women through women's therapy, consciousness-raising groups and feminist interaction to re-establish their self-esteem than they have been lead to believe – even than the theorisation of feminist therapists may lead to believe. What is needed to bring this about is that with each other's encouragement they try it.

A further drawback to feminist therapy, though this may gradually be disappearing as therapy centres develop, is that it remains class-bound. Nationally, far more middle-class women than working-class women are participating in it. Our contact with women involved in community work and social work suggest that the central ideas in feminist therapy are also being introduced gradually to women from a wider class background through social work practice. This is mainly being done through the formation of a variety of women's groups established by these workers (see, for example, Donnelly, 1986; Malek, 1985). The danger to be guarded against here is that through 'a social work' plan, feminist therapy may become adulterated into something that women would experience for the sake of helping them to cope with the status quo, as opposed to women voluntarily using it in their search for a way beyond prevailing emotional conditions.

The main body of literature on feminist therapy does not as yet incorporate a black perspective. For black women, the quality of their emotional well-being is mediated by their experience of racism and their responses to it, whilst that of white women is not. As we have said before, this means that black women have to tackle the impact of racism on their development simultaneously with that of sexism. Lorde makes the effect of racism on black women's development clear when she describes an incident of everyday life in an Underground train – a white woman ensuring that her coat is not touched by a black child sitting next to her:

The revulsion on the white woman's face in the subway as she moves her coat away and I think she is seeing a roach. But I see the hatred in her eyes because she wants me to see the hatred in her eyes, because she wants me to know in the only way a child can know that I don't belong alive in her world. (Lorde, 1984, p. 72)

Racism also affects the ways in which women offer resistance to the damage being caused to their emotional development whilst seeming to continue to live through modes of domination and subordination. Morrison describes the means whereby black women do so as follows:

Everybody in the world was in a position to give them [black women] orders. White women said, 'Do this.' White children said. 'Give me that.' White men said, 'Come here.' Black men said, 'Lay down.' The only people they need not take orders from were black children and each other. But they took all of that and re-created it in their own image. They ran the houses of the white people, and knew it. When white men beat their men, they cleaned up the blood and went home to receive abuse from the victim. They beat their children with one hand and stole for them with the other. (Morrison, 1986, p, 128)

Moreover, Lorde goes on to add that such experiences of racialised rejection not only damage relationships between black women and white women; they also adversely affect relationships between black women; leaving substantial anger and pain between them. Black women, particularly in America, have been engaging with the impact of racism in their therapeutic interaction and recognise that this aspect of their experience comes between them and has a significant impact on the therapist-client relationship. As Lorde says:

> For two Black women to enter an analytic or therapeutic relationship means beginning an essential uncharted and insecure journey . . . So this territory between us feels new and frightening as well as urgent, rigged with detonating pieces of our own individual racial histories which neither of us chose but which each of us bears the scars from. And those are particular to each of us. But there is a history which we share because we are Black women in a racist sexist cauldron, and that some part of this journey is yours, also. (Lorde, 1984, pp. 161–2)

## THE VALUE OF WOMEN'S RELATIONSHIPS

Besides addressing the detail of women's emotional well-being, feminist therapy and writings in women's experience and psychology have reinforced a general trend within the women's movement: to lend enhanced status to relationships between women. This challenges the idea that such relationships are necessarily subordinate or inferior to women's emotional engagement with men, or more trivial than men's relationships with each other. Instead, sisterhood (that is, loving as opposed to divisive relationships between women) has been increasingly valued. Women have recognised that they can share their experience more profoundly, more intimately and more sensitively with other women than with men. In the process they can create relationships that are just as profound, intimate and sensitive as those with men, if not more so (see Cartledge and Ryan, 1983; Ernst and Maguire, 1987). For feminists, lesbianism is no longer lodged in the realms of the psychopathological but has been increasingly recognised and legitimated as an intensely expressive form of relationship in its own right by substantial numbers of women (Hanscombe and Forster, 1982; Lorde, 1974) within the women's movement. This development has reinforced the idea that women are freed from the need for men to ensure they gain such experience. Whether lesbian relationships are more egalitarian in themselves is hard to deduce. Some accounts of

lesbian relationships and the controversy over lesbian sadomasochism (Ardill and O'Sullivan, 1986) indicate that the women concerned
are grappling with problems of dominance and subordination as
characterising their most intimate experience with other women
(Chambers-Brown 1983; Egerton, 1983; Ardill and O'Sullivan,
1987). Meanwhile, a common relationship centred around women
as opposed to men has started to gain increasing stature. Female
single parents began to speak out to the effect that, poverty and
social stigma apart, they find theirs to be a rewarding existence.
Their children feel that this is the case too (Segal 1983). Black
women have also propounded the importance of the idea of fulfillment through a variety of family forms (Lorde, 1984; Wilson, 1977;
Parmar, 1982).

## 'ROMANTIC LOVE' AND A LOVING ALTERNATIVE

Feminist attention to the realities of women's emotional experience
has also revealed that while romance may be one of the most
ecstatic emotional experiences for women it is also one of the most
injurious in terms of welfare. In doing so, it has identified the
following pitfalls – the widespread acceptance of romance as a
route to women's exploration of freedom and self-expression leaves
women vulnerable to existing social pressures; that while romance
may seem to be a gesture of self-assertion it is not an all-conquering
force, but constrained by everyday realities; that unjust suffering
may be seen as an acceptable and unavoidable part of romance.
Various feminist studies (see, for example, Winship 1978; Sarsby
1983) have shown how 'women's' and 'girls' magazines, though
experimenting with versions of the 'new woman', set out to reinforce
the idea that women's future is to move through romance to
domestic subordination – an already powerful motif in our society.
The degree of influence such publications exert on their readers is
not clear and it would be wrong to assume that women are influenced
in the directions of what they read. However, even if the influence
of magazines may be peripheral, studies which have canvassed the
views on marriage, romance and their own and other women's
futures held by young girls themselves present a bleak picture of
women's fatalism concerning their own potential (McRobbie 1978;
Sarsby 1983). The prominent view among working-class girls

emerges as being that their future welfare in terms of material resources, social position and emotional and sexual life depends on marriage (Sarsby 1983).

Women are aware of how the reality of marriage can be grim because of the double standards concerning the loss of personal freedom that ensues from their dependence on men:

> He had her in tears this morning. He won't let her go over the doorstep. He always thinks she's going to go off with another man. And me mum's not like that at all. All she wanted to do was to go to the ladies sauna, up at 'Manyana' with her sister and me cousin. And me dad! he went about with a face like fizz all day, so that she ended up not wanting to go. It's not fair. Just 'cos she looks young and pretty. He works with about fifty women and me mum never says 'Who's Lizzie then?'. She never bothers but he goes mad thinking she goes out looking for someone else. (Mungham quoted in McRobbie, 1978, p. 107)

Although seeing it individually as grounds for not being caught out, they may also be aware of the sufferings under this system of women who haven't got a man:

> I've got this auntie – Auntie Elsie, she's ever so nice but she never got married. So she misses out on a lot of things really. I mean she goes around with my mum and all the family and them, but well, she just sort of has to watch. Know what I mean? I don't want to be like her. (McRobbie, 1978, p. 105)

Despite the degrees of understanding, the impression is that the majority of working-class girls interviewed acquiesce in their future lives taking this form. Among young women from all class backgrounds who have been interviewed there is no impression of large scale rebellion on the part of young women seeking marriage or cohabitation with men more on their own terms, or challenging the idea that marriage or cohabitation are really in women's interests. Where studies do document girls' resistance to following conventional patterns in heterosexual relationships, the evidence from the girls themselves suggests that they are struggling against a general trend:

> As a working class teenager at a secondary modern school, I went along with my mates in believing in true love and the romantic dream ... It began to seem to me that romantic love was an illusion ... Having done away with the myth of Mr Right, the next step was to question the myth of the perfect marriage. A lot of my mates seemed to see only as far ahead as their white wedding and honeymoon, but I was less starry-eyed ... I only had to look around to see unappealing examples of what those years could contain. (Hemmings, 1982, p. 104)

For young black women, the situation is even more complex in that racism, by closing off the economic opportunities available to black men, means that a black woman's attachment to a black man does not guarantee even the same level of economic security that a young white woman expects to achieve through the marriage contract. Thus the position of young black women reflects the way in which racism and sexism combine to seriously jeopardise the quality of their lives. However, black women have a long history of their own to refer to in resisting their subjugation as women within their own community milieu, and this has been given increased prominence by black feminist activists in debates not only with black women, but also with white women (Lorde, 1984; Biswas, 1986).

Romance, both historically (see Harrison, forthcoming) and in the present, can represent an oppositional stance on the part of women against male power and/or the status quo. For example, a woman might choose her own lover rather than consent to an arranged marriage (Harrison, forthcoming). She might fly in the face of convention 'in the name of love', thereby rejecting a 'suitable' match or a steady husband. However, such actions do not necessarily free her from male domination or a subordinate status. She may find herself the subject of social stigma, under the thumb of her freely chosen lover and/or rejected in due course in conditions of material hardship (Wilson, 1983).

While not mounting a sustained attack on the phenomenon, feminist writings have also documented the tendency for women to accept suffering as an inevitable part of romance and the depressing outcome of this (Dobash and Dobash, 1980; Caplan, 1986). That they love someone is put forward – in fact we would suggest has been put forward by most women at some time or another – to justify enduring the most questionable treatment, and several social pressures coalesce to make it very difficult to tackle such a situation. In lives which may otherwise be very lonely and drab, to end a relationship, however awful, which once shimmered or occasionally shimmers may seem tantamount to ending the only chance of that sort of ecstatic experience. To bolster this impression, there is a lot of pressure on women to believe that a woman's existence on her own is hard going. Moreover, the evidence suggests there is a good deal of truth in this being the case (Bickerton in Cartledge and Ryan, 1983). No openly agreed code of what constitutes decent behaviour in emotional and intellectual terms within subsisting relationships exists between women, let alone between men and women (Eskapa, 1985). As a result, there is little by way of collective support to fall back on to encourage its existence. Feminist attention to what can and does go on in the name of romance therefore performs a useful service. It sets before women and men the question of what they are prepared to tolerate for themselves and for others.

Some feminists have gone on to argue against the trend of romantic relationships, and indeed against the trend of social relations generally, with their preoccupation with ownership, be it of mates, family, friend, goods, services or status. Instead, as in the case of Simone de Beauvoir (1970) and Germaine Greer (1971) they have argued for non-possessive love as the authentic form of love to strive for. By this they mean love that doesn't lead to women attempting to possess a man or to yield to being possessed. These writers argue that otherwise 'love' is, in fact, a reflection of fear – fear of lacking a personal identity. Therefore, one has to 'have someone' or else one is nothing. Alternatively, there is the fear of being alone if one does not 'have' someone. As Simone de Beauvoir says:

Even if they can choose independence, this road [that is, love] seems the most attractive to a majority of women. It is agonising for a woman to assume responsibility for her life. (de Beauvoir, 1970, p. 655)

Germaine Greer comments that:

> It might be a better world . . . if people did not think in terms
> of catching people's love but of loving them. 'I got him', is
> nonsense in terms of love relationships, and so is 'I lost him'. If
> we could stop thinking in terms of capital, we would not have to
> fear the loosening of the captives' bonds and our failing beauty,
> and he would not have ulcers about being outstripped or belittled.
> (Greer, 1971, p. 159)

If it became established, this pattern of non-possessive loving
would end the problem of women and men remaining confined in
relationships compromising their own needs or forcing others to
compromise theirs in the name of keeping the relationship going,
that is maintaining hold of the possession. It would also offer a
chance of being loved for one's own sake rather than for the hidden
agenda in 'romantic love' – the security that one offers.

Despite these advantages, it is very hard for women to adopt the
approach suggested by non-possessive loving. First, men generally
bring greater material resources and status to a relationship. Even
if a man's social status is not higher than a woman's her social
standing remains particularly dependent on her having a 'stable
relationship' with a man (Segal, 1983; Kishwar, 1986). Without a
long-term male partner it is still difficult for women to engage in
heterosexual relations in an unstigmatised way. Even if they do so
they may well feel guilty or inhibited about getting sexual relief for
its own sake (Kitzinger, 1985). While lesbian relationships are
gaining in legitimation they remain deviant in public discussion:
compared with male homosexual relationships they are also doubly
stigmatised as being commonly regarded as somehow subsexual.
While work on rape and domestic violence suggests it is an illusion
(Brownmiller, 1976; Dobash and Dobash, 1980), a relationship with
a man is also seen as bringing protection from other men (Hanmer
and Saunders, 1984). Having a man around and/or in the house,
makes uninvited intrusions or assaults from men seem less likely.
Racism makes the situation even more dire for black women.
Because in white society all black family forms are presented as
pathological and deviant (Carby, 1982; Parmar, 1982; Dominelli,
1988), the position of black women is problematised whether or

not there is a man involved with them and their children (Lorde, 1984).

Beyond these problems, the existence of non-possessive love could still result in bad treatment for women. In a society already constructed to men's advantage, non-possessive love is likely to be used by them to further their interests. Men can and do employ women's demands for non-possessive love as a rationale to engage in practices and relationships that go against the feelings of women in question, as opposed to respecting them; for example promising to engage in child-care responsibilities, but leaving them for the woman to sort out when the going gets tough (Achilles Heel, 1983).

A further condition for a loving relationship is needed beyond non-possessiveness – that love, either between the two individuals concerned or in terms of others beyond them, should not enforce or reinforce subordination. If relationships result in subordination we suggest that they should not be dignified with the name of love. This means that love between two people centred on the accumulation of status, power and goods and the diminution of other relationships, such as friendship, comradeship and love of children other than one's own, as secondary, is questionable. Equally, if a relationship between a couple is maintained at the price of compromising the integrity of either partner or denying their existence at times, whether they are a wife, husband or lover, then that cannot be a loving relationship, but instead a destructive or self-centred activity.

This still leaves the problem that romantic love can seem all-important: what else has the power to generate such a massively rewarding experience? Therefore, we tend to seek it, setting aside all other considerations, and to have to relinquish it is to feel that one is moving into the abyss.

Goodison (1983) has offered one answer, suggesting that we 'fall in love' in a wide variety of situations far from the socially recognised romantic or sexual ones and argues for greater recognition of this. Our view is that, sadly, we experience an even more powerful set of inhibitions. We do not simply fail to give adequate recognition to varied instances of falling in love, instead we only allow ourselves to construct a specific set of feelings amounting to 'falling in love' in a narrow range of situations. Our answer is that potentially any contact with any other human being or group of human beings has the same radiant power. There is no problem with our experience of romantic love as such, except that it has been narrowed down to one type of relationship. In the process, the opportunity to love as we are able has been denied, our ability to do so has been truncated and other loving relationships have been downgraded.

## A FEMINIST/ANTI-SEXIST APPROACH TO MEN'S EMOTIONAL WELFARE

Following feminist initiatives in counselling and writing there are now a few slender accounts of men's emotional experience by men trying to counter patriarchal assumptions. These confirm that the men in question see male demands as tending to predominate in intimate relations with women (Festau, 1975). However, they recognise that the resulting relationships centred on dominance and subordination are not only injurious to women's needs but also stultifying for the men concerned (Tolson, 1977). Therefore egalitarian relationships might more truly meet emotional needs of both men and women. For example, Reynaud writes as follows on men's role in marriage:

There is actually no love which is possible in a relationship of appropriation, and there can be no question of a human relationship between two people when one of them is being considered as an object. A man gets impoverished pleasure from possessing a woman, a pleasure which bears no comparison to that which two free individuals could experience together. (Reynaud, 1983, p. 97)

Tolson comments on heterosexual relationships:

One 'theme' that did crystallise out of one men's group, was the recurring problem of couple relationships . . . We were in favour of women's independence but felt threatened by it. We wanted to renounce our aggressive role, but felt bound to it. We were tired of disputes and petty squabbles, but had no power to stop them. Even though we were searching for a unified sexuality, we still felt impelled to 'perform' – and to watch ourselves performing . . . The 'nuclear family' was a trap, both for women and for men because it demanded polarised gender roles 'assertive/submissive', 'decisive/uncertain', 'detached/dependent' etc. (Tolson, 1977, p. 138)

Giving weight to such writings is not to ignore the phenomenon of the 'dominated' man in a relationship with a woman. But we would make the following points. One should examine whether a man became 'dominated' on his terms, that is, in reaction against the conventional dominant male role failing to meet his emotional needs (McLeod, 1982). Like his counterpart the 'dominating' woman, being dominated as the hallmark of his emotional existence doesn't necessarily represent a liberated state, but rather compliance to the pattern of one or other hierarchical roles as being the option in emotional relationships – a situation likely to have characterised his upbringing (Metcalfe and Humphries, 1985).

While men's sexual needs are still accorded primacy over women's, this can still fail to meet their emotional needs in intimate relationships. Contemporary accounts of 'minority' sexual activity among homosexual men (Weeks, 1981) or of covert male sexuality within prostitution (McLeod, 1982) or clandestine homosexual relations (Humphreys, 1975) are starting to indicate that the conventional heterosexual mode of male sexuality, the dominating 'macho' male, massively inhibits men's emotional expression. The emotional experience of black men in society is also mediated by racism. It has problematised their sexuality by denigrating it for being overly emotional and over-active in its expression (CCCS, 1982; Hiro, 1971). Moreover, black men have found their right to family life denied through immigration laws which prevent their families from coming to Britain to join them (CRE, 1985), or allowing them to support their families overseas (Plummer, 1978; Gordon and Newham, 1985).

Men have also begun to discuss the way in which, although their material interests may be fostered by their distance from the demands of child-care, they are thereby also cutting themselves off from one of the most creative and rewarding experiences (Hearn, 1983). Besides the emotional gains for men, greater exposure to nurturing human life in an intimate way might result in men being less prone to accept the stereotype of their prime role in destroying loving relationships through aggression. They might also have a more profound appreciation of the creative labour involved in child-rearing and thereby share more fully in women's vested interest in this not being destroyed. By freeing their own emotional development, men might also adjust their scales of what was acceptable human damage – with far-reaching consequences. As the Feminism and Non-Violence Study Group (1983) have commented:

> When a soldier or civilian is killed, twenty years or more of the fruits of one women's labour is destroyed ... Men too have suffered (though not been oppressed by) sexism. Society has kept them at arm's length from the magic of human life and this separation has had very dire consequences. It has meant most men are more likely to see human beings as expendable, and can be conned into feeling a sense of glory in dying for their loved ones, people or country. (Feminism and Non-Violence Study Group, 1983, p.11)

## EMOTIONAL LIBERATION FOR CHILDREN

Existing forms of care through the family and its substitutes are so thoroughly imbued with hierarchy and possessiveness mediated through gender (Barrett and Mcintosh 1982), it is difficult to point to alternatives and weigh the benefits that children may derive from them. Nevertheless, feminists have begun to map out the ways in which children generally are victims of inequality in their relations with their parents – as opposed to being the victims of isolated cases of parental pathology. Feminist studies of incest (Nelson, 1982; Ward, 1984; Dominelli, 1986) have shown that it is a widespread practice, not just the preserve of the perverted few. Such studies have also indicated that, in keeping with the general dominance of male sexual demands, children are viewed as appropriate sex objects, mainly as a consequence of male parental power over them.

At the same time, work is being done to elucidate how girls are being brought up to accept the role of subordinate carers (Eichenbaum and Orbach, 1984, Belotti, 1975) and boys to assume a role of superiority in their relations with women (Arcana 1983; Belotti, 1975). In such accounts a central thesis is that mothers'

part in this process is highly influential and that it is important that
as feminists, women should both resist and counter what is going
on:

> Rejection of the traditional mother role is part of our task.
> Another part is acceptance – the acceptance of our sons into our
> daily lives. By now everyone has considered the idea that small
> boys and young men should know how to make beds and wash
> dishes, sweep, dust and do the laundry ... But there is less
> agreement about bringing men into the rest of our lives – the
> parts outside, or beside the role that would make all women into
> housekeepers. (Arcana, 1983, p. 247)

Extensive work on what anti-sexist child-care means in detail
has yet to be done. Some accounts exist of play groups and nurseries
run along anti-sexist lines (see, for example, 'Policy Statement',
NCC, 1985). Work to cultivate young women's assertiveness
is mostly confined to the adolescent age group (Curno *et al.*, 1982)
and does not involve young children. Nevertheless, the authors
have encountered support groups for parents trying to tackle the
problem of how to bring up boys as well as girls in a non-sexist
way (Skelton, 1984). As discussed in Chapter 2, the object lesson for
children, of child-care not being primarily 'women's business' and
a low-status activity, depends on the nature of the provisions
set before children. Publicly endorsed and financed child-care
provisions drawing on the labour of men and women is of critical
importance here (David and New, 1985).

However, as yet, feminists have failed to grapple with the issue
of women's routine use of physical violence in child-care. For
example, smacking or the threat of violence is commonly employed
by women to control their children's behaviour (Newson and
Newson, 1976). By doing so, day in day out, they are reinforcing
the patriarchal principle that force legitimately underwrites hierarchical relations, as these descriptions from the Newsons' study of
common child-care practices illustrate:

Foreman's wife:
'They need a little bit – what they say about smacking, you can't
give them all their own way. I mean you've got to have them a

little bit frightened of you, haven't you? I think you have anyway.'
Sales rep's wife:
'Well usually I think I use my hand, but if I have a stick I can wave it about and it has a great effect but I don't like smacking with a stick. (Do you sometimes?) Yes, I have smacked them with it sometimes on the bottom.' (Newson and Newson, 1976)

It might seem risky for feminists to draw attention to this phenomenon. Feminist work to date has concentrated on women as the victims as opposed to the perpetrators of violence, would focusing on women's violence to children undermine this analysis? We would suggest that such fears are groundless, that a feminist analysis brought to bear on this situation would elucidate that it amounts to women, yet again, being under the constraints of sustaining and reproducing patriarchal relations as part of the process of socialising children. Given the way in which the legitimation of authority through the use of physical force runs throughout our society it is not surprising that women employ such an approach as a 'normal' part of the way in which they bring up their children. If women addressed this question, the issue of where the pressures on woman to behave in this way derive from would begin to be opened up, and immediate benefits for children's welfare might accrue in terms of a less violence-prone existence. The chances of children being brought up to respect non-violence might also be increased. It would also mean that women would not only be rejecting violence when inflicted against them, but also when they were in a position to inflict it, as, in this case, *vis-à-vis* the children in their care who occupy a comparatively powerless and dependent position in relation to them. This lesson is of crucial importance as women contemplate exercising greater power but in an egalitarian way.

All the activities and focal points of interest described here should not be viewed as amounting to an arcane corner of feminist studies in child-care. If feminists are concerned to establish egalitarian relations, they amount to an enormous and unavoidable task for them to address: how can children be 'brought up' neither to treat others as subordinates or objects, nor to submit to being treated as such? We see that the key to starting on this project as lying in the central focus of the theory and practice of feminist counselling, that is, women themselves questioning and breaking out of the emotional subordination to which they have been subjected. Thus, for us, addressing the question of how women's emotional needs can be met also has inescapable beneficial consequences for children and men.

# 4
# Creating a Feminist Statutory Social Work

## INTRODUCTION

As described in previous chapters, a feminist stamp has by now been placed on three major dimensions of social work practice – the definition of social problems; organising to promote welfare; and the specific consideration of emotional problems. Meanwhile, feminist initiatives have begun to make inroads into a fourth dimension of practice – statutory social work. In analysing the potential and significance of this work, we discuss the contribution made to feminist analysis by radical and Marxist critiques of statutory social work's social control role, as the precursors of a feminist approach. We then set out what we see as the nature and achievements of feminist action to date regarding statutory social work. Finally, we discuss the necessary conditions for such work to develop to a point where statutory work as we know it is a transformed into a truly feminist social work.

## THE CONTRIBUTION OF RADICAL SOCIAL WORK AND THE MARXIST CRITIQUE

Statutory social work purports to be *the* state enterprise that has people's personal welfare as its central concern. Moreover, the material and operational resources statutory social work incorporates, such as day nurseries, homes for the elderly, residential child care facilities, domiciliary services, counselling, aids, adaptations and money have enormous potential for assisting people's well-being. Nevertheless, the emergence of 'radical social work' and the sets of ideas embodied in the CASE CON critique of the late 1960s

and early 1970s (Bailey and Brake, 1975) began to point out that
statutory social work was prejudicial to people's welfare in the first
place in terms of the basis on which its services were offered. While
the ideas embodied in such work were diffuse, ranging across a
number of publications and initiatives, they had the following
central thrust: social work help was not offered on the basis of
clients' own definition of need, but with the aim of their rehabilitation towards conventional norms of behaviour. This was despite
lack of evidence that the desired rehabilitation was achieved by
this means, and in the face of clients' needs possibly meriting
assistance in their own right on humanitarian grounds. Writers on
radical social work pointed out that the problems that social work
clients faced were defined as proceeding from their individual
inadequacy rather than as having any origin in widespread social
conditions. Therefore the social work help which was proffered
stigmatised social work clients in terms of labelling them as personally deficient and unable to cope. In the process social work also
fulfilled a diversionary function, drawing attention away from the
social origins of the problems it addressed. Moreover, through the
exploration of personal circumstances in detail that characterised
report writing and supervision, social work was invasive of personal
privacy and represented a threat to civil liberties (Whitehouse,
1985).

While raising such awkward questions about the benevolence of
statutory social work in practice, the radical social work critique
had its own limitations. Having defined statutory social work as
possibly pernicious it provided no solution to this dilemma in the
form of a programme for transforming statutory social work into
an activity that would secure rather than subvert social justice.
Instead it reached either for a switch to forms of community action,
or for the 'drop out' solution – that the way out of social work's
shortcomings was to avoid practice of it – radical non-intervention
(Schur, 1973). The problem with the first type of solution, epitomised
by statutory social workers squatting with their homeless clients,
was that while undertaken with integrity, it did not grapple with
the problem of the extent to which statutory social work as an
institution might be capable of change. It therefore left the practices
of the agency it was criticising untouched. The problem with radical
non-intervention as a solution was twofold. Unless it gained mass
appeal among the statutory social work profession who had a vested

interest in their own employment, its challenge was unlikely to stop the practice of social work in its tracks, and secondly, if social workers were to do nothing, that would include not addressing actual need amongst clients – hardly a gain for their clientele. The radical social work critique, while urging the prioritisation of poverty as a problem and referring to the structural origins of social work clients' problems, also failed to develop the explanatory power of its analysis to account for *why* statutory social work was fulfilling a pathologising diversionary role (Webb, 1981). Meanwhile, feminists such as Elizabeth Wilson (in Bailey and Brake, 1975) were trying to inject a feminist component into the analysis being developed by radical social work. However, this intervention remained a token presence rather than a central feature of the overall analysis.

That work has been undertaken through Marxist critiques of social work such as in the writings of Corrigan and Leonard (1978), Bolger *et al.* (1981), Simpkin (1979), and Walker and Beaumont (1981). They have set out how social work is a state agency in a society where the state is underwritten by vested interests in maintaining deep-rooted, class-based inequalities. Therefore it is not surprising that social workers operate to maintain this status quo in various ways. These include defining social problems as originating in individual defects rather than in profound inequalities in the distribution of material wealth and power, carrying out forms of intervention as if this were the case, and using their power of persuasion and constraint to induce people to accept and cope with their lot under such a system.

While making this point Marxist writers have brought out that the clients of statutory social workers are aware of their policy function and do not necessarily regard them as their first choice to turn to for help (Bolger *et al.*, 1981). But at the same time, in Marxist critiques there is an appreciation in their own terms of the possibilities for constructive practice in statutory social work. In the first place this turns around an acknowledgement of the opportunities that social work provides for contact between those experiencing class inequalities at first hand and those possessed of a Marxist analysis of them. As reflected in proposals for practice, this can mean, as Corrigan and Leonard (1978) advocate, that social workers imbued with a Marxist understanding should encourage their clients in contrary circumstances to reflect on the social origins of their problems. This is seen as a means of lessening the stigmatisation of clients as individuals by encouraging them to view their own achievements more positively – as struggling against odds for which they were not to blame. Such an approach displays a sensitivity to individuals' worth. But, beyond this, Marxist writers' analysis of the development of practice in a statutory setting has distinct limitations. As exemplified in Corrigan and Leonard's work (1978) but also, for example, in Bolger *et al.*, (1981).

Marxist social work writings do move into developing detailed accounts of the forms action can take in their appreciation of the dialectical identity of state agencies, that is, as incorporating to a degree the possibility of struggles against dominant class interests as well as perpetuating those interests. This dialectical struggle is personified in the presence of Marxist social workers within social work agencies. Unfortunately, the prescriptions for practice that such social workers should undertake are confined in Marxist social work writings to what is possible within social work agencies pretty much as they stand. Perhaps the reason for this is that Marxist writers regard statutory social work agencies as part of the state apparatus aimed at controlling people, which by definition cannot be transformed within the current social configuration. In this way Marxist writers produce a very limited series of proposals which contradict their egalitarian intent because they are still hemmed in by the social control function of existing statutory agencies. For example, Hilary Walker and Bill Beaumont writing on a desirable approach to the client, suggest:

We should adopt an open and honest approach with clients so they can be clear about our role and relationship with them. Clients should be aware of the constraints operating on us – that we are supervised and accountable – and the implications of this for them. They need to know that written records may be subject to inspection and that reports prepared on them may have wider distribution and be forwarded to a prison or hostel. They need to know the possible dangers which might arise from total honesty. The idea of 'contracts' may be popular with your colleagues and in your agency. However, the surface appearance of equality in 'contracts' masks the unequal relationship between clients and probation officers. Clarity includes recognition of the power relationship between you and your clients. (Walker and Beaumont, 1981, p. 176)

Bolger *et al.*, comment in a similar vein:

> In the short run the social worker can move towards these experiences of democracy by sharing the realities of their situation. We believe that nearly all children in care would respond to an objective explanation of the role of the social worker and the law. They would appreciate that the social worker is actually near the bottom of a hierarchy and is constrained by law and would be obliged to take certain steps if certain circumstances arose. (Bolger *et al.*, 1981, p. 104)

Through seeking to argue against such conditions as being a problem Mike Simpkin actually reveals the limitations of a 'Marxist practice' in an otherwise untransformed setting:

> Since social work is at best a flawed and limited way of helping people, and at worst descends to sheer deception, and since clients as a whole are neither organised nor possessed of much political weight, some Marxists have suggested that radicals should leave social work for other sectors of the economy. This position is the reverse of the belief that social work can alter the world and equally myopic. Within the employment opportunities which are open, social work seems as legitimate an occupation as many others provided that its limitations and contradictions are fully recognised. (Simpkin, 1980, p. 159).

By consigning statutory social work to reinforcing middle-class ideology and agency norms, a Marxist approach fails to develop forms of social work practice which incorporate sensitive work at an individual level, take account of both personal experience and broader social conditions, respond to grass roots activism, utilise the resources of local and central bureaucracies in the pursuit of egalitarian aims.

Marxist texts *per se* have also failed to integrate an account of oppression on the basis of gender centrally into their analysis, and consequently into their formulations for practice. This gap has been acknowledged by Walker in a way that is applicable to the whole of the Marxist position. She comments on her earlier work written with Beaumont from a Marxist perspective in a chapter on women's issues in a subsequent collection of essays which by its presence, to use Marchant and Wearing's phrase (1986), 'at least ensures an element of feminist analysis'. Walker writes:

> Our analysis in 'probation work' was essentially class based and did not address itself sufficiently to the oppression of women as a group nor to the dimension of sex within a class analysis. (Walker in Walker and Beaumont, 1985, p. 67)

The outcome of this tendency in Marxist writings has been to undermine the importance of women as the prime actors in social work operations. The issue of the hierarchical social relations that women are subject to as the majority of clients, carers and social workers, with their crushing consequences for personal welfare, is not addressed in any consistent fashion. Going on from this, neither women's own potential for challenging such a situation nor initiatives undertaken by women feminists both within statutory social work and from feminist 'bases' outside social work, have been examined in detail. Latterly, under feminist pressure and influence, writers such as Peter Leonard have registered that such oppression is an important issue in theorising about social work (Leonard, 1984) because of the way in which social disadvantage along gender lines surfaces in the presence and experience of clientele. But even here there is no developed account of how a feminist practice is being developed, and might be developed further, to begin to rectify such a situation.

Moreover, both Leonard (1984) and, for example, Walker and Beaumont (1985) as cited above, are still in the grip of adding an analysis of gender on to or into a class analysis of oppression and worrying about which should take precedence in the process. To quote from Walker:

> Tension surrounding this theoretical issue will run through this chapter since, while a class analysis of society does not fully explain women's oppression, neither is assigning women to a single class satisfactory'. (Walker in Walker and Beaumont, 1985, p. 67; see also Wilson, 1980)

The possibility of a resolution to this problem through a non-hierarchical approach to how various forms of oppression are viewed is not entertained in Marxist writings, that is, being prepared to acknowledge the full force of different forms of oppression whatever their nature, be it classism, racism, sexism, heterosexism or ablebodiedism, as opposed to seeking to rank them from the outset. Consequently, the creation of a truly comprehensive account of forms of oppression is not arrived at, and in keeping with this, neither is the question opened up of the form that a statutory practice might take which gives equal weight to different social divisions.

## THE DEVELOPMENT OF FEMINIST STATUTORY SOCIAL WORK

Feminist analysis of statutory social work also proceeds from a critique of its social control role but without denying the importance of class or other social divisions aims to take adequate account of gender. In doing so it has set out how women who predominate as clients, carers and workers suffer from the sexist nature of the organisation and practice of statutory social work (Wilson, 1977; Dale and Foster, 1986; Finch, 1984; Brook and Davis, 1985; Dominelli, 1983, 1984). Feminist analysis has elaborated how this is no accident, given that statutory social work agencies are state agencies in a patriarchal capitalist society where women's main role is seen to be that of discharging domestic labour in the interests of reproducing and maintaining male primacy on the labour market (Wilson, 1977).

Dealing first with women's roles as carers or clients it is indisputably the case that 'a substantial part of statutory social work is concerned with the provision of respite or auxiliary care in the form of day centres for groups of different ages or having a variety of needs; helpers on a sessional basis; short-term fostering; and home helps to carry out a range of domestic labour. But by its definition and construction, respite or auxiliary care reinforces the notion that women should hold the prime responsibility for providing care of the very young or the infirm irrespective of the impact of this on their welfare. Statutory social services do not aim either to lift such a burden from women or to be the means of its being discharged collectively through comprehensive day care and night watch provision available as a right to all. Nor to couple it with policies linking such provisions to the demands of anyone holding a job in the labour market so that meeting the responsibilities of caring for others becomes truly compatible with waged work, thereby freeing men to play their part as well. Meanwhile, analysis informed by a feminist perspective has set out the serious damage to women's welfare caused by their being the prime carers and to indicate its exacerbation when cuts are made in existing forms of respite care. Louise Rimmer and Jennie Popay, referring to Marcia Hunt's survey of women's employment opportunities, argue as follows:

> Responsibility for elderly or infirm dependents can affect whether or not someone is able to work outside the home at all or it can affect hours worked or their choice of employment ... women responsible for the care of elderly or infirm persons were less likely to be working than others, and if they were working they were less likely to be working full-time. One in six part-time workers with these responsibilities said she was compelled to work part-time because of her responsibilities. And over a fifth of all working women with these responsibilities said that their employment was affected in some way – mainly by being forced to take time off work. (Rimmer and Popay, 1982)

Hughes *et al.* (1980) and many others (for example, David and New, 1985; Bruner, 1980; Clarke-Stewart, 1982) make a similar point with reference to the lack of existing day care provisions for the under-fives:

> The long term career and earnings losses for all mothers, because of child care responsibilities they carry, are enormous, and go far beyond any actual loss of earning while staying at home to care for young children. (Hughes, 1980, p. 32)

Meanwhile, in a fashion which is still socially acceptable, families' incomes are depressed by the loss of women's earning power through caring for dependants at home. Losing an income because women work at home can cause substantial numbers of families to fall below the poverty line (Tizard and Hughes 1976; Webster 1984).

Beyond consideration of women's material resources and their careers lies the problem of the strain and stress inflicted on them by the 'round-the-clock' care of dependants. It is on record that women suffer considerably, along the lines described by this woman who first cared for her elderly mother-in-law and is now looking after her own elderly mother:

> 'My husband said it should be my job; conscience said it should be my job; bloody-mindedness and some shred of self-respect (not even as I washed her skinny bottom did mum-in-law trouble to hide her loathing of me) said anything but my job . . .'

> 'I love my mother dearly, but I have no illusions about the cost of that love. Her comfort has been gained at the expense of my life. The only release is her death and what do I do then? Who will employ a middle-aged woman, assuming that there's anything left of that woman to employ?' (*Guardian*, 1983)

These stresses in turn hold dangers for the recipients of women's care. Trendy, heartless slogans such as 'granny bashing' fail to do justice to the excruciatingly mixed emotions which boil when people want to care, and feel they ought to care, but are at the end of their tether in terms of their own human resources (Phillipson, 1982; Bonny, 1984). The same phenomenon is identifiable in accounts of parents driven to distraction by the demands of child-rearing unsupported by collective care (Hughes *et al.*, 1980).

Cutbacks in the resources that do exist to offer support to carers in the situations we have been describing can produce acute distress. As Chris Phillipson (1982) argues:

> Contrary to popular belief, there is little evidence that the welfare state has undermined the commitment of the family towards its older members. Unfortunately, it is much more likely that the present round of cuts will place intolerable strains on daughters and sons attempting to care for elderly parents. By cutting back on holiday provision and day care schemes, essential means of support for a single daughter or working mother may be removed (Phillipson, 1982).

Moreover, the emphasis on providing services at minimum cost, which characterises resources that continue to exist, can result in extensive suffering on the part of users. The following extracts from a routine hunt a for good child-minder by a young black woman are not unsympathetic towards the problems faced by women working as child-minders. However, they bring out the appalling treatment children may be exposed to as a result of good day care provisions being supplanted by what the policy-makers themselves agree is inferior quality care in the interests of a 'low cost' approach (DHSS/DES 1976). The deleterious position in which women and children may be placed, as official concern for quality is replaced with one aimed at juggling balance books, is revealed in the following account:

> In September, due to extreme economic hardship I started to work – my first job as a supply teacher. Derek was 2 months. I went to Social Services and I asked for him to be put on the day nursery waiting list. I worked part-time averaging £50 gross, but this varied. I did not always get the work. Derek was cared for by a neighbour for £8 a week, until one day he came home with a cigarette burn on his hand . . . I went back to Social Services. They said they had no place. I asked around but I could not afford to pay the going rate £15 – £17 per week. I heard of a minder who charged only £10, but was a bit of a religious fanatic . . . I went back to Social Services and asked to see a social worker. She agreed to do what she could. I found out afterwards that my file said I might be abusing him because I had removed him from so many minders. I wrote a furious letter and questioned why he was at risk, and why hadn't they taken any interest in my case before. This time I was given a hand-picked priority minder. When we got to her place there was a child asleep on the floor, no blanket, no pillow. She claimed he couldn't sleep anywhere else, and she wasn't even concerned about it. I was expected to leave my child there. Papers were filled in. I was horrified at the assumption that my desperate situation meant that I was incapable of any standard of child care, and would accept anything. I refused. (Penn, forthcoming).

If and as carers/clients do finally break down as a result of the demands placed upon them, then total care can be provided through social services departments for their dependents, but as such it is highly stigmatised, either as a last resort in the case of the elderly or the disabled, or as the extreme symbol of family failure in terms of reception into care for children. Meanwhile, across the past two decades, with some acceleration as a result of being in keeping with Radical Right ideology, the policy of community care, that is, of care centred in families as opposed to institutional provision, has built up. As Janet Finch's work has demonstrated, community care or care within families should be decoded as 'care by women who bear the prime responsibility for it' (Finch, 1984). While the families or women concerned may receive some financial compensation, policies such as the total reliance on foster care for children, as now embarked upon by some local authority social services departments, are powerful reinforcers of the ideal of reliance on women within the home as the main carers.

It is not an exaggeration to describe the characteristic and most high-profile (and highest priority) work on the part of statutory social services with clients at present as the pursuit and surveillance of parental failure (Parton, 1985). In terms of working contact and assumptions informing practice this can more specifically be written as maternal failure (David and New, 1985). Social services departments are kept at this task in a climate of fear, by intense public pressure arising from the pillorying of social services departments and individuals in the media if they fail to spot and relieve instances of child abuse. In the process, as many commentators have pointed out, money is diverted from preventative resources such as day nurseries and specialised provision generally for the infirm (Biggs, 1987; Hyde and Deacon, 1986). Social workers have to and have to be seen to discharge more of a policing role, which undermines what personal support they might offer as counsellors in response to early cries for help. Personnel and funds are withdrawn from community action which is stimulating the development of supportive networks in the community in the interests of meeting the priorities of statutory work (*Guardian*, 1983). These developments, both actually and symbolically, powerfully underline the idea that whatever else, women must discharge their maternal role within the home.

Other common practices within statutory social work encourage the idea that where male dominance is supported by the integrity of the family conflict with women's personal welfare, then it is women's personal welfare that must suffer. So studies of the subject still produce accounts of women receiving little active support from social workers to leave situations of domestic violence (Pahl, 1985).

Where girls are the victims of incest the tendency is still for statutory workers to reach for family therapy techniques to bind the family together as the highest priority (Dominelli, 1986).

Beyond this, young women are still being processed into care in the way young men are not, because their sexual 'promiscuity' threatens to escape family control (Smart and Smart, 1978). Social work supervision at all stages of the operation of the criminal justice system has also been reported as centring its efforts on trying to foster and inculcate adherence to the routines of domesticity amongst women offenders (Heidensohn, 1985; Dominelli, 1983).

In making this critique of statutory social work practice, we do not wish to give the impression that feminism is resistant to any controls being placed on individuals' behaviour. But a feminist theory and practice of social control proceeds from rather different premises than that currently prevailing in statutory social services. What a feminist approach is seeking to do in the first place is to sort out the ways in which women's behaviour is controlled to the detriment and subordination of their welfare. In keeping with this principle, a feminist approach to statutory practice may be more 'controlling at times than that uninformed by a feminist perspective. Thus, for example, in cases of child sexual abuse a feminist approach might consider it important to consider the separation of the daughter and the father while a more 'liberal' family therapy approach might work towards keeping the family together in a way that appears less disruptive but which might represent a greater sacrifice of the daughter's interests.

At the same time, a feminist approach to issues of social control, in our view, does not represent simply taking the part of women over and above the interests of others. This can be illustrated in relation to the physical abuse of children by women. In this, there appears to be a conflict between the interests of the woman in terms of her 'right' to have her children with her and those of the children in terms of their right to physical and emotional well-being. Feminists such as Wise (1985) have tried to resolve this issue by prioritising the interests of the children over those of the mother. We take the view that the situation requires a more complex response than this, because responding as Wise does endorses the subordination of the interests of the woman concerned. We believe that feminists are not in the business of fostering relations of subordination at any point in their work. Feminist practitioners need to concentrate on working out how to create ways in which the interests of both parties can be kept on an equal footing. In the case of a mother abusing her children, this may mean that the social worker has to separate the mother from the children. In doing this the social worker would be engaging in protecting the interests of the children whilst at the same time trying to convey to the mother that her behaviour without condoning it is not reflective of her own individual pathology (see Chapter 3), but rather sadly indicative of characteristics of social relations prevailing more generally in respect of parents and children (Valentine, 1987). At the same time, it is incumbent on feminist social workers to convey the same message to their agencies and beyond. In this way the false forms of social control centring on the definition and response to child abuse as a matter of the pathology of a small number of parents, may be unravelled.

Besides drawing attention to the operation of discrimination on the basis of gender in the lives of the social-work clientele, feminist analysis has by now begun to unpick the interlocking net that traps women – the majority of workers – in the lower reaches of statutory social work's organisational hierarchies. Earlier feminist work (for example, Wilson 1977) introduced the existence of such a phenomenon into critical debate. Subsequent work such as that of Brook and Davis, (1985), Dale and Foster (1986) and Skinner and Robinson (forthcoming) had analysed various tendencies and practices that go towards constructing such a situation whilst providing, as in the case of Skinner and Robinson's work, an account of feminist training initiatives designed to challenge and change this. These writers have pinpointed the way in which the managerialist form into which social services departments were re-organised twenty years ago has fitted male-dominated career patterns and assumptions, and facilitated men's establishment in greater numbers in the upper reaches of these organisations. In addition, day-to-day working relations and men's and women's assumptions about women's appropriate place and roles in the organisational hierarchy, together with the general handicaps in terms of education, training, self-confidence and family responsibilities with which women face career opportunities, are all discussed in terms of their subordinating effect on women as workers.

## CHARACTERISTIC FEATURES OF FEMINIST SOCIAL WORK PRACTICE IN STATUTORY SETTINGS

Against such an agenda for change, feminist initiatives in practice by now amount to an identifiable, extensive and widespread programme of action. This includes the impact of feminist work from bases external to statutory social work on statutory practice itself; direct practice from a feminist perspective with clients in statutory social work on a one-to-one and small group basis; feminist social workers' support groups; trade union action, and attempts to tackle the male-dominated management pyramid. We discuss the hallmarks of such efforts in turn before going on to analyse their cumulative significance. We shall discuss the importance of a feminist stamp on working relations for social work generally in Chapter 5, but we include discussion of it here as developed in statutory social work because it forms such an integral feature of feminist efforts to make an impact on social work practice in this sphere.

Initially the greatest impact on statutory social work came about through the resources created in feminist networks and campaigns external to social work itself. Thus women victims of domestic violence who might be statutory clients, for example, as a result of the development of Women's Aid, at least came to have *some* possibility of safe, alternative emergency accomodation and a chance of slightly better treatment before the law and at the hands of local housing departments in the longer term (Binney *et al.*, 1981). Women personally active in the women's movement in women's groups, women's centres, campaigning on feminist issues, and moving through training (Donnelly, 1986; McLeod, 1982) have also as a result sought to invest their energies as feminists in their jobs as statutory social workers – leading into the range of feminist initiatives discussed below. In this process feminists in social work education have promoted active interest in developing feminist practice either on their own initiative or in response to student demand (Brook and Davis, 1985; Marchant and Wearing, 1986) through constructing courses specifically on feminist practice incorporating work in a statutory setting. The evidence is that such initiatives now exist on a national and international basis (Women in Social Work Network, 1986; Marchant and Wearing, 1986; Women's Caucus of the International Association of Schools of

Social Work, 1984). As a supplement to this work, feminists in social work education have also acted as a means of providing further support as women engage with the demands of practice from a feminist perspective in what may be a hostile work environment. This has taken various forms: for example conferences (Warwick Feminist Social Work Practice Conference Group, 1979); university-originated support groups (Brook and Davis, 1985); and the production of printed material, for example *Directory of Women*, (1986).

In terms of direct practice with clients, there is evidence by now of feminist work in terms of individual counselling and group work being undertaken as an integral part of statutory social work by women workers around the country (Hale, 1984; Wise, 1985; Brook and Davis, 1985; Donnelly, 1986; Evans, 1985). The evidence is usually in the form of case studies produced by the workers involved even where feedback in terms of direct quotations from the clients concerned is drawn on, the selection of the material remains in the individual worker's hands. We are not suggesting at all that the veracity of the accounts should be treated as suspect but merely point out that the material available on this issue has to be treated cautiously. It also represents a good argument for the development of more systematic analysis in this area.

While accounts of one-to-one counselling from a feminist perspective relate to clients in greatly differing situations (see, for example, Wise, 1985; Hale, 1984; Marchant and Wearing, 1986) we would suggest that the following account by Judith Hale, a statutory social worker deliberately setting out to work from a feminist perspective, bears the hallmarks of such practice.

The official brief for the statutory social worker considered here (Hale, 1984) was to supervise an older son who was home on trial having been in care for most of his life. His mother, Margaret, in her thirties, had had him and another child in the context of two 'failed relationships' and now had two very young children in a marriage that seemed much more stable. We would argue that Hale's work exemplifies many of the strengths of feminist one-to-one practice in a statutory setting:

1.  Without disregarding the statutory brief, from the outset Hale as the worker gave central importance to the welfare of the woman concerned in her own right, as opposed to doing so as

a mean to the end of equipping her to service the needs of other people. In practice this meant paying attention to what could be done to relieve Margaret's low self-esteem and feelings of depression.

2.  The problem was redefined in a way that sought to avoid automatically stigmatising the woman as individually inadequate and took account of the possible social origins of the difficulties that had arisen. Thus it was not assumed that the client had fallen down in respect of women's roles but the possibility of those roles making unreasonable demands on women was embraced. As Hale commented:

> A reading of Margaret's case file dating back to her teens – produced the impression of an irresponsible inadequate woman who had sacrificed the welfare of her children in her hedonistic search for pleasure ... The file was read by the author with the stance maintained throughout contact with her, that she had been the victim of a restrictive upbringing related to her gender and that the early years of her adult life had represented a search for loving, stable relationships and a secure home.

3.  The worker than set out to develop forms of interpersonal interaction between herself and the client in keeping with an egalitarian feminist stance. This meant she presented herself as a resource to be drawn on by the client to maximise her personal and material resources in the interest of her own welfare. This was as opposed to the social worker presenting herself as the bearer of superior analysis, superior models of behaviour, or superior understanding which she then sought to induce the women to accept. The two specific forms such intervention took were the worker herself providing Margaret with a brief respite from child-care through playing with the younger children herself. Secondly, through discussion, setting out the way in which the demands and difficulties Margaret had faced in past and present relationships have much in common with women's experience generally, and acknowledging Margaret's achievements in the face of this.

4.  Hale, as the worker, did not seek to place a feminist perspective on a pedestal above other analyses of oppressive social condi-

tions, nor to treat it as a panacea for all problems. So, for example, the importance to Margaret's well-being of her present husband providing 'in a calm and steady manner a caring and supportive relationship' compared with that of other men in her life, was acknowledged.

5.  The indications are that the client benefited from intervention undertaken from a feminist perspective in two critical respects: first, by gaining increasing feelings of self worth; and second, thereby being enabled to be more active in securing her own welfare. In the process she was able – albeit on a very local basis – to dissolve some of the constrictions of her gender role. As Hale writes:

> Margaret recently observed she had never felt so contented. She related this directly to the fact that she had never felt that anyone liked her and, more importantly, since she had a very low opinion of herself she had felt that this evaluation was deserved. Her new self-confidence has enabled her to establish more social contacts and she has recently enrolled her toddler in a daily play group.

6.  Hale's work also reflects a characteristic weakness in the way in which feminist practice on a one-to-one basis in a statutory setting tends to be conceptualised and carried out. She both sees and accepts feminist practice on a one-to-one basis as being carried out within the confines of a statutory practice predominantly discharging a social control role (see also Wise, 1985). Her argument in justification of this situation is that because statutory work at the one-to-one level will be carried out anyway, at least by undertaking work from a feminist perspective where possible 'a feminist practice will better serve the clients than the alternative which they would, in any case receive' (Hale, 1984).

In response to this question whether it is any solution to feminists to leave the matter at accepting that the effects of their practice will be overwhelmingly countered by sexist policy and practice in their agency and the sexist tendencies in the majority of the workers in their organisation.

Arnon Donnelly's account of feminist group work in a statutory setting (Donnelly, 1986), we would argue, can also be taken as a general example of feminist practice in this respect. Its characteristic features are also similar in several ways to those of feminist one-to-one work in a statutory setting as discussed by Hale. Again, there are many points in her work which we would wish to endorse and which we would argue typify other such feminist efforts, for example in Marchant and Wearing, (1986); Falk, (1986). Donnelly's (1986) monograph concerns the development of a group on a bleak housing estate initiated by two women social services department workers, in which she participated as a student. The points we wish to highlight in respect of her work in a statutory setting are the following:

1.  The original aim was to use group work to promote the welfare of the women concerned for its own sake and thereby in this instance to break through the tendency of statutory social workers to concentrate on helping women to cope as carers for others. As Donnelly describes the workers' intentions:

    Stella and Alison, believing that women are frequently held responsible for whatever goes wrong in a family and that social work intervention does a grave disservice to women by often defining them only in terms of their relationships to men and children felt that to work with women in their own right was valid.

2.  The problems the women faced were redefined away from their being personally inadequate to their having to cope with daunting personal and social conditions as a result of 'the subordinate social position obtaining from their gender ... exacerbated by life circumstances of intense economic and social deprivation'. Indeed, Donnelly's contact with the women led her to conclude that in order to survive, 'extraordinary, even superhuman, efforts' were demanded of them.

3.  The prime aim of the practice of the group was consciousness-raising, that is, to provide a means for women to share the difficulties they faced and the common features of these. This was in the hope of disowning feelings of isolation, building self-esteem and enhancing women's capacity to take action to foster their own welfare.

4.  The evidence from Donnelly's account is that to a great degree the women group members found that genuinely helpful co-operative non-competitive social relations were established within the group. Members' contributions tended to be valued equally, they seemed to invest their efforts equally in the group and provide support generally. As one group member commented: 'We were surprised to know how many of us had the same problems and helped each other by talking about them.' At the same time hierarchical divisions to do with 'differential class and material resources were present as exemplified by the workers' very self-conscious decisions not to stay too long in the group in case they inhibited other members' initiatives'.

5.  In common with other accounts of feminist group work (McLeod 1982; Falk, (1986); Evans, 1985), Donnelly's (1986) work brings out that the provision of continued emotional support was vital, whatever other activities the group undertook. The reason for this was the appreciation that besides its being important in its own right, women chronically had to cope with such heavy demands on their emotional resources that without such support their capacity for activism would have been seriously undermined.

6.  The indications from women's accounts of the group were that they gained considerable benefit in terms of feelings of self worth, and also in terms of an enhanced ability to assert their right to decent treatment – as these two thumbnail accounts respectively illustrate:

> Debbie: 'Sometimes you get the odd one that starts crying because they're upset about what we're talking about and we all go and comfort them and bring them back in and then they're alright after we've had a talk to them ... Because they don't feel embarrassed, you see, bursting out crying because we all know what it's like.'
> Jean: 'There's quite a few have had dealings with the social security and doctors and they just think they can walk all over them, and in fact when they start with the people that are in the Women's Group, they find out that people start saying, 'Well why've I got to do this?' They seem to be

answering them back whereas ... they didn't have the confidence until now.'

7.  Donnelly does discuss the issue of how feminist action in statutory social work may possibly be on a collision course with official policy through challenging the status quo in terms of its treatment of women. But her solution is that possible conflict can be sidestepped by social workers' 'pump-priming' feminist initiatives and then ceasing to be involved as they develop.

Where we would take issue with Donnelly (1986) is in her avoidance of how the problem of possible conflict between feminist small group work and agency aims may be resolved. In this she reflects the general absence of discussion of this issue in the literature relating to statutory social work (see Brook and Davis, 1985; Marchant and Wearing, 1986). A further problem with her approach is that the feminist social workers' commitment to the women with whom they are working and the successful maintenance of valid projects may, for whatever reason, require the continued presence of the feminist workers concerned.

In order to sustain their own efforts as they try to work from a feminist perspective, women workers in a statutory setting have developed their own support groups of like-minded colleagues (Brook and Davis, 1985). There is no systematic register of such groups but the authors' practice and teaching contacts suggest that although the size of the respective groups may be small, numbering perhaps no more than half a dozen or so members, they exist throughout the country.

The strength of interest in feminist social work practice has also been reflected in the holding of a number of national conferences drawing on such support groups, with attendance running into several hundreds (Hale 1984). Accounts of such groups (Brook and Davis, 1985; Evans, 1985) and the authors' own knowledge indicate that their function is to help group members work together to clarify the aims of a feminist practice, to review the outcome of their efforts; and to lend support and endorsement to specific feminist projects. While providing collective solidarity, not surprisingly they are also characterised by controversy in terms of working out the nature of a feminist perspective, and a fluid identity as members move into new working situations or develop new working interests.

This process is reflected in the following summary of the progress of a local support group in a personal communication to the authors:

> Launching feminist practice at all had depended in the development of a women in a social work feminist support group. Across four years involving twenty or so women it provided a forum where the principles of feminist practice were hammered out, where as individuals women developed their understanding of their own gender oppression and support each other as they struggled to develop feminist practice within their work. The support gradually dissolved as participants' need for intense initial explorations of their own experience and feminism was met and as the locus of their interests and efforts moved in some cases beyond the confines of statutory work into related fields where more progress seemed possible, such as unions, women's therapy and the local Labour Party. Meanwhile, ties of friendship had remained for many members and a further support group involving other women has recently been established fulfilling the same sort of role (Cherry, 1984). (See also Brook and Davis, 1985; McLeod and Dominelli, 1982.)

The type of work such groups undertake may be exemplified by two such groups in authorities local to the Warwick course where both authors teach. In the first group, an ex-student of the course, determined to maintain her commitment to feminist practice, has played a key role in developing and sustaining a support group amongst female colleagues across several years. Besides providing a continuing forum for discussion of feminist issues, it has also been working to improve the low status of home-care workers within the authority and plan to develop a women's centre locally. Management's response to such groups is somewhat variable. The impression the authors have gained in relation to this first group is that it remains quiescent, with powers in reserve to be applied if and when the group becomes more powerful and questioning of the authority's practices. For example, while the group is still allowed to meet in work time, the senior managers of the authority have begun to express an interest in being informed in a systematic way as to what is on the agenda at meetings. In the other authority, a group of probation officers established a women's support group within the service. This has recently been given recognition by senior management by being given the opportunity to comment on policies in terms of their impact on women's interests. The overall impression is that women in social work support groups are fulfilling a useful role in fostering the maintenance and spread of feminist practice across a wide range of authorities.

Meanwhile, women workers in both the probation service and social services departments have been working in the issue of promoting better working conditions for women through trade union activity. The issues they are tackling indicate the entrenched nature of sexism not only in the employing organisation, but also in the unions themselves. To illustrate this, in 1984-85, we asked feminists active in their unions in the local social services departments and probation offices to describe the issues they were raising. These were as follows: within the National Union of Public Employees (NUPE) a women's committee was being set up to look at what was preventing women from being involved in union activity; and feminists in the local probation service were active in the Women in the National Association of Probation Officers (NAPO) Group recently formed to promote the interests of women within the union. They were also active in NAPO locally in terms of promoting initiatives undertaken by the National Equal Opportunities Committee, concerning such issues as improving maternity agreements, applying guidelines for dealing with sexual harassment and equalising superannuation conditions and the position of homosexual and lesbian officers.

Besides feminists initiatives aimed at improving general working conditions, a range of work has now begun which tackles the issue of the disproportionately small number of women in management positions in statutory social work (Skinner and Robinson, forthcoming). This has concentrated on training schemes designed to alert both women and management to the issue, to challenge stereotypes which reinforce the view that such a situation is appropriate and to institute positive action programmes to promote women's entry into the senior management in greater numbers. The specific questions that are being addressed can be illustrated by referring to the project that Jane Skinner and her colleague were engaged to undertake in a local statutory social services department (Skinner and Robinson, forthcoming). As a result of their investigation, Skinner and Robinson perceived the block that women experienced in entering managerial ranks was at the 'entry into management point'. They describe their discovery in the following terms:

> Whilst women comprise a majority in almost every service delivery post, including those of social worker, they are in a minority at the first level of management – the team leader or other supervisory post. As this is the first rung of the management career ladder this situation was agreed to be of crucial importance in reinforcing the continuance of female under-representation in management overall'.

Skinner and Robinson's account of the project to tackle this problem illustrates that gains in consciousness of sexism on the part of its perpetrators and preparedness to tackle it on the part of women can be made through work specifically aimed at addressing it. The male managers involved were 'surprised at the extent of their own discriminatory practices towards women promotees'. The women main grade workers felt the course had helped them 'to recognise and assess their own abilities and skills, together with building confidence'.

While the determination of trainers carrying out such work remains undimmed, it is clear from their own accounts of what they are up against that the odds against equality of opportunity along gender lines are still enormous. As Skinner and Robinson (forthcoming) comment:

> From the many connections we have, and contacts made with us by a range of women within the social services industry – it remains the exceptional employer who is taking any positive action. Yet every agency about which we know has a grossly unbalanced staff – both in gender and race terms.

Such work also reveals that women's disadvantaged position in the social services job hierarchy represents the fusion of a number of broad social conditions which require change beyond its own remit or scope. These are women's prime responsibility for child-care, the ideology of male dominance and female subordination introjected at a personal level and the prevalence of managerialism as the organisational form for which the educational and social system has groomed men from birth.

The evidence for two further characteristics of feminist practice in statutory social work is barely discernible due to their very early stage of development – but their importance is such that we should refer to them. These are the development of anti-sexist practice and the fusion of feminist and anti-racist practice respectively. Our teaching experience during the past two years leads us to testify that, though limited in number, there are male students heading for statutory employment who have an interest in and have worked on developing anti-sexist practice during their training. It is not yet clear whether their intention to carry this forward into practice has occurred and, if so, to what effect. Contact and discussion with women in women and social work groups and with feminist trainers indicates that there is recognition that any feminist must endorse and work to further anti-racist practice. Unfortunately, it seems to be the case that both in training and in practice, amongst the majority of white feminists at least, feminist and anti-racist practice have developed almost as separate disciplines. Our impression is also that in respect of male trainers and practitioners concentrating on developing anti-racist practice, it is the exception rather than the rule that they give central importance to gender issues. It seems that at the moment the business of developing statutory social work practice that deals simultaneously with both gender and racial oppression has fallen largely on the shoulders of black feminists. For example, black women were responsible for challenging both racist and sexist practice in one local authority nursery known to the authors and pushing for the implementation of anti-racist and anti-sexist policies, although the social services department was promoting both anti-racist and anti-sexist policies at the time (personal communication to the authors).

In assessing the achievements of feminist practice in statutory social work, which *has* to be done if one is to work out what can be done next, we are drawn to some sobering conclusions. As discussed above, both in theory and in practice the position of women as workers and clients has now been problematised in terms of their gender. Going on from this, there is now a network of initiatives extensive in both organisational and geographical terms which has tackled this issue and is continuing to do so. The indications are that in terms of the women involved as clients and workers on an individual and small-group basis, it has promoted welfare in terms of boosting emotional well-being, securing some material gains and encouraging efforts to place rights and needs on an equal basis to those of men. In the process, feminist initiatives have lent their weight to co-operative, non-hierarchical modes of working. This is in keeping with their basic analysis and has taken the form of, for example, lessening the authoritarian role of social workers, and welcoming collaborative work addressing more than one social division, whilst insisting on the importance of addressing gender issues.

Unfortunately, existing evidence also indicates that as yet feminist practice within statutory social work remains a minority activity with limited impact on overall policy and practice. Thus the isolation felt by feminist workers has been commented on by writers while discussing the importance of developing feminist practice (Wise, 1985). Paradoxically, this is also testified to by the declared need for presence of women in social work groups. Meanwhile, trade unions remain a target for feminist efforts, for they do not provide an unqualified source of support. Additionally, a male dominated employment pyramid persists. Reflecting and compounding the limited nature of feminist influence is the fact that while practice bearing a feminist identity is being carried out, documentary evidence (Hale, 1984; Wise, 1985; Donnelly, 1986; Evans, 1985; Falk, 1986; Brook and Davis, 1985; Marchant and Wearing, 1985), together with our own discussions and contacts with statutory social workers, indicate that the *same (feminist) workers* are still engaged in work reinforcing various forms of social control of women, with all the inegalitarian implications of this. Feminist probation officers, for example, are not organising against the social injustice of using imprisonment for women – and by extension for men – when as the most extreme social sanction we have, it is employed for the most part in the case of crimes of petty theft (Lea and Young, 1984). Nor are feminist probation officers thrusting before the public the evidence piled up in their case records as to women's material deprivation and lack of power to alter this (Dominelli, 1983).

With the exception of a few social services departments, where as the results of the activities of individuals and groups attempting to raise feminist issues concerning child abuse in social services, feminists have still not applied a feminist perspective to the monolithic bureaucracy relating to the prevention and detection of child abuse which dominates social services fieldwork. The lessons of the suspect nature of the social conditions in which children are reared, and the overwhelming burden of child-care on women, our tolerance of violence as a determinant of social relations are accessible in feminist thought (see Chapter 3). Nevertheless, there is as yet no strong feminist presence within social services practice pressing for consideration of the possible benefits of applying this perspective. Instead, up and down the country, feminist as well as non-feminist workers are operating child abuse procedures rooted firmly in the idea of the psychopathology of parents as the root cause of the problem.

We find existing feminist theoretical responses to this dilemma unsatisfactory. Brook and Davis do not address the issue directly and in this way they fail to set their account of feminist practice in a statutory setting in a useful context. At the point at which they write about it, its identity is that of a hard-fought-for fringe activity of limited influence whose analysis is spot on but whose power to change conditions in the direction of that analysis is very limited. Is that how it is doomed to remain? They offer no answer. The response that Hale (1984) and Wise (1985) offer we find unfeminist in its fatalism, that is, that feminist practice can be fitted into a predominantly unfeminist or anti-feminist work setting (see above). The non-solution represented by Donnelly's (1986) work is to acknowledge and appreciate that feminist work in a statutory setting and the main aims of the agency may be on a collision course, but for the workers to opt out before that collision occurs (see above).

CREATING A FEMINIST STATUTORY SOCIAL WORK

Our starting point is that the development of feminist practice within statutory social work is essential. Only by engaging with the demands of social work in what remains one of its major settings, that is, in terms of resources, powers, numbers of workers and clients, can the discipline of feminist social work as a discipline continue to progress. Otherwise, the extent to which it is possible to develop such practice, fused with statutory agency work, remains untested and unknown and its potential benefits closed off to large populations. The attempt to develop feminist practice within statutory social work as its given context is also vital because otherwise it is impossible to deduce how feasible a project this is and the nature of the limitations in practice. While making this point it is important to acknowledge the extent of the continued reliance of feminist work in a statutory setting on feminist action external to it. Thus the ideas of problem redefinition that feminist statutory social workers are working to, for example, owe much to the work of feminist sociologists (see Finch and Groves, 1983) and workers in management studies (see Marshall, 1984). Therapeutic interventions owe a great deal to writings and practice emanating from feminist therapy, and the context of group work has drawn much from feminist work generally on health issues, domestic violence and the development of women's centres.

Unlike Donnelly (1986), our view is that feminist practice within statutory social work is not necessarily on a collision course with the overall policy and administration of the agencies in which it is occurring. It depends on the political complexion of the local and central state governing those agencies. Therefore feminist workers do not *have* to choose between career suicide, to do feminist social work only 'after hours', or follow it only as a 'learning' experience on a course. Nor does feminist practice in a statutory setting have to remain highly circumscribed. To the extent that local and central government reflect a feminist presence, then feminist practice within statutory social work can be underwritten and promoted in a major way.

We are discussing this issue in the context of a regime with a substantial majority in central government and also very powerful base at the local level, whose programme as discussed earlier (see also Chapter 6) is antithetical to feminist aims. Its policies are operating to subordinate women in the labour market, for example the changes in maternity provisions for women, and the entitlements of part-time women to employment protection legislation. These are rendering women more susceptible to entrapment in the demands of domestic labour. Their message is all the more readily received as, besides economic compulsion, it is accompanied by ideologies that endorse such a scenario as reflective of the natural order. Thus in demanding change consistent with feminist principles and drawing on the support of the local and central state to underwrite it, we may seem to be appealing to a far-off hope. In response to this we would say that there are examples from recent history in respect of specific issues, of the powerful impact that endorsement on the part of the local and central state can have in the furtherance of feminist objectives. These examples demonstrate how the same effect extended across a range of issues would transform statutory practice as we know it into a truly feminist enterprise.

The first example concerns the Greater London Council (GLC) which on the basis that it was a vital service to underpin women's rights, through its Women's Committees over three years (1982 – 85) boosted the provision and development of local authority day care by funding more than two hundred projects in London amounting to a 12 per cent increase in existing day care places (GLC, 1984). At present, a Cinderella provision as regards virtually all local authorities, local authority day care for the under-fives is concentrated on providing a remedial service for parents and children 'at risk' or on providing what is universally acknowledged to be a poor quality, low cost (that is to local authorities) service in the form of child minding (David and New, 1985; Mayall and Petrie, 1977). The ideology underpinning either inadequate provision or its dearth is that a women's place is appropriately within the home looking after infant children, irrespective of the detrimental effects on the welfare of all concerned (Browne and France, 1986).

The GLC initiative backed the institution of increased funding for a gamut of collective day care provisions for the under-fives, ranging from well-resourced local day nursery care to specially organised provision for the under-twos, to mobile day centres and after school care. As an integral part of the project, decisions about the types of projects to support were arrived at on the basis of widespread consultation with women's groups throughout London. Parental involvement was built in to undertake some of the management of the day care facilities. The development of anti-racist, anti-sexist practice was underwritten in terms of staffing policies, practices and equipment. In a few years it was demonstrated that where the political will exists in the local state to promote women's welfare, and links into it the welfare of children, substantial funding and policies central to feminist aims can be developed. Far from being at odds with each other, work at what is normally treated as being on the lowliest level of local authority practice and local state policy were fused to promote feminist practice in a striking way.

The history of the ultimate dissolution of the GLC itself (Campbell and Jacques, 1986; Livingstone, 1987) demonstrates how susceptible local state power is to central government control. As will be discussed in Chapter 6, the general tendency of central government is still characterised by a weak or spasmodic espousal of feminist aims, if not marked by policies generally running counter to them. Nevertheless, there have been a few moments when central and local state and statutory social work practice have been unified in temporary coalitions which have resulted in promoting feminist aims. These moments demonstrate both that such an alliance is possible and the powerful effect it can have in furthering feminist goals. One such instance occurred through the PROS campaign to end direct imprisonment for soliciting by women working as street prostitutes (McLeod, 1982; see also Chapter 2). The moment that legislation went through Parliament these forces were synchronised; there was cross-party support for the measure, the Government not wishing to pressure MPs against voting for it because unity had to be maintained in public because of the Falklands crisis. Numerous local probation administrations had permitted and endorsed work supportive to the PROS campaign in agency time. NAPO, the probation officers' union, was affiliated to the campaign: individual probation officers had played key roles in the development of local organising groups. Working from a feminist perspective they had wanted to end the scapegoating of women prostitutes as the originators of prostitution through the criminal law. Although the change in the law has not ended all forms of such oppression of prostitutes for example, imprisonment for fine default resulting from charges of soliciting has continued – it does illustrate the way in which power can accrue from having firm political support for such initiatives firmly lodged at local state and central government levels.

We suggest that these examples and the preceding discussion also illustrate how, for feminist influence to be all pervasive in statutory social work, local and central state endorsement also require the contribution of a feminist presence in terms of the definition of problems to be worked on, in direct social work practice, the organisation of working relations, grass-roots campaigning and providing emotional empowerment on a feminist basis.

We argue that the creation of such conditions, including local and central state endorsement, is not impossible, only extremely difficult (see Chapter 6). But as a result, all the hard work of feminists in respect of feminist statutory social work to date can be consolidated and developed. And in the process, their efforts can be transformed from a promising minority activity into a truly feminist statutory social work – both complementing and being complemented by feminist social work and feminist action more generally.

# 5
# Creating Feminist Working Relations In and Through Social Work

As indicated in the Chapter 4, social work as a profession is one site of women's inequality in the labour market. Moreover, women's position in the labour market generally, while marked by several gains across the past decade in terms of legally endorsed rights – such as in equal opportunities legislation and in terms of the development of various practices such as positive action against sexual harassment – has undergone a deterioration during the recent recession and through the onset of 'radical right' policies. There has been a relatively high rate of increase in unemployment (Coyle, 1984), a decline in the percentage of male income earned (Aldred, 1981; Armstrong, 1984) and the erosion of certain employment rights relating specifically to women such as the right to re-employment after maternity leave (Dale and Foster, 1986). In such a situation one cannot look to any generalised improvement in working conditions for women which will also benefit women social workers, and social work agencies' characteristic organisational forms still tend to be marked by dominance and subordination in a way which is detrimental to the interests of women social workers.

But it is not only the position of women social workers that is problematic in terms of their material conditions. The poverty of the majority of their clients – who are women claimants either at home with dependent children, or single parents, or the elderly, or carers – is increasing in absolute terms (CNCW, 1979; CPAG, 1987; Bonny, 1984; Wilson, 1987; Stallard et al., 1983). At the same time, social workers' practice in relation to women clients' material conditions remains questionable. As described in Chapter 4, the tendency in statutory social work is to respond to women clients in a way that maintains their location in the domestic sphere with all its limitations in terms of personal income. In addition, voluntary and community work initiatives (with certain exceptions) are not centred on securing and maintaining better working conditions in terms of waged labour – see, for example, the ACW collection of articles (Curno *et al.*, 1982). Such concerns are thereby relegated to a peripheral status.

Feminist social workers prepared to recognise the importance of women's material conditions in terms of their welfare, and committed to doing something about this, are therefore faced with a daunting set of issues to tackle. We would argue, however, that there are lessons to be drawn from feminist initiatives on working relations, within and beyond social work, as to how these issues can be addressed. In the remainder of the chapter we suggest that the following strategies, taken together, amount to an informed and constructive feminist social work practice in terms of working relations:

1.  The recognition of the problematic nature of women's material welfare and employment conditions;
2.  The promotion of women social workers' welfare as workers;
3.  The promotion of women social work clients' and client groups' material welfare;
4.  Fostering awareness of the common material interests between women social workers and clients;
5.  The contribution of 'independent' feminist social work organisations;
6.  An appreciation that the achievement of feminist working relations in social work needs the contribution of a feminist thrust in other spheres, notably a feminist political presence.

We end by suggesting that the benefits of such strategies are also in children's and men's interests.

## RECOGNITION OF THE PROBLEMATIC NATURE OF WOMEN'S MATERIAL WELFARE AND EMPLOYMENT CONDITIONS

Our starting point is that in order to do justice to the importance of the issue of their own material welfare and that of the women they work with, women social workers must not be lulled into a false sense of security about 'progress' in this respect.

Marxists have argued that by entering the labour market and becoming waged workers, women can achieve both their independence *and* equality with men (Engels, 1972; Cox, 1974; Wickham, 1978), but despite the fact that women have entered the waged workforce in significant numbers, (reaching 40 per cent of the waged workforce in Britain) their experience of waged work has not resulted in their liberation (Coote, 1980). Though women enjoy the opportunities for socialising provided through their jobs, their accounts of their experiences in the workplace have been bleak. Feminist scholars have substantiated the personal hardship women endure in their working lives, including the daily humiliations heaped upon them through sexual harassment (Benn, 1983), and uncovered evidence demonstrating women's disadvantaged position in the workforce generally (Mackie and Pattullo, 1977). These revelations have come about because feminist research has questioned the male-centred norms inherent in workplace organisation, perpetuated through traditional social science analysis of the working environment, and demonstrated the importance of gender as a crucial factor which mediates, and is mediated by, existing working relations.

Feminists have also challenged the Marxist assumption that women's domestic labour is unproductive, contributing only 'use value' (see Seccombe (1974) for an account of this position). Molyneux (1979) has criticised Seccombe's analysis for treating 'women' as historical categories and therefore failing to grapple with women's work in the home as producers, reproducers and consumers. Dalla Costa and James (1972) have argued that women's work in the home is both productive and essential to capitalism. The Wages for Housework Campaign has demanded that women be paid for their domestic labour as a practical way of making this point. Socialist feminists have been less convinced that this is an appropriate way of handling the issue as it carries within it the danger of trapping women more firmly into being responsible for all domestic work. Instead, they have sought ways which can link the fact that women work both at home and in the workplace. Thus feminists have redefined traditional concepts of work to include both paid and unpaid labour.

Taking gender as the starting point for their work, feminists in the West have shown how women are systematically discriminated against in employment (Armstrong, 1984; Aldred, 1981; Michelson, 1985; Stallard *et al.*, 1983). Women have been shown to occupy primarily those jobs with little status and low pay. In Britain, for example, despite the decade that has elapsed since the promulgation of the equal pay and anti-sex discrimination legislation, the gap between men's and women's wages has been widening since 1979 (Aldred, 1981). Women's earning capacity is only 73 per cent of men's (National Economic Survey, 1983). A major reason for this state of affairs is that 75 per cent of lower paid workers are women (Key, 1983), located mainly in the clerical and retail trades, the textile industry, catering and domestic work, hairdressing, and virtually the whole of the service sector. Even in professional occupations, women occupy the lower ranks, for example as general practitioners rather than consultants in medicine, as field workers rather than managers in social work. Women are, therefore, still engaged primarily in nurturing and caring jobs which have become defined as 'women's work', replicating the tasks they undertake in the home (Beechey, 1977; Howe, 1986). Moreover, whilst Marxists have failed to recognised that women's entry into waged labour does not free them from their domestic responsibilities, feminists have revealed that women workers have, in fact, two jobs – an unpaid domestic one at home and a paid one in the workplace, and have coined a phrase to describe their situation – the 'dual career' women (Rappoport and Rappoport, 1978). Men, on the other hand, tend not to experience similar demands: characteristically, their arrival home signifies the end of their working day, not the commencement of another shift. Feminists have argued that women's progress in the workplace is being hampered by their being used as a reserved army of labour which is drawn into and out of production as the economy demands (Adamson, 1976; Beechey, 1977). What makes it possible for women to be used in this way is the construction of their lives around their primary responsibility – that of caring for others.

Ironically, the pressures on women to work often stem from their caring responsibilities. As the cost of maintaining a decent standard of living within the family increases, the two-income family is becoming essential in practice if not in ideology (Eichler, 1983). This makes a mockery of the idea of a 'family wage' earned by the man (Barrett and McIntosh, 1980) on which wage negotiations and the idea of keeping women out of work are founded. In fact, a women's wage is now so central to the family economy that if women did not go out to work, family poverty would quadruple (*Families in the Future*, 1983). By making such information available, feminist scholarship has challenged the notion that women work for 'pin money': their earnings are now largely essential to the livelihood of their families. However, women's lack of substantial earning power in the labour market, and the failure of the state to make up for it by guaranteeing everyone a reasonable income, accounts for much of the poverty endured by single-parent families headed by women. Poverty in modern society is mainly a female problem, hitting older women and single-parent families the hardest (Stallard *et al.*, 1986; Nett, 1982).

Feminist research has also revealed that, by adding to the tempo and stress in their lives, carrying the 'dual career' burden has held unacceptable costs for women. Being increasingly tired through overwork, their mental and physical health has suffered. Furthermore, the 'dual career' burden has severely constrained the opportunities and energies women have available for developing and enjoying relationships with their children (Calvert in Brook and Davis, 1985). Besides exposing the gendered basis of the stratification within the labour force, feminists have also indicated the demeaning and subservient features which characterise working relations between women and men as subordinates and superiors at work. 'Women's work' within office chores. for example, making the tea, is something that women workers, regardless of their status, tend to be expected to undertake on top of their normal duties. Sexual harassment, ranging from mild verbal attacks aimed at undermining women's sense of confidence as workers, to actual physical assaults on them, is intricately woven into the daily pattern of women's working lives (Stanko, 1985). But these indignities have tended to be ignored as private matters which women have had to handle on their own if they did not want to 'make fools of themselves'. Such incidents were treated as individual problems, and were not made into a public issue until feminists turned them from private woes into a social concern, by organising campaigns aimed specifically at challenging traditional perceptions of the quality of women's life at work (Benn, 1983; Whittington, 1986).

We would argue that women have put up with the limitations of their position at work because of their concern to ensure the well-being of their families, and also because waged work provides them with social contact which contrasts favourably with the isolation they would otherwise endure at home. In other words, feminists have demonstrated that despite the inhumane nature of the labour hierarchy, the exploitative basis of personal relations between superiors and subordinates under the wage contract, and the destructive forms that power relations in the workplace assume, a major attraction of waged work for women is that it compares favourably to the appalling circumstances and drudgery under which they carry out domestic tasks (Gavron, 1966).

In making gender a matter for serious deliberation in the workplace, feminists have sought to redefine the nature of work. Central to their project in doing so is the desire to make employers consider their employees as whole persons with a life outside work which impinges on their activities in the workplace, and which is in turn affected by what happens in the workplace. Particularly important in this respect is their attempt to get employers to accept the fusion between their employees' private lives and responsibilities emanating from it, for example child-care, and their work-related ones. For women to be able to fulfil their obligations *vis-à-vis* their children, for example getting them to school and tending to them when they are sick, and remaining within the workforce on an equal basis with men, several demands had to be made. These are, to challenge the organisation of the working day with its rigid starting and ending points (TUCRIC, 1980); to question the organisation of work itself for its dependence on the pressure of a particular individual in a given post (TUCRIC, 1980); to contest women being confined to the lower end of the employment ladder and their virtual exclusion from leadership and managerial positions (Aldred, 1981; Armstrong, 1984); to attack employer indifference to women's family commitments (Aldred, 1981; Michelson, 1985; Armstrong, 1984); to demand changes in society's expectations concerning men's involvement in domestic life (David and New, 1985); and to argue for women's right to control their own fertility (NAC, 1978).

As a result of feminist organisation in the trade union movement, political parties, autonomous feminist groups, positive action initiatives, networks and campaigns, feminists have been able to initiate a number of changes in workplace organisation. They have been able to legitimate flexible working time thereby circumventing the formerly rigid hours of work which barred women from fulfilling their domestic duties and this aspect has been developed further with other innovations such as job sharing, allowing individuals to share a post and enables them to meet their familial duties whilst maintaining their foothold on the employment ladder (Whitehouse, 1985). Women's climb up the career ladder has been fostered through programmes which aim to instil gender awareness in existing male members of staff, particularly those involved in management, and build confidence among women employees (McLeod *et al.*, 1986). These initiatives have been coupled with the promulgation of equal opportunities policies which attempt to remove systematic discrimination against women in the way in which jobs are advertised, the places from which prospective employees are recruited, the handling of interview procedures and the questions asked of women in the interviewing panel, the support offered to women once they have succeeded in obtaining the post, and the encouragement of women already in position to progress in the organisation (Women Working Project, 1987). In addition, feminists have highlighted the importance of safeguarding women's health. But feminists have raised this concern beyond the traditional one of health and safety at work, where care has been taken to ensure that safety procedures are upheld in relation to wearing protective clothing, handling equipment appropriately and using caution around hazardous substances. Feminists have broadened health and safety at work issues to encourage employers to take a preventive role in protecting women's general health, for example, screening women workers for cervical cancer. Through work in this area, feminists have also questioned the low priority given to men's health and safety at work. For too long, men have compelled to put up with dangerous conditions and hazardous substances which imperil their health because of the tyranny imposed by their role as the 'sole bread winner': men have often accepted intolerable conditions at work because of their need to 'provide for their family' (Dominelli, 1986b).

Whilst these achievements are commendable in that they have challenged previous conceptions of working relations, there is a catch in them – they can be used to *intensify* the economic exploitation of women, whether they are introduced as gestures of goodwill by enlightened employers or adopted out of expediency by more cynical employers. Both enlightened and cynical employers have found that women's performance at work has improved, and productivity increased, as a result of more benevolent employment practices. For example, the productivity of women who have access to workplace crêches has risen because they are able to concentrate more fully on their job, knowing that their children are safe. This in turn augments employers' profits (Allenspach, 1975), but productivity increases through these means have not yet resulted in increased pay for women. The means of facilitating women's entry into the labour market whilst they carry domestic responsibilities do not necessarily operate in the best interests of the women. This has been the case, for example, with regards to the flexibility provided for women through flexitime and job-sharing. Women's take-up of flexitime and job-sharing has reinforced the idea that caring for children and other members of the family is women's responsibility instead of one that is shared amongst all members of society – young and old, men and women alike (David and New, 1985). For what it has done, rather than promote the idea that women should be relieved of the burden they carry in fulfilling their 'dual career', it has perpetuated it (BWU, 1985) because the role of men in domestic situations has not changed.

Our conclusions, therefore, are that a feminist analysis is essential to uncovering the pitfalls that beset women's welfare in any work setting. Moreover, we conclude that the process of placing a feminist stamp on working relations is both far from complete and subject to reverses – but that any modest gains that have been achieved from a range of feminist initiatives. In the light of these conclusions, we would suggest that the issue of women social workers' as workers has to be confronted by feminist social workers. We now go on to discuss what women social workers stand to gain from pursuing the main strategies feminists have developed in social work and beyond, to promote women's interests in working relations.

## THE PROMOTION OF WOMEN SOCIAL WORKERS' WELFARE AS WORKERS

The greater part of our discussion will concern women statutory social workers, as they make up the majority of social workers and are employed in the bureaucracies that have a monopoly over social work provisions. But it is also important to consider the employment conditions of women workers in voluntary agencies and community work units, because their employment in these work settings does not exempt them from problematic working conditions. Systematic analysis of the work setting of women social workers in community work agencies and the voluntary sector is sparse (Dixon, *et al.*, 1982; Hopkins, 1982). Ironically, the voluntary and community work sector provides workplace situations in which women can rise through the ranks more quickly and achieve managerial positions to a greater degree than in large welfare bureaucracies; the reasons for this are as yet unanalysed in the literature. However, in our opinion, they are unlikely to lie in institutionalised sexism being less prevalent in these organisations, but rather in the fact that men find working in such agencies a less attractive proposition in terms of pay, working conditions and career advancement opportunities. We would also suggest, from our working contacts through teaching and practice that the position of women workers in the voluntary sector, with its precarious funding, is particularly vulnerable. It is characterised by the job insecurities that cluster around women's employment by small companies, often on fixed-term contracts and with no clear promotion path (MSC, 1986). It is also our impression that commitment to the ideals of the voluntary agencies concerned leads many of the women workers to discount their exploitation in terms of excessively long irregular hours worked, and for low pay. While the employment 'pyramid' in such agencies may be tiny, our impression is that despite the fact that it may be easier for women to reach managerial positions in these settings, the tendency is for the highest positions to be male-dominated. In view of these characteristics it seems most important that feminist social workers in statutory settings develop links locally through support groups and union groups with women in voluntary and community work settings, to review and assist in their raising pay and conditions issues.

We turn now to the position of British women workers in statutory settings. In Chapter 4 we indicated how the gendered divisions of labour prevail and how women have been primarily confined to the lower levels of organisations (Howe, 1986). To do full justice to the entrenched nature of the institutionalised sexism that dominates working relations, it is also necessary to set out how the organisational development of the past twenty years have been heading towards masculinisation and is continuing in this direction. More women workers are to be found in those areas of social work which are seen as areas of 'woman's work' where the caring aspects of the job are to the fore, for example, residential care with the elderly, whilst men workers are more likely to be found in areas in which the male values of 'control' dominate, for example in probation work (Howe, 1986). In addition, the penetration of corporate management techniques into the welfare arena in the past two decades has resulted in social work becoming more and more concerned with managerialist issues such as improving efficiency, expanding technical resources, being cost-effective, and running the enterprise on a scientific basis (Howe, 1986; Walton, 1975). The intensification of managerial control and bureaucratic intervention in social work, with its attendant growth of male managers, can be termed the masculinisation of social work and has become most evident in the post-Seebohm era. Some feminists argue that the reorganisation, of social services in 1974, following the Seebohm Report with its greater emphasis on male managerial norms, has caused a deterioration in women's standing at the top reaches of the profession (Wilkes, 1981; Skinner and Robinson, forthcoming). We would suggest that what has happened as a result of the restructuring of social work in 1971 is a process of professionalisation which has attempted to rid social work of its 'Lady Bountiful' and voluntary worker image and replace it with one based on a scientific model of efficiency, cost-effectiveness and predictable service delivery. The drive to professionalise social work in a manner more akin to that prevailing in the medical profession has represented an attempt to increase the status, pay and influence wielded by social workers, and the creation of large unified departments headed by men managing the vast resources contained within them has been a central feature of this. In organisational terms, a gendered rationale has emerged for the allocation of work roles according to these criteria. Men have been located in posts in which they could perform most effectively – managing resources, and women have been placed where they were best able to work – with the clients. Thus, women who had been in charge of agencies before reorganisation found themselves demoted as a consequence of it (Howe, 1986). But more significantly, for women as workers, this has meant that women, who have been more concerned with the quality of service delivered to the client, have often found themselves at odds with a managerial thrust which is more worried about how to best allocate resources and 'balance the books' (Wilkes,

1981) than ultimate outcome for clients. This situation has made working life particularly difficult for feminist social workers whose general orientation is one of challenging the bureaucratic approach to social work.

In Chapter 4 we also set out how three types of initiative within statutory social work agencies are nevertheless putting women's interests on the map, that is, trade union action, positive action and training programmes, and women in social work support groups, and evaluated their respective strengths. We would now like to go on to argue that in terms of developing strategies to improve women's position as workers, it is vital that all three sorts of initiative are pursued, and in a complementary way, otherwise the leverage that women can exert as workers in their own interests is undermined. Thus we noted that women in social work networks still remain very reliant on management discretion. Trade union endorsement of their efforts is therefore important so that in the event of discriminatory practice on the part of management against one of their members, industrial action can be considered. Equally, women in social work support groups may provide essential preliminary encouragement to women to take focus on and take up feminist issues related to the workplace, and thereby enhance their subsequent involvement in trade union activity (see pp. 121–4). Women in social work support groups may again provide the vital impetus for positive action programmes and training programmes to be considered by management. At the same time, what emerges as the concern of members of such support groups to foster more egalitarian working relations, may enable them to act as a useful lobby in terms of training programmes geared to promote women's entry into management. Women in social work support groups may be best placed to raise the issue that such training programmes should not become mere vehicles for ambitious women irrespective of their commitment to women's welfare generally; nor feed into the acceptance of managerialist organisational practices as being a 'good thing to get into' irrespective of the lack of hard evidence that they have actually produced benefits in terms of the quality of the caring services provided by statutory agencies (Skinner and Robinson, forthcoming). The combined efforts of trade union, positive action/training programmes and women in social work support groups also seem the least that is required to tackle the position of the three most disadvantaged groups of women workers in statutory social work: black workers, residential workers, and care assistants. Otherwise the brief of such feminist initiatives in practice reduces to the élitist one of promoting the interests of white (Certificate of Qualification in Social Work) CQSW-trained field workers.

In addition to feminist initiatives within statutory social work, it is important to discuss the attempts to make local authorities as employers more responsive to women's needs and interests, as they are the ultimate sources of control over funding and policy in terms of social services departments, and likewise in a major way in respect of the probation service. The local state as an employer of women does not have a consistently good record in terms of serving women's interests. For example, local government has been responsible for some of the appallingly low wage levels women endure in the service sector, such as those for cleaning in schools and acting as 'dinner ladies' (Webster, 1984; Armstrong, 1984). But within the local state in Britain, for example, the formation of Women's Units has been the major vehicle through which, by engaging with Labour councils espousing municipal socialism, fem-inists have attempted to challenge working relations. The Women's Committee Support Unit in the Greater London Council (GLC), the Camden Council's Women's Unit, and the Birmingham Council Women's Unit are three well-known examples. Other local authori-ties have chosen to deal with these issues through the appointment of Equal Opportunities Officers for Women, for example in Leeds and Sheffield. The main objectives of the women's units have been to identify areas in which women's needs were not being met, for example in relation to lesbian women's and disabled women's transport needs (Camden Women's Unit); foster initiatives that would meet identified needs, for example the provision of self-defence classes (Birmingham Women's Unit); find novel ways of working with women, for example setting up women's forums for women residents to have direct contact with women councillors (Camden Women's Unit); and by placing women in charge of the women's units, give women the opportunity to work in settings which would not devalue their contributions. As the represent-ational aspects of the work of the women's units will be discussed in Chapter 6, we will consider only those aspects relating to working relations here.

Whilst these initiatives constitute major steps forward for local authorities in that through their existence and practice they are publicly acknowledging that women do experience specific problems not encountered by men, they are seriously flawed. Firstly, there is the question of their future being assured. The demise of the GLC has led to a substantial reduction in the financial resourcing available to feminist community groups, and indicates the centrality of having government support for feminist initiative in the form of funding. Secondly, there is the problem that these responses may be mere tokens: the axing of the Birmingham Women's Committee following Labour's reduced share of the vote in the 1987 local elections demonstrates that the commitment to feminist initiatives can be more apparent than real (Whitlock, 1987). There is a very real concern that women will be made scapegoats in adverse electoral situations and that this could result in the loss of recent feminist gains in the workplace, such as equal opportunities policies, training schemes, child-care programmes, safety and women's health projects, and research on women's needs (Armstrong, 1987). Moreover, feminists have questioned the extent to which one Equal Opportunities Officer with responsibility for all women employees in a local authority undertake all the work which needs to be done in order for women to achieve equality at work (TUCRIC, 1983). The response is also a token in so far as to does not acknowledge the fact that inequality between men and women at work is not limited to 'employment' issues pure and simple. Third, there is the question of serious under-resourcing of the women's units: for example, in 1984 the GLC allocated £500,000 to the London Women's Unit for all its initiatives in London. Fourth, since this funding is provided under Section 137 of the 1972 Local Government Act, its future is shaky, as central government can decide to withdraw such funding at any time. The abolition of the GLC suggests that this is no small threat under the aegis of an administration that is not pro-feminist and is adamantly against municipal, or any other form of, socialism. The continuation of women's groups which were formerly supported by GLC funds has become extremely insecure as a result of the abolition of the GLC and only those groups which have secured funding from other sources have survived. Last, there is the problem of feminists working within frameworks established by hierarchical institutions: many of the schemes endorsed by the women's units cannot further feminist aspirations for egalitarian social relations at work because the Units are constrained largely to placing women within existing structures which are hierarchical and bureaucratic in their orientation (Coke, 1987).

## THE PROMOTION OF WOMEN SOCIAL WORK CLIENTS AND CLIENT GROUPS' MATERIAL WELFARE

Starting with statutory social workers in terms of their material welfare, the majority of women clients fall into two groups. They will either be without paid employment, living in relative (that is, actual) poverty (Townsend, 1980) and caring for dependents, or they will be without paid employment, living in relative (that is, actual) poverty and in a state of dependency due to infirmity or old age. Taking the first group: the trend of practice undertaken by both feminist and non-feminist in response to this situation is quietist, that is one which does not challenge the *status quo*. At worst, it concentrates on assuming that women 'manage' their role as carers irrespective of the damage it does to their material welfare (Dale and Foster, 1986) and at best it incorporates an element of welfare rights work in order to maximise their income as claimants. Without disparaging the importance of such welfare rights work, we would like to suggest that just as a benefits check should move to become a routine element in social work practice, so should a review with the woman concerned, about training and career opportunities. This is not to assume that the solution to a woman's materially disadvantaged position has to take the form of a job, or that she would necessarily choose that, nor to blind oneself to the low pay and questionable working conditions it could lead to: it is to draw on existing feminist work which has challenged the assumption that 'unemployment' is not such a problem for women in the way that it is for men and which has set out its corrosive effects on women's welfare. It is also to urge feminist social workers to consider using and developing the resources to which they have access, to open up the possibility of employment as a realistic option for women clients.

Writers such as Coyle (1984) have shown that since 1977 half a million women have come 'out of the market', and the opportunities for women to re-enter full-time employment since then have been limited. While women's coping response to unemployment may have been to become full-time housewives or mothers there are several ways in which this may have problematic consequences for their welfare. In Angela Coyle's sample, a number of women had children after becoming redundant but 'in motherhood women face many of the problems of unemployment, isolation, boredom, and the loss of their wage' (Coyle, 1984), and they not only missed their wage as working women, but also the sense of identity and purpose it gave them. As one woman commented:

> You don't miss it straight away you see, you've got your redund-ancy money . . . Then I got everything done and I got bored. I couldn't stop all day in a house. I wouldn't like to spend all day in the house cleaning up, every day forever. (Coyle, 1984)

In addition, where women did have male partners, unemployment tended to confirm the woman in the role of domestic servant because there was now more time available for it and less justification in terms of 'job demands' to avoid it. As one woman who was interviewed said:

> Well everything's done now when he gets in. He knows his meals will be ready on time and he can just sit down for the night. (Coyle, 1984)

Drawing on the concerns of such work and bearing in mind the resources that statutory social workers have access to, we would like to suggest that the following programme of action is considered in relation to unemployed women clients. First, raising the issue of training and career opportunities with the women themselves and drawing on local agencies providing resources of advice and infor-mation on these issues. Second, organising groups in which women can participate on a voluntary basis, to provide useful moral support as these issues are considered collectively. Third, by lobbying management through union action and women in social work support groups, for such amenities as day care provisions and home help assistance to be more readily available to women resuming work. Fourth, seeing and carrying out counselling support as the women concerned re-engage with training or employment as being as legitimate a focus for interpersonal intervention as 'emotional' issues. Fifth, being prepared to develop ways of working with male partners to enhance the chances of their supporting the women concerned in their efforts. Finally, and alongside such action, developing contacts with whatever are the local examples of the increasing range of women's employment or re-employment projects (BWU, 1986b) to establish local agencies as a possible source of recruitment. This adds up to a formidable amount of work, indicating the need for a collective initiative in the nature of a 'resuming work programme' endorsed by the local union or women in social work support group. But the amount of new and additional work entailed is an indication of the extent to which conventional statutory practice veers away from dealing with women's unemployment as an issue, despite the serious consequences to the welfare of the women concerned.

As we said earlier (see p. 134), voluntary agency and community work initiatives have with few exceptions tended to be sucked into dealing with non-employment issues as far as the women are concerned. The main reasons for this seem to lie in the daunting conditions women have to face in an underesourced way in their lives 'at home'. Therefore action on housing campaigns, play facilities, health and nursery resources is desperately needed (see Mayo, 1977). But unemployment also tends to be handled in a sexist way: for example, one author's experience on an MSC Area Manpower Board suggests that agencies which take women's unemployment on to their agenda as a women's issue, tends to do so primarily in ways which simply train women to do 'women's jobs'. Where there are exceptions to this, as in the establishment of feminist community initiatives specifically geared to training women in particular skills in non-stereotyped ways, women's response in terms of their numbers and the degree of enthusiasm for the woman-centred approach of the projects tend to be very positive (see Collins et al., 1978).

Where feminist community work initiatives have been developed on employment issues, they have also given the lie to the impossibility of organising women who are not already in trade unions. This is very significant for women's welfare as employees because women in such conditions are probably the most vulnerable workers. So British feminists initiated campaigns on homeworking, for example the Leicester Outworkers' Campaign (LOC), attracting significant numbers of homeworkers into their ranks. These campaigns were then able to influence both the Trades Union Congress discussions on homeworkers, and push the National Union of Hosiery and Knit Workers into taking a more active part in the affairs of women working from home. Working together, these three bodies have attempted to affect a clarification of the status of homeworkers – as either employees or self-employed people, through their influence on the legislation process. The issue is an important one for women, as the determination of their status will affect their employment rights (Hopkins, 1982).

In terms of promoting the material welfare of women who are dependents, either through infirmity or ageing, feminist statutory social workers would seem to face an even more daunting task, and augmenting two sorts of provision seems fundamental. The first is disposable income to defray the expenses needed to make good the shortfall in availability of adequate shelter, heat, food, transport and social intercourse recorded as virtually the standard conditions for the elderly (Phillipson, 1982). The second is the provision of substantial paid care thereby relieving carers and those cared for alike of the sufferings accumulating as the result of round-the clock care falling on a woman relative with only brief respite, which has again emerged as a commonplace life experience (Finch and Groves, 1983).

In their day-to-day practice, feminist statutory workers may at most be in a position to log the needs they encounter and their agencies' shortfalls in meeting them as evidence to be taken up by groups lobbying specifically on these issues (for example, Age Concern). But at the same time, if women organising within statutory social work were specifically to espouse the cause of women dependants (for example the elderly) it could add to the raise the minimalist standards to which the local state and political parties work. This would be a long-term project, but an encouraging parallel lies in the community work field. Here the National Child-care Campaign has been instrumental in lobbying the GLC to raise the priority it gave to day care arrangements for the under-fives in its policies, and in lobbying within the Labour Party to begin to include a systematic comprehensive policy for under-fives provision in its manifesto (personal communication to the authors).

FOSTERING AWARENESS OF THE COMMON MATERIAL INTERESTS BETWEEN WOMEN SOCIAL WORKERS AND CLIENTS

Just as it is important for women social workers to appreciate *as workers* the *generally* problematic nature of women's working conditions as a target for action, so it is critical that they view the resources that state social work may provide as equally essential to underwriting their own material welfare as well as that of their women clients. For in this way maintenance of such resources, their destigmatisation, and even their expansion, can become a target for collective action as being in social workers' own, as well as those of their clients', interests. To work through one example of this: Jane Calvert in Brook and Davis (1985) provides the following instance of the double burden of working and caring as typical for a woman parent working from nine in the morning to five at night:

> Typically she will get up at 7:00 am to feed and dress the children. This will be seen as her job, since her husband's role is that of the breadwinner and he does not have the social skills necessary to do these jobs. She will get the children out of the house by 8:15 am to be dropped off at a friend's or child minder's before setting off for work. Any lunch break will be spent shopping for the family. Arrangements will have to have been made for children's lunches and for picking them up from school and minding them until the mother returns. After collecting the children she will return home at about 5:45 pm when she will feed the family and if she is lucky get the children ready for bed by 7:30 pm. Next she will have to do the washing, ironing and housework. She will probably have finished this by 10:00 pm and the rest of the time is her own. If any of these arrangements break down then she will have to go sick or get to work late. At work she is likely to be constantly tired and to be seen as unreliable. School holidays will of course present even further complications. (Calvert in Brook and Davis, 1985, pp. 84 – 5)

This description could, in fact, stand for any woman social worker in these circumstances. In this case, one can see immediately how the development of after-school care schemes, also running during school holidays, would be a crucial resource. If the children are of pre-school age, for this social-worker mother as well as her clients, the provision of good day nursery facilities would remove the dilemmas associated with the price of employment being the use of what is frequently, through no fault of their own, substandard care provided by childminders (Mayall and Petrie, 1977). In fact, the availability of such care might make all the difference between the choice to move into paid employment or training or not, because as has been documented, woman hesitate to do so for fear of bad day care affecting their infants' welfare (Tizard and Hughes, 1976). This is not to mention the current government stipulation of the child-care 'availability test', that is, mothers have to demonstrate that they have access to adequate child care facilities if they are to be treated as genuinely seeking work. Again, if the social worker had an elderly or infirm relative at home it is most likely that she would do the bulk of the caring. In this case the state of local provisions in terms of respite care, night sitters, day care centres and home helps might make the difference as to whether or not the social worker could continue in employment at all, or reduce her career chances by moving into part-time work, or possibly wreck her own health through total exhaustion. While it might seem to be moving into the realms of fantasy, a look at the hours this woman is working, besides providing a case for some equitable gender divisions of labour, would also seem to make a good case for the home help services to be put on the same footing as street lighting. The positive consequences for women's mental and physical health in terms of avoiding exhaustion might be as significant as those proceeding from what is already recognised as a public health service.

## THE CONTRIBUTION OF 'INDEPENDENT' FEMINIST SOCIAL WORK ORGANISATIONS

The size of the working population and the scale of the resources involved have made it important to discuss the forms feminist struggles have taken to change working relations in social work organisations not originally established as feminist initiatives. But these work settings can be characterised as still dominated by relations of subordination and labour hierarchy – albeit constraining feminist enclaves, such as women in social work support groups and women's units. It is therefore, also important to assess the significance of feminist efforts to create autonomous workplaces as an integral feature of feminist social work. This is because these initiatives offer the opportunity to examine the additional gains that can accrue from the more wholesale development of working relations along feminist lines in particular work settings.

'Autonomous' feminist workplaces have covered a broad range of enterprises both 'within' and beyond social work, while tending to be small in size. In Britain, these have included commercial activities in publishing, for example *Spare Rib* collective; clothing co-operatives, for example, Ragged Robin; autonomous spaces for women linked to services provided by existing public organisations, for example, health centres for women and well-women clinics; independent voluntary organisations, for example, rape crisis centres; women's therapy centres; and restructured 'traditional' workplaces, for example the Lee Jeans Co-operative. The main features of these initiatives have been their attempt to work collectively and reduce the impact of social divisions, (of race, disability, age, and hierarchy in all its manifestations, including pay, status, and skills); their recognition of the equal worth of the different contributions individual people can make; their reduction in the division between the management and the workers; their attempt to eliminate the division between the demands of the workplace and those of family life; their commitment to both worker and consumer involvement in the decision-making processes; and their woman-centeredness which makes what happens to working women a highly visible concern of the enterprise.

We would like to take the example of the British Women's Aid Federation refuges as indicative of how these aims work in practice and what the shortcomings of placing a feminist stamp on working relations through these organisational forms may be. The network of women's refuges which formed the Women's Aid Federation was originally created to provide a response to women experiencing domestic violence. This legitimated women's right to reject such treatment, did not stigmatise them for being subjected to it, and located the problem in patriarchal social relations which cast women as the appropriate victims of violence. In the first place the refuges have been established as women-centred and controlled spaces, thereby providing safety for women who have been abused by men. Refuge workers' critique of the professional stigmatising response has led them to attempt to reduce the divisions between the 'professional' workers and their 'clients' by encouraging women who have been subjected to domestic violence to adopt the roles of workers and act in collective ways with one another. Enabling all group members to learn skills from one another, such as knowledge of supplementary benefits and effective strategies in dealing with the Department of Health and Social Security (DHSS) has been one way of maximising both material and personal resources as well as providing for more equitable relationships by reducing the power that those who have 'professional' skills and expertise might exercise over those who have not (Binney *et al.*, 1981). Working in this way also ensures that women give to others as well as take from them and so interpersonal relationships tend to become less hierarchically structured (Pahl, 1985). The focus of the interaction between 'the worker' and the woman she is working with is on enabling the woman who has been abused to decide for herself what she would like to do with her life, and provide her with the skills, confidence and support she needs to achieve these aims, whether they relate to material conditions, such as obtaining housing or benefits or gaining work, or 'emotional' issues, such as deciding whether to return to a male partner (Binney *et al.*, 1981). In approaching the situation on this basis, feminists take account of the way in which working and personal lives mesh with each other.

Such characteristics indicate that when feminist forms of working relations are allowed to develop, they cater for women's interests in a variety of important ways. Their freedom to do so may have been achieved through sidestepping the tight bureaucratic controls existing in state welfare agencies, but without being consistently underwritten by substantial resources in terms of material and personal which only a feminist presence in local and central government could ensure, their effectiveness is severely constrained: the quality of the material conditions they provide is problematic and their future rendered uncertain. Thus rape crisis centres frequently only have sufficient funds and volunteers to open for a few hours a week (see Bangor Rape Crisis Centre, 1987). Women are repeatedly on record as finding the physical squalor of refuges, resulting from overcrowding in dilapidated property, intolerable (Pahl, 1985) and ventures such as women's therapy centres – which have to close waiting lists of hundreds because the demand is too great for staff, funded on slender, short-term budgets, to cope with (BWTC, 1986b) – still face a future where funding is not guaranteed.

Meanwhile, it is important not to paint too glossy a picture of the extent to which the establishment of more feminist forms of working relations dissolve all social divisions. Class divisions are still keenly experienced in such initiatives (Pahl, 1985) and black women who have used such resources are on record as being confronted by racism (see Guru, 1987). Such experiences have prompted black feminists, for example, to establish battered women's hostels specifically aimed at meeting the needs of black women. However, these provisions are also unable to meet existing demands for their resources. For example, in the London area, there are only four refuges specifically earmarked for Asian women (GLC/WEG, 1986). Limited provisions of this nature leave the needs of other black women unmet, and it means that the racism prevailing in refuges used and staffed primarily by white women continues unabated (Jervis, 1986). There is also a tendency in the autonomous feminist organisations we are referring to not to attract older women to make use of their services (*Spare Rib*, 1980). This does not necessarily occur because these organisations are inherently ageist, but it may well indicate that they need to pursue positive action policies to reach older women, if their needs are not to be marginalised.

## UNDERWRITING THE ACHIEVEMENT OF FEMINIST WORKING RELATIONS IN SOCIAL WORK

In relation to promoting the conjoint material welfare of women as workers and clients in the ways we have been discussing, it is clear that any efforts by social workers would need to be underwritten by feminist initiatives in other spheres for them to make headway. Feminist work on social problem definition, on women's right to an emotionally fulfilling life, (as opposed to one designed to subordinate her needs), feminist campaigns to maintain care provisions, all come to mind. But political pressure from a feminist presence in the local and central state by government is also crucial for raising issues about women's working roles. For example, the post-war history of the stigmatised and under-resourced nature of day care for the under-fives is also a history of the assumption consistently informing governmental policy, of whatever party political complexion, that such care is properly women's prime, unpaid, responsibility in the home (David and New, 1985). The only consistent challenges to this have come from municipal authorities who have been responsive to feminist arguments concerning the centrality of day care for under-fives in terms of women's welfare as workers.

Central and local government policies have also emerged as shaping and sustaining the male-orientated managerialist thrust of latter-day social service departments. In relation to this, our discussion has indicated that a feminist presence in local authorities and central government generally is required to provide the necessary policy backing to consolidate feminist initiatives within statutory agencies and within certain local authority settings to promote decent working conditions for women. Discussion of the material welfare of women clients and women social workers swiftly uncovered questions about the need for profound changes in policies to income maintenance and the collectivisation of 'care' if women's material welfare and emotional well-being was not to be sacrificed.

Therefore we would suggest that for feminist social workers an interest in the development of a feminist political presence, and consideration of how it might be supported is as relevant to an interest in women's working relations as an interest in women's working relations is relevant to 'social work' practice.

## THE BENEFITS OF FEMINIST WORKING RELATIONS FOR CHILDREN'S AND MEN'S WELFARE

We would argue that by now feminist scholarship relating to women's material welfare and working conditions has demonstrated that the attempt to split women's and children's interests in this respect is a nonsense. There is no evidence that children suffer from the provision of good quality day care (Tizard and Hughes, 1977; Nairne and Smith, 1984; Browne and France, 1986; David and New, 1985). There is every evidence that such care is only provided in a general way when it is endorsed by the state through central government policies radiating into local measures and backed by adequate state funding (Nairne and Smith, 1984; Browne and France, 1986). There is also evidence from other European countries with similar economic conditions to our own that complementary measures relating to working conditions such as paternity leave, shorter working days and statutory parental leave enable both parents to participate adequately in the labour market to secure the dual income now essential to the family' material comfort (Eichler,

1983) and to participate adequately in the care of their children (David and New, 1985). What is good for women in terms of the working conditions and relations we have described feminists as reaching for, is good for children, whether they are the children of social workers or of their clients.

In as much as men become carers through a partner's infirmity or choose to involve themselves in care of dependents, then any improvements in the 'woman's role' in this respect clearly hold advantages for them too. For example, feminist action on maternity leave had resulted in some local authorities and voluntary agencies providing parental leave which enables men to take time off work when their partners are giving birth. Feminist initiatives on securing women equal pension rights with men in terms of leaving pensions to their dependents, for example, widowers, if they come to fruition, will also benefit men. But what about affluent male social work managers enjoying the prestige and material rewards of their status? Surely, it is not in their interests to support a feminist approach to working relations. We would suggest that they ponder on the contradiction hitherto implicit in this chapter. Men occupying such a position are engaged in social work as a profession, to promote welfare. Are they happy that the managerialist role they occupy is at such a cost in terms of the material and working conditions of the majority of workers in their agencies? Are they content that the agencies to which they are dedicating their lives are partly failing to meet material needs of clients on the vast scale we have outlined in this book?

# 6
# Developing Together: a Feminist Political Presence and Feminist Social Work

To conclude our discussion we now want to look specifically at the relationship between feminist social work and the development of a feminist political presence. As we see it, a feminist political presence in local and central government is crucial to feminist social work having any established future. After discussing this, we will review the current nature of such a feminist political presence and the extent to which it has come under attack from the dominant political regime and we will then go on to consider some of the ways in which work might be developed to strengthen feminist action in local and central government, and the contribution that feminist social work can make to such initiatives.

In concentrating on considering feminist work in relation to well-established political institutions such as local government, central government and existing political parties, remaining largely within national boundaries, we are not naively assuming that political power lies with those political forms alone. We are also keenly aware that any national government has to make its compromises with foreign powers, and with multinational companies and financial capital securing their power through their control of resources and wealth rather than through electoral consent. Nevertheless, we would suggest that to begin with both the local and central state hold access to considerable power which is being used to shape social and material conditions. Ignoring the possibility of using that power in feminist directions renders feminism an idealist pursuit. In considering the development and expansion of a feminist political presence we are not overlooking the fact that it is affected by a host of interconnecting forces beyond electoral politics that impede the growth of and support of a feminist political programme amongst women. These comprise ideological, material and institutional constraints that women come up against, which have been examined throughout our earlier discussion. Nevertheless, we regard the development of a feminist political presence in electoral politics as an important route whereby women can gain access to local and central state power in ways that may actively promote women's welfare.

In discussing feminist politics, however, we are also talking about an activity which in our view transcends the party political arena. Feminist politics is about dissolving the separation between the decisions that are made within the public realm of electoral politics, which people primarily affect when they cast their votes, and all the other decisions which profoundly affect people's lives, but which are not made by their elected representatives (Dominelli and Jonsdottir, 1988). Feminists posit a different understanding of power relations from that referred to in conventional political discussion, maintaining that one cannot totally have a division which separates public or institutional power from personal power exercised by individuals. Moreover, as the state intervenes in every aspect of our lives, through legislation, welfare agencies, law enforcement agencies and local authorities, the separation of the two is untenable. It is this belief, that politics permeates every social interaction, which enables us to conclude that a feminist political presence must actively percolate through the whole range of social organisations and interaction. Moreover, such feminist political presence will in turn be shaped by the gamut of activities undertaken in the name of feminist action, including feminist social work.

## UNDERWRITING THE FUTURE OF FEMINIST SOCIAL WORK

We would argue that the fate of what we have singled out so far as the five main elements of feminist social work – the definition of social problems, the development of feminist campaigns and networks, feminist therapy and counselling, feminist statutory social work and feminist working relations, has demonstrated the importance of feminist aims and practices characterising action in what are recognised as the main public political arenas: local government and central government.

To these aspects of feminist social work in turn, it is by now apparent, for example, as discussed in Chapter 1, that the work of problematising women's primary location in domestic labour has not been a once-and-for-all gain of the contemporary women's movement. Instead, the growth in power and popularity of conservative ideologies and the cutbacks in state provisions in the wake of successive Tory administrations has lent increased legitimation to the idea that it is an expression of individual choice and freedom to be cared for where possible 'at home'. The consequences for women as carers are thereby marginalised in public debate and the issue of their welfare as a priority has seemingly to be refought from scratch in reaction against such trends as the withdrawal of state funding from the child-care element in the school day, the increased 'throughput' in hospital care and the reduction in support services for the elderly (Armstrong, 1984).

Meanwhile, seemingly well-established feminist grass-roots networks and organisations such as the Women's Aid Federation face what seems like a war of attrition through funding difficulties. In 1986, this organisation, which has pioneered action on domestic violence around the world, faced the total collapse of its research effort, a future primarily dependent on volunteer labour and the dissolution of its administrative infrastructure because of the uncertain nature of central government funding (personal communication to the authors).

The indications are that feminist therapy is meeting a widespread need amongst women for relief from crippling damage to their emotional well-being (Ernst and Maguire, 1987). The damaged state of women's mental health also remains a massive problem for the National Health Service. However, there is as yet no central or local state backing for a network of feminist therapy centres and as a consequence its work continues to be funded on a shoestring. Where it exists it is treated as an annexe to local authority health provisions (BWTC, 1986).

As discussed in Chapter 4, feminist practice in statutory social work remains an esoteric specialisation as opposed to reflecting systematic policies emanating from local government bureaucracies. As was demonstrated in Chapter 5, women have been inexorably pressed back into the home and out of the labour market as a result of the recession with all its attendant consequences for their material and emotional welfare. This runs counter to and undermines the equal opportunities initiatives begun in the early 1970s – but there is no national policy to address the specific issue of women's unemployment (Armstrong, 1984).

The curtailment of effective feminist social work activity in each of these spheres has a knock-on effect on the rest. Thus, for example, the weakening of the refuge network makes it more difficult to produce evidence of the nature and extent of domestic violence as a social problem. Shortage of resources is hampering the efforts of personnel engaged in women's therapy centres to disseminate their ideas into feminist circles in statutory work because their time for such work is so circumscribed. Pressures on statutory social workers to place work with women in a residual category in terms of work priorities reduces the chances of women's circumstances being highlighted through their practice as requiring attention. Also, in a circular way, if forms of feminist social work are not underwritten by a feminist political presence, the women concerned are less likely to promote feminist political work. For example, it is only as women working in local government bureaucracies begin to experience the benefits of positive action by women's committees or women's units that they are likely to develop a vested interest in their continuation.

THE NATURE OF A FEMINIST PRESENCE IN CONTEMPORARY POLITICS

*The local state*

At the level of the local state, the experience of British feminists is illustrative of the host of problems women engaging in social change in women's interests can encounter. Here, feminists have had patchy success, with some local authorities being more convinced than others of the importance of getting rid of gender oppression. The Women's Committee Support Unit in the GLC and the Camden Council's Women's Unit are perhaps the best-known example of local authority attempts to take on board the 'women's question'. Although both Camden Council and the GLC have established their women's committees in response to pressure put upon them by feminist Labour councillors, they have also developed close links with the London Women's Liberation Movement by using public meetings as the forums in which policy on matters of interest to women have been initiated. Other local authorities have attempted to deal with the problems women experienced as workers, and as members of the community by appointing Equal Opportunities Officers for women, for example in Leeds and Sheffield, as already mentioned (TUCRIC, 1980). The briefs given to these officers have included examining fully the treatment and prospects of female local authority employees and suggesting proposals for equalising opportunities between men and women workers; looking at the needs of women as consumers, particularly in housing design and transport; lobbying on behalf of women; and providing women with information about existing facilities and services.

Though these initiatives constitute major steps forward for local authorities in that they are finally publicly acknowledging that women do experience specific problems not encountered by men and that discrimination against women does occur, we have serious reservations about the amount of work both the women's units and Equal Opportunities Officers can do to eliminate gender oppression in a context where so many of these initiatives are now under attack as a result of the Conservative Party's political power in central and local government. As we know, the GLC's Women's Unit as such no longer exists: the Birmingham Women's Unit is experiencing difficulties since the Women's Committee, a major avenue for its access to and influence upon the elected members, has been axed (see p. 143); and the Camden Women's Unit is facing increasing hostility from the Conservative opposition on the council (GLC/WEG, 1986). In addition, the third term of a government committed to public expenditure cuts as the means of controlling inflation, and the reinforcement of women's position as mothers responsible for the care of their children (Minford, 1984), is unlikely to produce significant gains in the resources local authorities have available for funding projects specifically earmarked for women. Despite these reservations, we believe that the initiatives undertaken through women's units and Equal Opportunities Officers do represent important avenues through which feminists have utilised their employment in local authority settings to advance women's position, and improve somewhat women's material circumstances.

The women's units, like Equal Opportunities Officers, have been given wide-ranging briefs aimed at eliminating discrimination against women and improving their position. The Birmingham Women's Unit, for example, have covered sexual assault, women's self-defence, and the role of the police in relation to crimes committed against women as well as the more usual issues connected with local authorities as employers and providers of traditional services. Feminists working in these units have tried to prioritise women's interests across all local authority departments, involving local women of all races, creeds and philosophies in their activities, and with the aim of transforming the hierarchial decision-making processes of local government. In order to meet their objectives, feminists have had to develop alliances with women who were interested in women's issues (but who did not identify themselves either with feminism or the women's movement), trade unionists, trade councils, councillors and activists in political parties, in particularly the Labour Party. In addition, feminists in the women's units have tried networking on both a national and international basis through various committees concerned with issues around women's rights, for example, the Women's National Commission, the Association of Women's Committees and the European Parliament Committee on Women's Rights. They have also tried to meet the twin objectives of making councils more accountable for the services they provide to women and involving women through working groups, open meetings and conferences more fundamentally in making decisions about the quantity, quality and nature of the services they require (Camden Women's Unit Report, 1982). Women attending these group meetings and conferences are entitled to evaluate the services being provided by the local authority and put forward proposals for changes. However, this attempt to democratise decision-making and expose it to the wishes of the broader collectivity of women has been problematic. For as these forums have no legal standing within the confines of the local authority decision-making hierarchy, they cannot control the voting behaviour of councillors. Lacking formal powers for mandating councillors on specific proposals, the women concerned have had to hope that their persuasive powers are strong enough to influence elected representatives when it comes to taking formal decisions on their behalf. The process has therefore relied heavily on the power of personalities, and on the ability of groups to present their cases and this has subverted the emphasis that feminism places on participatory democracy. Moreover, the councillors' role in the management committee has also been used by unsympathetic councillors to block feminist initiatives aimed at eliminating gender oppression.

The potential gap between those who hold the power to make decisions and those who try to influence their decision-making through open forums has already surfaced in relation to the working groups. Initiated by local feminists, these have taken the form of open meetings between local women residents and councillors to discuss issues and policies of interest to them. The working groups have been used by the women's units as mechanisms through which power is devolved downwards. They were intended to represent those sectional interests in the community which normally receive little attention, for example the needs of disabled women, lesbian women, black women, adolescent women and older women. However, these working groups have often put forward controversial and radical demands, which have embarrassed right-wing Labour councillors and delighted the Conservative opposition – for example, Camden Women's Unit's demands for hostels and refuges in King's Cross for prostitutes: Camden Council's endorsement of the working group's demands in the form of making funds and resources available for their implementation was picked up by the popular press which then used hostile stereotypes of fallen/bad women to construe such moves as Labour's mishandling of public money, and accused it of making grants to 'unworthy' and unrepresentative groups such as homosexuals, lesbians and prostitutes (Camden Women's Committee Report, 1982). In Birmingham, the Labour-controlled council abolished the Women's Committee and sacked women councillors who were chairing major council committees in Housing and Social Services as well as the female chairperson on the Women's Committee because it was nervous of being labelled a 'loony left' council for endorsing the policies advocated by the Women's Unit (*News on Sunday* (1987) p. 13). This demonstrates the precariousness of the position women's units can find themselves in because these are neither formally vested with legislative and executive powers in their own right, nor is there a guaranteed commitment to their presence within the local state or central government.

Feminists are also worried that if they end up being co-opted into the local state bureaucracy, they will be used primarily to identify and fill gaps in existing provisions for women rather than to transform the nature of those provisions and the processes whereby decisions about them are reached. But if feminists lose their radical thrust at local level it will also be more difficult for them to get the local state to influence central government policies in a direction which affirms the allocation of power and resources to women (Camden Women's Unit Report, 1982).

These experiences suggest that the position of feminists operating within local state structures is fairly fragile. They have secured some improvements in the position of women and this has been contingent on their developing appropriate support networks both inside and outside these structures and utilising them effectively in pursuit of their goals. Even when they have managed to achieve this, there is no guarantee that those politicians espousing a feminist stance who are in control of the local state apparatus will respond positively to their demands or underwrite their continued existence within it. This in turn points to the importance of establishing a feminist presence in political parties and within central government. It is this issue we shall now consider.

## Feminist social action within political parties

To date, political parties in the West have been mixed in their response to women's demands for recognition of the special problems foisted on them by society's definitions of women and their roles. We will examine the situation as it currently exists in Britain to highlight both the potential for and limitations of feminist activity on this front. The Labour Party has the most positive record in this respect and as such is the most powerful political party to do so, but even its history is chequered in this respect. It has had some remarkable women organising female members and established a Women's Section as early as 1908 when the Women's Labour League was admitted to the Labour Party and finally merged with it in 1918. However, the Labour Party remains very much a male-dominated party. Its leadership is male (though there was one unsuccessful female contender who stood for the deputy leadership in the 1983 leadership election); most of the candidates standing for parliamentary elections have been drawn from the 'A' and 'B' lists which are overwhelmingly male; and the candidates selected to stand for the bulk of the safe parliamentary seats are male. But Labour is trying to eliminate some of the discrimination in selection procedures and is encouraging women to stand as candidates; it has also reserved five seats on the National Executive Council for women nominated from the Women's Section. In addition, during the 1987 general election, the Labour Party committed itself to establishing a Ministry for Women which had the responsibility of overseeing provisions and policies concerning women and working towards the achievement of equality between the sexes. However, the practical outcome of such moves is limited and there is considerable hostility to some of these 'positive' measures from both male and female members. Opponents to the creation of special facilities for women argue that women have already achieved equality in the Party and that women's low profile arises because they fail to get involved in its activities. Whilst some Labour women reject the pathologising of women for their failure to achieve prominence in the Party, they maintain that women do not need special measures to do so. They contend that women are able enough to compete with men on their terms and win if they are sufficiently motivated (personal communications to authors). Others see Labour's commitment to improving the position of the working class generally as providing sufficient safeguards for women. Even the radical leader of Sheffield City Council has opposed women-only organisations in the Labour Party. He stated, 'I wouldn't want women to organise separately. It is bound to divert energy and commitment from other things. We're all in this together, if one lot goes down, we all do' (Ashurst, 1987). Besides this, the Labour Party did not win the 1987 general election. Even if it had, feminists have doubted whether the much publicised 'Ministry for Women' would eliminate gender oppression. Ashurst (1987), for example, criticises the Labour Party for packaging 'women's issue' in a way that marginalises women's interests. In fact, she considers the creation of a separate ministry for women as a way of entrenching male power and privileges. She says that:

> Women who are asking for more than a bit of freedom from the kitchen sink pose a . . . threat. One way of containing this threat is to separate male and female political spheres. We get childcare and the domestic front whilst they get the 'big' issues that deal with the economy, industry, employment and defence. (Ashurst, 1987, p. 47)

Female Labour members of Parliament are still few in number.

Although ninety-three women candidates stood for Labour in the 1987 elections, only twenty-one gained seats. The position of black women is even less represented than of white women. It was not until the 1987 election that Britain's first black woman (Labour) MP was elected. The paucity of women in the house of Commons is largely attributable to the fact that most of the women candidates stood in seats unwinnable by Labour. Of those women who have managed to get into the House for Labour, even fewer have been invited by their male leaders to assume ministerial positions, particularly at Cabinet level. For example, only two women have reached these heights during the period since the second world war Avowed feminists seem to have had an even worse fate. They have not yet made it to the higher corridors of ministerial power, although some have recently been promoted as key figures for the proposed 'Ministry of Women'. However, as mentioned earlier, the amount of power this ministry would have had if Labour had succeeded in winning the election is doubtful (Ashurst, 1987).

Labour's record on policy is also patchy in terms of seeming to be more pro-feminist when in opposition than when in power. When in government, Labour's progress in improving women's material circumstances gives way to arguments about costs, as economic considerations gain ascendancy over political commitments. So, although Labour introduced the Equal Pay Act, it gave employers a period of five years in which to adjust to the idea. Supported by the Confederation of British Industry (CBI), employers used this period to find ways of evading or avoiding the provisions of the Act through the numerous loopholes it provided. Labour did not implement its policies on child-care provisions and child benefit because of the high costs involved. Most of the findings of the Finer Report, aiming to improve the financial position of mothers and particularly those in charge of single-parent families, were virtually ignored. Even though Labour passed the Sex Discrimination Act in 1975, it excluded much of government activity from its scope, for example, taxation, social security, pensions and immigration law. Yet these are areas which cause a great deal of hardship to women and are a major source of discrimination against them because they operate so heavily against women's welfare.

This account demonstrates that both integrated and separate provisions in the Labour Party have only helped women achieve limited gains in placing a feminist stamp on the Party. Economic exigencies override concerns about women's liberation during critical periods in the economy, and its socialist commitments to protecting the interests of the working class fail to defend women's interests either as members of the working class or as a significant proportion of the population which does not own or control the means of production. What the evidence of Labour's poor performance on the women's issue also highlights is its powerlessness as a national political party with a weak mass base when it comes to confronting the real owners of the country's resources and the real wielders of the power that comes with that ownership – the international financial, commercial and industrial bourgeoisie. The response of the most recent Labour Administration in relation to the public expenditure cuts provided ample demonstration of this weakness. At the time, Labour complied with the International Monetary Fund's demand for the slashing of public expenditure by placing the major burden of this on the welfare state, leading to a drop in employment opportunities for women in state employment and a reduction in welfare services which women were expected to meet within the confines of the family (Dominelli, 1978).

The current state of a feminist presence in the other minority political parties in Britain must be considered as they might in theory offer a promising means for advancement. However, a review of the situation in practice indicates that this is not the case. The SDP/Liberal Alliance has not got a much better record in respect of women holding positions of power than has the Labour Party; while a women remains as President of the SDP, the important leadership role is held by a man. Similarly, the Liberal leader is male. Although fielding a greater number of women candidates than the other two major parties in the 1987 election (*Labour Research*, 1987) there are only two Alliance women MPs. Otherwise, while the Alliance did not espouse a Ministry of Women in the 1987 election, many of the Alliance policies on women approximate to those held by Labour, for example those relating to child benefits and pensions (see *Woman*, 1987, p. 21).

The record of left minority parties, for example the Socialist Workers' Party, and the Workers' Revolutionary Party, has not impressed feminists because of their emphasis on the supremacy of class oppression over other forms of oppression. In fact, their performance, particularly with regard to feminists within their own ranks, and their insistence that women's liberation would be the automatic outcome of the revolution putting the working class in power, formed the basis of the feminist critique of the Left (*Feminist Review*, 1986). Feminists have therefore demanded that socialists and Marxists take on board, both politically and personally, the specific subject of the oppression of women (Rowbotham *et al.*, 1979).

The Communist Party (CP) lost a number of its prominent feminist members when they grew disillusioned with its failure to respond meaningfully to women's issues and to give them the priority they deserved. Its authoritarian structures, sexist practices and refusal to give women's issues priority over economic concerns convinced many feminists that it was appropriate either to leave the CP or not join it in the first place. Yet, CP policy endorses many feminist demands, including those covering equal pay, abortion, the provision of child-care facilities, and the socialisation of domestic labour. Communist Party intellectuals have also contributed to the development of feminist theory and practice through their writings and involvement in community politics and trade union activities. However, the strength of the CP's impact as party is weaker now than it was during the Minority Movement of the 1930s.

Although the Green Party (the former Environment Party) has a small following, its leadership is collectively organised and it includes issues of major concern to women within its Manifesto, for example peace and the protection of the environment. The potential of the Green Party to attract a large number of followers is difficult to asses. A major factor limiting the electoral growth of the Green Party is that other parties, particularly the Labour Party, have picked up on a number of issues which they see as major attractions, for example the question of animal rights and defence.

*Feminist social action within an autonomous political party*

Our account so far indicates that as yet no parties on the left in British politics have a very developed feminist stamp. In theory, a possible solution to the conundrum of how to achieve power within existing party political structures but without relinquishing feminist aims lies in the formation of an independent feminist political party. This has not yet been developed in Britain but has been created, for example, in Iceland, and we shall now consider the opportunities created by feminist action following this tack. While making allowances for different social and economic conditions, the experiences of Iceland's feminist party is instructive for feminists thinking along these lines elsewhere.

Kwenna Frambothid (KF), the Icelandic feminist party, was formed at a mass meeting of women called in November 1981 by a small group of feminists who felt frustrated with the Icelandic feminists movement for its failure to substantially alter women's position in the country. The women concerned decided to form a feminist party which would follow feminist collective principles with the short-term aim of influencing the electoral process at the local level and using any position within it to highlight the oppression of women in Iceland and to press for provisions promoting women's welfare. Kwenna Frambothid candidates stood for the May 1982 elections in Rekjavik and Akureyri and the party gained 11.7 percent and 18 percent of the vote respectively, resulting in the election of two councillors in Rekjavik. The position of the KF councillors in Akureyri was different from that of Rekjavik because the election of a hung council made them feel compelled to join the left-of-centre coalition, so their feminist political edge rapidly became blunted. Therefore we will focus on the activities of the Rekjavik group.

Within a very short time, KF women, in association with other women who were interested in women's condition but were not party members, had established a number of feminist ventures, for example a feminist newspaper, a woman's centre, a refuge, and a organisation for working women – the Organisation of Women in the Labour Market (SKV) which was a major initiative attracting working-class women to the feminist movement. However, within a year of its formation, ideological rifts amongst KF women led to a split which resulted in the formation of another political party – Kwenna Listin (KL). The rifts revolved around the question of the nature of feminist politics and the extent to which feminists could become involved in electoral politics without reneging on feminist principles. The disagreements between the women on this score were profound: the KF women felt that feminists could only have a limited role in electoral politics, whilst KL women felt that the importance of doing something about women *as women* gave them a larger political role which included their standing for parliament and being less concerned about the political philosophy held by the women who joined their ranks. Thus, KF came to be considered a feminist party whilst KL became a women-centered women's party. Kwenna Listin went on to win three seats in the national elections of 1983, and nine seats in the parliamentary elections of 1986; Kwenna Frambothid candidates did not run in either of these elections. In fact, the struggle within KF, amongst women who wanted to join KL women and stand for the 1986 elections and those who did not, became so bitter that KF folded up as a party, whilst those women who wanted to stand for parliament did so through the aegis of KL (Dominelli and Jonsdottir, 1988).

With regard to the lesson feminists can draw from Icelandic experiences, it would seem that the organisational device of the formation of a feminist party alone is insufficient to solve the problem of gaining political power on feminist terms when feminists are still in a political minority. Instead, such a development in isolation would seem to run the risk exemplified by the fracture of KF and KL. If women want party political power in the short term they may have to disown feminist principles that are now in the ascendancy. If women want to maintain such principles, they run the risk of not being able immediately to gain political power by mounting a party programme. In either case, a feminist political party becomes a weak vehicle for establishing feminist political power.

## Feminist political action beyond political parties

Our discussion has revealed that a significant number of feminists in Britain (as in Iceland) remain dissatisfied with both existing political institutions and the response of all left political parties on the issues nearest to their hearts. In Britain, their attempts to discover fruitful ways forward have taken two main forms. The first, popular in the early 1980s was the possible development of forums to unite different segments of the left. This was epitomised by the Beyond the Fragments Conference of 1980 (Rowbotham *et al.*, 1979). But such public stagings of possible unity have not led to the creation of a consistent force to be reckoned with. Second, a substantial number of feminists have responded to the political vacuum on the left and its resistance to grappling with personal sexist and heterosexist practices by focusing on separatist autonomous organisations for women which are more concerned with providing for welfare in relation to specific issues rather than being involved in any form of electorally-based politics. Particularly prominent in this context is the work of radical lesbian feminists. But such women-only initiatives cover a vast range of issues from groups such as Women's Arts Projects to the Greenham Common Peace Camp to Rape Crisis Centres. These groups do play a 'political' role in challenging institutions symbolising male power, for example the media, the nuclear arms race, and the primacy accorded to male needs. However, their treatment of what is 'political' reflects an attempt to link the issues of the power individual men hold over women, directly with the issue of the patriarchal power men exercise over women as a gender through control of society's power and resources. They leave the political organisation of society in terms of its electoral machinery outside the scope of their analysis. While such an approach has been influential in stirring public consciousness and framing public debate, we feel this view, which amounts to sidestepping powerful political structures in society, misses a valuable opportunity for feminists to consider how they might influence the development of social relations further in progressive directions.

Beyond women actively involved in such groupings are other women whose numbers are impossible to quantify but on the evidence present in this book alone are considerable, who on an individual basis as a result of engagement with feminist activity are embodying feminist aims in their social relations in a way which is important to them and are keen to continue to do so, or to alert other women to the belief in this. Research of the longer-term effects of woman's contact with the services provided by feminist enterprises as diverse as publishing, battered women's refuges or women's therapy centres is sparse – but it might yield a systematic account of this phenomenon which confirms the power of its influence. For example, in the research of the outcomes of feminist therapy which one of the authors is currently undertaking, she has found that the work of four women counsellors has enabled dozens of women 'ex-clients' to face up to the emotional demands of their lives up to a couple of years later with what they recognise to be new-found emotional self-esteem. Moreover, they are also keen to do what they can to foster the development of women's therapy centres so that other women can benefit (McLeod, 1987b). Such allegiance to feminism does not, however, either necessarily nor readily translate into formalised political support for a feminist programme through voting or party political membership. Even if it did, our foregoing discussion indicates a consistent feminist programme for it to support seems some way away in terms of any party political agenda.

### 'The opposition party'

Ironically perhaps the strongest case for the importance of developing a feminist presence in local and central government in Britain is made by referring to the record of the Party serving under the first woman Prime Minister. The Conservatives staunch endorsement of patriarchal relationships and familial ideology has produced a devastating decline in the fortunes of women as post-1979 legislation and public expenditure cuts have wiped out a number of earlier feminist gains. Conservative Cabinet Ministers have in the meantime busied themselves with reinforcing traditional notions of domesticity and femininity, and have produced a depressing catalogue of women's material losses under Tory stewardship (*Labour Research*, 1983). One of the most telling illustrations of the political attack that feminist aims and gains are currently under is provided by an analysis of the erosion during the Conservative Administration of the measures achieved through the 1970 Equal Pay Act and 1975 Sex Discrimination Act. These include:

(i)     a widening gap between male and female earnings; female wages declined from a high of 75.5 per cent of male wages in 1977 to 73.9 per cent of male wages in 1982 (*Labour Research*, 1983);

(ii)    losses in maternity leave provisions and protection for pregnant women through changes in the earlier legislation: changes introduced under the 1980 Employment Act make it more difficult for women to get their jobs back after pregnancy; the notification requirements for women to return to work have been tightened and made more complicated; and a women's right to her old job back has been reduced to 'suitable alternative employment', with the power for the employer to dismiss her if she refuses to accept a 'reasonable' offer;

(iii)   a disproportionate rise in female unemployment as public expenditure cuts have savagely reduced services – three-quarters of those losing their jobs in the public sector are women;

(iv) an increase in the caring burden that is borne by women at home as support services decline through nursery closures, and cuts in home help services, day centres for the elderly and homes for the handicapped;

(v) a heavier burden for the low paid (*Labour Research*, 1983): this affects women workers who form the bulk of the low paid – male workers who form the bulk of the highly paid benefit from tax reductions accruing to those in the high income brackets;

(vi) a reduction in the rights of part-time workers, the majority of whom are women, moreover the Conservatives have abolished some Wages Councils and curtailed the powers of the minimum wages machinery attached to low paid industries which have offered unionised women workers a modicum of protection, for example, those aged under 21 have been excluded from being covered by Wages Council protection, affecting mainly women who form the bulk of the low paid, and the remit of Wages Council has been limited to setting minimum requirements for holidays and holiday pay;

(vii) the introduction of the 'availability for work' test through forms UB41 and UB671 make obtaining work for women whose child-care arrangements allow them only to undertake wage labour on a part-time basis more difficult. Women are now compelled to demonstrate that their child-care arrangements enable then to undertake full-time work (WWAF, 1978) Women who cannot meet these requirements are deprived of unemployment benefit even though they have the requisite contributions, because they are considered unavailable for work. Moreover, it provides an extreme example of how the ideology of familialism is reinforced. Women who would rather go out to work are forced back into the home, and dependent on a man's income through either cohabitation, marriage or prostitution. Enforcing women's dependence is absurd given the significance of women's earnings to the 'family' income. It is even more nonsensical in the face of statistics indicating that only 8 per cent of all family units include a mother, father and dependent children;

(viii)   the perpetuation of specific discrimination against married women. Although the Conservative Government's refusal either to give housewives easy access to the Non-Contributory Invalidity Pension or to allow married women entitlement to the Invalid Care Allowance have had to be modified as a result of a European Court ruling that such activities constituted discrimination on the grounds of sex and marital status, the Government has affirmed its recalcitrance in respect of married women's rights by denying them access to the Community Programme by making only those who have been on benefit eligible for such work. The Government's stance on this issue continues to reflect the view that the woman, in her role as wife, mother and daughter should be caring for her invalid husband, handicapped children and aged parents for nothing, as a 'labour of love';

(ix)   an exacerbation of the insecurity prevailing amongst black women. Black women's settlement rights have deteriorated substantially as immigration rules have tightened and the 1981 Nationality Act has taken effect (Cohen, 1981; CCAB, 1983); Commonwealth women can no longer acquire patriality or register as British citizens through marriage. Foreign-born women who are British citizens cannot bring foreign-born husbands and fiancés into the country. Furthermore, wives can be deported if their husbands are deported even though they have not contravened any law themselves; and

(x)   a greater intrusion into the lives of poor women by the state, through the DHSS and Social Security Services departments, and by employers who have been given rights to administer provisions under the Family Credit Scheme and Social Fund as specified in the Social Security Act of 1986 (LSSC, 1986).

THE FUTURE OF A FEMINIST PRESENCE IN POLITICS AND THE CONTRIBUTION OF FEMINIST SOCIAL WORK

Our starting point, coming from a background in feminist social work, is that we are not surprised that a feminist presence in local and central state government is at such an early stage of development and suffering reverses, but neither are we daunted by this. For we would suggest that the lesson from feminist action on any gender-related issue, for example, rape, incest, women's labour or women's emotional welfare is that gender-based inequality permeates social relations in a profound way. Thus it is to be expected that feminist gains in any one sphere may be slow and halting because one is dealing with such powerful vested interests. Applied to local and central government politics, this means that the faltering nature of such progress is not sufficient evidence in itself to conclude that a substantial feminist political presence will never be developed.

But having said this, it is no excuse for inaction: for just as a feminist analysis and practice rejects conservative determinism as represented by the idea that women are intended by nature to be subordinate through their gender, so it also rejects a fatalistic 'law of history' approach, guaranteeing that one day seemingly insoluble social inequalities will be resolved in a truly classless state. Instead, feminists appreciate that gender equality has to be created by their efforts; having the 'correct' analysis alone does not ensure that it will happen. This feminist spirit is well summarised in Skinner and Robinson's reflections regarding training in social services departments:

> We have no ready-made recipe for a quick and easy change. But we know from experience of the last years as trainers and women who are/have been managers, that significant and positive change can occur when two or three prime movers set out to achieve movement – even against the odds. We leave to those who believe the current situation to be equitable and efficient, lengthy explanations of the problems associated with generating change. We shall continue to engender, encourage and assist those taking positive action. (Skinner and Robinson, forthcoming)

On the basis of our preceding discussion, we would suggest therefore that there is still 'all to play for' in both negative and positive senses in terms of developing a feminist political presence. Beginning with the local state, our discussion in this and previous chapters indicates that a feminist stamp on policy and provisions at the local government level is vital to underwriting a score of policies and practices in women's interests. Therefore this should remain a site for feminist intervention. But this in turn means that work to develop a feminist party political presence has to be continued because again, as our earlier discussion illustrated, this is essential to the maintenance as well as the development of feminist action in local government. While there is feminist representation in party political activity, its weak condition indicates that it is crucial to seek ways of developing it; we would suggest that there are existing resources in feminist practice and principles which could be drawn on to achieve this.

First, feminists concerned to build feminist interest in and support for engagement with local and central government activity should develop negotiations with feminists primarily concerned with action in groups devoted to specific issues, on the following basis. The fate of such groups during the past decade indicates that unless their efforts are endorsed at both central and local levels material resources are likely to be curtailed and their future placed in jeopardy. Therefore their active support through voting, lobbying or organising to maintain and increase the number of feminist candidates is vital. Equally, women who may have, or stand to benefit from, feminist amenities underwritten by local or central government funding, which as we have previously argued could represent an enormous number, could justifiably be appealed to on the same basis.

In turn, the groups and individuals appealed to would have the right to expect that 'their' candidates would adhere to implementing feminist aims if supported and elected. In this way one would be working towards the fusion that the Icelandic women's party failed to achieve, of building up the numbers of feminists in power through party politics whilst adhering to feminist programmes. The evidence of the increased number of women voting for Labour in the 1987 General Election (*Guardian*, 1987) suggests that women are increasingly prepared to endorse those elements of feminism which were presented to the electorate. We are inclined to think that if women, including non-feminist women, are offered programmes that are of relevance to them, they will support them. Certainly, the experience of KL in Iceland is that when a 'women's programme' was placed before the electorate, it succeeded in capturing 18 per cent of the national vote, male voters included (Dominelli and Jonsdottir, 1988). This suggests that some men will also back activities aiming to improve the position of women.

In addition, the indications from the social work enterprises we have reviewed are that feminist principles and practices – when followed – constitute a political programme that attracts allies from an even broader constituency. The principle of not prioritising the importance of various social divisions, while not denigrating the importance of any, once battled out, has been the basis of alliances between feminists and those confronted by racism, ageism, hetero-sexism, ablebodiedism, and men concerned to dissolve sexist pract-ices. There is evidence of the feasibility of such alliances in the work undertaken by black feminists whose struggles against racism and sexism have involved them in making across-the-board alli-ances within the black community and amongst those outside it supporting their aims (see Lorde, 1984). This point was reiterated by Angela Davis in her speech in London on International Women's Day in 1986:

I think this is a period where we must increasingly acknowledge the interconnectedness of our struggles. It is impossible to formul-ate an accurate view of women's oppression without taking into account the economic dimensions of our oppression, without of course understanding the critical role played by racism, and without understanding their relationship to the global battles for peace. (Davis, 1987)

Therefore, in feminist action one may have in practice the unifying principle which left-wing parties have yearned for in theory under the title of a broad democratic alliance and thereby potentially and gradually a great swathe of support, as and if feminist political organisation develops further.

Meanwhile, feminist action is coming of age in respect of the issue of state control of resources, having pressed for their use in women's favour through the women's units. We would suggest that the recent development of campaigns and networks ranging from Greenham Common women to miners wives campaigns and work to promote women's welfare as workers marks a new and critical phase in the women's movement, while opening up a further vast sphere of operations. This is that feminists have now begun to be politically aware of the importance of the direction of material resources as reflecting social justice in terms of gender, which is now seen as too important to be 'left to men' while constitutional or domestic issues or simply equal access to job opportunities are pursued. The target is a long way off but it means that ultimately the operations of international capital are now in feminist sights (Davis, 1986).

Moreover, taking together the testimonies of women throughout this book, the hallmark of engagement with feminist action is that it is reflected actively in the personal working and public life of the individual concerned. We would suggest, therefore, that any 'gain' for feminism is not a matter of superficial political allegiance but qualitatively already goes beyond what major political parties achieve in terms of their more numerous supports.

Finally, there are indications that as feminist social work develops it can contribute to strengthening a feminist presence in party politics at a central and local level. In the first place there is evidence that feminist work in terms of uncovering social problems has made and can make its mark on party political programmes. It was noticeable in the 1987 general election, for example, that following many years of work on the part of feminist activists and scholars (see Hanmer and Saunders, 1984) the Labour Party placed centrally in its manifesto, as a specific issue, the tackling of violent crime against women. Meanwhile, a plethora of grass-roots campaigns and networks ranging from women's therapy to women's art groups to day care initiatives have demonstrated gender-based need and created organisational structures that have been in a position to have local authority or government funding channelled their way, thereby making it possible for such resources to be directed towards meeting women's interests at ground level.

The documentation of the outcomes of feminist therapy and feminist counselling (Eichenbaum and Orbach 1985; Ernst and Maguire, 1987) is gradually building up. It indicates that there are definite gains from such work in terms of the release of women's emotional energy, development of self-confidence and supportiveness to other women. Moreover, these gains are also constantly building up the population of women actively engaged in promoting their own and other women's personal welfare along anti-sexist lines (Donnelly, 1986; Ernst and Maguire, 1987). In this way also, therefore, feminist work relating to the most intimate corners of experience is gradually creating a supportive tendency for feminist initiatives to draw on at the macro-level.

In addition, the development of a feminist professional presence in statutory social work means that any resources coming into those agencies to tackle social injustice rooted in gender stand some chance of being used in that way. Finally, feminist initiatives on working relations running throughout the social work field have not as yet transformed social work agencies into models of working relations in terms of gender. For any sympathetic administration, however, they have marked them out as prime sites for work on the betterment of women's material welfare as clients and workers.

Feminist social work has the capacity to make a major contribution to the welfare of women, children and men. We hope that this will encourage your support and involvement in it.

# Bibliography

Achilles Heel Collective (1983) *Achilles Heel Special Issue on Masculinity*, no. 5. (London: Achilles Heel Collective).

Adamson, O., Brown, C., Harrison, J. and Price, J. (1976) 'Women's Oppression Under Capitalism', *Revolutionary Communist*, no. 5, pp. 1 – 48.

Ahmed, S., Cheetham, J. and Small, J. (1987) *Social Work with Black Children and their Families* (London: Batsford).

Aldred, C. (1981) *Women at Work* (London: Pan).

Allenspach, H. (1975) *Flexible Working Hours* (Geneva: International Labour Organisation).

Amos, V. and Parmar, P. (1984) 'Challenging Imperial Feminism', *Feminist Review* no. 17, Autumn, pp. 3 – 19.

Andrews, B. (1982) 'Violence in Normal Homes', unpublished Research Paper (Department of Social Policy and Social Sciences, Royal Holloway and Bedford New College, London).

Arcana, J. (1983) *Every Mother's Son – The Role of Mothers in the Making of Men* (London: The Women's Press).

Ardill, S. and O'Sullivan, S. (1986) 'Upsetting an Applecart: Difference, Desire, and Lesbian Sadomasochism', *Feminist Review*, no. 23, pp. 31 – 58.

Armstrong, J. (1987) 'Comment', *Everywoman*, June, p. 38.

Armstrong, P. (1984) *Labour Pains: Women's Work in Crisis* (Toronto: Women's Press).

Ashurst, F. (1987) 'Women on the Margins', *Spare Rib*, no. 179, June.

Bailey, R. and Brake, M. (1975) *Radical Social Work* (London: Edward Arnold).

Bailey, R. and Brake, M. (1980) *Radical Social Work and Practice* (London: Edward Arnold).

Baker-Miller, J. (1978) *Towards a New Psychology of Women* (Harmondsworth: Penguin).

Bangor Rape Crisis Centre (1987) *Information Leaflet* (Bangor: Bangor Rape Crisis Centre).

Banks, O. (1981) *Faces of Feminism* (London: Martin Robinson).

Barker, H. (1986) 'Recapturing Sisterhood: A Critical Look at 'Process' in Feminist Organising and Community Work', *Critical Social Policy*, no. 16, Summer, pp. 80 – 90.

Barrett, J. (1986) 'Anti-Sexist Book Project at P.C.L. Nursery', *National Childcare Campaign Newsletter*, Sept/Oct.

Barrett, M. (1986) 'Eurocentrism and Feminism', *Feminist Review*, no. 21.

Barrett, M. and McIntosh, M. (1980) 'The Family Wage: Some Problems for Socialists and Feminists', *Capital and Class*, no. 11.

Barrett, M. and McIntosh, M. (1982) *The Anti-Social Family* (London: Verso).

Barrett, M. and McIntosh, M. (1985) 'Ethnocentrism and Socialist-Feminist Theory', *Feminist Review*, no. 20.

Bass, E. and Thornton, L. (1983) *Never Told Anyone* (New York: Harper).

BBC (British Broadcasting Corporation) (1986) *Who Would Hurt a Child? Childwatch* (London: BBC Publications).

BCDP (Batley Community Development Project) (1974) *Batley at Work* (Batley: CDP).

Beauvoir, S. de (1970) *The Second Sex* (Harmondsworth: Penguin).

Beechey, V. (1977) 'Some Notes on Female Wage Labour in Capitalist Production', *Capital and Class*, no. 3.

Beechey, V. (1980) 'On Patriarchy', *Feminist Review*, no. 2.

Bell, C., McKee, L. and Priestley, K. (1983) *Fathers, Childbirth and Work Opportunities* (Manchester: Equal Opportunities Commission).

Belotti, E. (1975) *Little Girls* (London: Writers and Readers Publishing Co-operative).

Benn, M. (1983) 'Isn't Sexual Harassment Really About Masculinity?', *Spare Rib*, no. 156, July, pp. 6 – 8.

Benn, M. and Sedgley, A. (1984) *Sexual Harassment* (London: Tavistock).

Bennington, J. (1973) *Local Government Becomes Big Business* (London: CDP).

Benston, M. (1969) 'The Political Economy of Women's Liberation', *Monthly Review*, vol. 21, no. 4, pp. 13 – 27.

Bhavnani, K. K. and Coulson, M. (1986) 'Transforming Socialist-Feminism: The Challenge of Racism', *Feminist Review*, no. 23, Summer, pp. 81 – 92.

Bickerton, T. (1984) 'Women Alone' in Cartledge and Ryan (eds) *Sex and Love: New Thoughts on Old Contradictions* (London: The Women's Press).

Big Flame (1980) 'Match of the Day – Sex v Class' in *Walking a Tightrope* (Liverpool: Big Flame Pamphlet).

Biggs, S. (1987) 'Quality of Care and the Growth of Private Welfare for Old People', *Critical Social Policy*, no. 20, Autumn, pp. 74 – 82.

Binney, V. (1981) 'Domestic Violence: Battered Women in Britain in the 1970s' in Cambridge Women's Studies Group, *Women in Society: Interdisciplinary Essays* (London: Virago).

Binney, V., Harkell, G. and Nixon, J. (1981) *Leaving Violent Men: A Study of Refuges and Housing for Battered Women* (London: Women's Aid Federation).

*Birmingham Daily News* (1986), issue 344, p. 2.

Biswas, S. (1986) 'Reworking Myths' in *Spare Rib*, no. 173, December, pp. 14 – 17.

Bolger, S., Corrigan, P., Dorking, J. and Frost, N. (1981) *Towards a Socialist Welfare Practice* (London: Macmillan).

Bonin, S. (1982) 'Experiences of Setting Up and Working on a Girls' Project' in Curno, A. *et al.*, *Women and Collective Action* (London: Association of Community Workers).

Bonny, S. (1984) *Who Cares in Southwark* (London: National Association of Carers and Their Elderly Dependants).

Bowl, R. (1985) *Changing the Nature of Masculinity – A Task for Social Work*, Monograph (Norwich: University of East Anglia).

Bramley, J. (1983) 'So Who's Looking After Granny', *Guardian*, 15 August, p. 10.

Bridges, L. (1975) 'The Ministry of Internal Security: British Urban Social Policy 1968 – 74', in *Race and Class*, vol. 16, no. 4, p. 376.

Brittan, A. and Maynard, M. (1984) *Sexism, Racism and Oppression* (Oxford: Basil Blackwell).

Brook, E. and Davis, A. (1985) *Women, the Family and Social Work* (London: Tavistock).

Brown, G. and Harris, T. (1978) *The Social Origins of Depression* (London: Tavistock).

Browne, N. and France, P. (1986) *Untying the Apron Strings: Anti-Sexist Provisions for the Under-Fives* (Milton Keynes: Open University Press).

Brownmiller, S. (1976) *Against Our Will* (Harmondsworth: Penguin).

Bruner, J. (1980) *Under Five in Britain* (London: Grant McIntyre).

Bryan, B., Dadzie, S., Scafe, S. (1985) *The Heart of the Race* (London: Virago).

Burman, S (ed.) (1979) *Fit Work for Women* (London: Routledge and Kegan Paul).

Butler, S. (1978) *Conspiracy of Silence: the Trauma of Incest* (New York: Bantam Books).

BWTC (Birmingham Women's Counselling and Therapy Centre) (1986) *First Report* (Birmingham Women's Counselling and Therapy Centre. Edgbaston, Birmingham 15).

BWU (Birmingham Women's Unit) (1985a) *Report to City Council*, 5 November.

BWU (Birmingham Women's Unit) (1985b) *Job Sharing and Equal Opportunities for Women*, 13 December.

BWU (Birmingham Women's Unit) (1986a) *Workplace Nursery and Crêche Provisions*, 28 February.

BWU (Birmingham Women's Unit) (1986b) *Report to City Council*, 3 June.

BWU (Birmingham Women's Unit) (1986c) *Women's Committee Training Strategy and Budget 86/87*, 13 June.

BWU (Birmingham Women's Unit) (1986d) *Council Strategy on Violence Against Women*, 21 November.

BWU (Birmingham Women's Unit) (1987) *Women's Festival – Review and Evaluation*, 21 April.

Calder, N. (1987) 'The Men's Group in Bristol' (personal communication with authors).

Calvert, J. (1985), 'Motherhood' in Brook and Davis (eds) *Women, the Family and Social Work* (London: Tavistock).

Cambridge Women's Studies Group (1981) *Women in Society* (London: Virago).

Campbell, A. (1981) *Girl Delinquents* (Oxford: Basil Blackwell).

Campbell, B. and Jacques, M. (1986) 'Goodbye to the GLC' in *Marxism Today*, vol. 30, no. 4., April, p. 6.

Campling, J. (1979) *Better Lives for Disabled Women* (London: Virago).

Campling, J. (ed.) (1981) *Images of Ourselves: Women With Disabilities Talking* (London: Routledge and Kegan Paul).

Caplan, P. J. (1986) *The Myth of Women's Masochism* (London: Methuen).

Carby, H. (1982) 'White woman listen! Black feminism and the boundaries of sisterhood' in *The Empire Strikes Back*, Centre for Contemporary Cultural Studies.

Carpenter, V. (1982) 'Working With Girls' in *Women in Collective Action*, edited by Curno *et al.* (London: Association of Community Workers).

Cartledge, S. and Ryan, J. (1983) *Sex and Love: New Thoughts on Old Contradictions* (London: Women's Press).

CCAB (Chapeltown Citizens' Advice Bureau) (1983) *Immigrants and the Welfare State: a Guide to Your Rights* (London: National Association of Citizens' Advice Bureaux).

CCCS (Centre for Contemporary and Cultural Studies) (1982) *The Empire Strikes Back* (London: Hutchinson).

Chambers-Brown, J. (1983) *Day-care* (London: Virago).

Chavetz, J. (1972) 'Women in Social Work', *Social Work*, vol. 17. no. 5.

Cheetham, J. (1972) *Social Work with Immigrants* (London: Routledge and Kegan Paul).

Cheetham, J. (1982) *Social Work and Ethnicity* (London: George Allen and Unwin).

Cherry, S. (1984) (personal communication to the authors).

Claimants' Union (1984) *Women and Social Security* (London: Claimants Union).

Clarke-Stewart, A. (1982) *Day-care* (London: Fontana).

CNCW (Canada National Council of Welfare) (1979) *Women and Poverty* (Ottawa: Canada National Council of Welfare).

Cockburn, C. (1977) *The Local State* (London: Pluto Press).

Cohen, S. (1981) *The Thin Edge of the White Edge* (Manchester: Manchester Law Centre).

Coke, J. (1987) 'Feminist Practice in a Local Authority Setting', seminar discussion in the Department of Applied Social Studies, University of Warwick, Summer Term.

Collins, W., Friedman, E. and Pivot, A. (1978) *The Directory of Social Change* (London: Wildwood House).

*Community Action* (1977) 'Fighting for the Under-Fives', no. 29, Jan – Feb, pp. 26 – 9.

*Community Action* (1980) 'Women and the Cuts', no. 48, pp. 19 – 25.

*Community Care*, (1986) 'Sexism Inside Social Work', 18 Sept.

CDP (Community Development Projects) (1977) *The Limits of the Law* (London: CDP).

Cook, A. and Kirk, G. (1983) *Greenham Women Everywhere: Dreams, Ideas and Action from the Women's Peace Movement* (London: Pluto Press).

Coote, A. (1980) *O Hear This Brother* (London: New Statesman).

Coote, A. and Campbell, B. (1982) *Sweet Freedom* (Oxford: Basil Blackwell).

Coote, A. and Gill, T. (1974) *Women's Rights: a Practical Guide* (London: Penguin).

Corrigan, P. and Leonard, P. (1978) *Social Work Under Capitalism* (London: Macmillan).

Coulson, M., Magas, B. and Wainwright, H. (1975) 'The Housewife and Her Labour Under Capitalism – A Critique' in *New Left Review*, no. 89, Jan – Feb., pp. 59 – 72.

Coyle, A. (1984) *Redundant Women* (London: The Women's Press).

Cox, O. (1974) *Caste, Class and Race* (New York: Monthly Review Press).

CPAG (Child Poverty Action Group) (1987) *Boundary Changes* (London: CPAG).

Craig, G., Derricourt, N. and Loney, M. (eds) *Community Work and the State* (London: Routledge and Kegan Paul with the Association of Community Workers).

Crane, P. (1979) *Gays and the Law* (London: Routledge and Kegan Paul).

Crawford, C. (1981) *Voluntary Social Action: Rape Crisis*, unpublished MA Thesis (University of Loughborough).

CRE (Commission on Racial Equality) (1985) *Immigration Control Procedures: Report of a Formal Investigation* (London: CRE).

Croll, E. (1983) *Chinese Women Since Mao* (London: ZED Books).

Cross, M. (1984) 'Feminism and the Disability Movement – A Personal View' in Holland, J. (eds) *Feminist Action* (London: Battle Axe Books).

Curno, A., Lamming, A., Leach, L., Stiles, J., Ward, V., Wright, A. and Ziff, T. (1982) *Women In Collective Action* (London: The Association of Community Workers).

CWU (Camden Women's Unit) (1982) *Annual Report* (London: CWU).

CWU (Camden Women's Unit (1983) *Camden Women's Committee Newsletter*, September.

Dale, J. and Foster, P. (1986) *Feminists and State Welfare* (London: Routledge and Kegan Paul).

Daley, G. (1983) 'Ideologies of Care' in *Critical Social Policy*, no. 8.

Dalla Costa, M. and James, S. (1972) *The Power of Women and The Subversion of the Community* (Bristol: Falling Wall Press).

David, M. and New, C. (1985) *For the Children's Sake: Making Childcare More Than Women's Business* (London: Penguin).

Davies, R. (1975) *Women and Work* (London: Arrow Books).

Davis, A. (1981) *Women, Race and Class* (London: The Women's Press).

Davis, A. (1987) 'A Class Approach to the Struggle Against Racism', lecture given in Hackney Race Relations Unit during celebrations for International Women's Week.

Delmar, R. (1986) 'Broken Agenda', *New Statesman*, vol. 112, no. 2887, 25 July, pp. 20 – 22.

Delphy, C. (1984) *Close to Home: a Material Analysis of Women's Oppression* (London: Hutchinson).

Department of Health and Social Security/Department of Education and Science (1976) *Low Cost Provision for the Under-Fives* (London: DHSS/DES).

Directory of Women (1986) *Working With Women in the Birmingham Area* (Department of Social Adminstration, University of Birmingham).

Dixon, G., Johnson, C., Leigh, S. and Turnbull, N. (1982) 'Feminist Perspectives and Practice' in Craig *et al.* (eds) *Community Work and the State* (London: Routledge and Kegan Paul).

Dobash, R. E. and Dobash, R. (1980) *Violence Against Wives: A Case Against the Patriarchy* (London: Open Books).

Dominelli, L. (1978) 'The Welfare State and the Public Expenditure Cuts', *Bulletin of Social Policy*, no. 1, Spring.

Dominelli, L. (1979) 'Racism: The Challenge for Social Work Education' in *Social Work Today*, 10(25), pp.27 – 29.

Dominelli, L. (1981) 'Violence: A Family Affair', *Community Care*, 12 March, pp. 14 – 17.

Dominelli, L. (1982) *Community Action: Organising Marginalised Groups* (Reykjavik: Kwenna Frambothid).

Dominelli, L. (1983) *Women in Focus: Community Service Orders and Female Offenders* (Coventry: University of Warwick).

Dominelli, L. (1984) 'Working with Families: A Feminist Perspective', British Association of Social Workers Annual Conference at Nene College, Northampton, April.

Dominelli, L. (1986) 'Father-Daughter Incest: Patriarchy's Shameful Secret', *Critical Social Policy*, no. 16, pp. 8 – 22.

Dominelli, L. (1986a) *Women Organising: An Analysis of Greenham Women*, Paper presented at the International Association of Schools of Social Work Congress in Tokyo, August.

Dominelli, L. (1986b) *Love and Wages* (Norwich: Novata Press).

Dominelli, L. (1986c) 'The Power of the Powerless: Prostitution and the Reinforcement of Submissive Masculinity' in *Sociological Review*, Spring, pp. 65 – 92.

Dominelli, L. (1987) 'Family Therapy is Not Feminist Therapy', *Critical Social Policy*, no. 20, Autumn, pp. 87 – 9.

Dominelli, L. (1988) *Anti-Racist Social Work* (London: Macmillan).

Dominelli, L. and Jonsdottir, G. (1988) 'Feminist Political Organisation in Iceland', *Feminist Review*, no. 27, Summer.

Donnelly, A. (1986) *Feminist Social Work with a Women's Group*, Monograph 41 (Norwich: University of East Anglia).

Donzelot, J. (1980) *The Policing of Families* (London: Hutchinson).

Doyal, L. (1983) *The Political Economy of Health* (London: Pluto Press).

Dreifus, C. (1973) *Woman's Fate: Raps from a Feminist Consciousness-Raising Group* (New York: Bantam Books).

Egerton, J. (1983) 'A Personal Account of the Lesbian Sex and Sexual Practices Conference', *Trouble and Strife*, no. 1, Winter, pp. 28 – 31.

Eichenbaum, L. and Orbach, S. (1982) *Outside in and Inside Out* (London: Penguin).

Eichenbaum, L. and Orbach, S. (1984) *What Do Women Want?* (London: Fontana).

Eichenbaum, L. and Orbach, S. (1985) *Understanding Women* (London: Penguin).

Eichler, M. (1983) *Families in Canada* (Toronto: Gage).

Elliott, M. (1985) *Preventing Child Sexual Assault* (London: Bedford Press).

Elliott, M. (1986) *Keeping Safe: A Practical Guide to Talking with Children* (London: Bedford Press/NVCO).

Ely, P. and Denney, D. (1987) *Social Work in a Multi-Racial Society* (London: Gower).

Engels, F. (1972) *The Origin of the Family, Private Property and The State* (London: Lawrence and Wishart).

Ernst, S. and Goodison, L. (1981) *In Our Own Hands: a Book of Self-help Therapy* (London: The Women's Press).

Ernst, S. and Maguire, M. (eds) (1987) *Living with the Sphinx – Papers from the Women's Therapy Centre* (London: The Women's Press).

Eskapa, S. (1985) *Woman Versus Woman* (London: Pan).

Evans, A. (1975) *Hours of work in Industrialised Countries* (Geneva: International Labour Organisation).

Evans, D. (1985) *Developing Feminist Groups in Statutory Practice: A Case Study of a Women's Group in 'Smalltown'*, unpublished MA/CQSW dissertation (Coventry: Department of Applied Social Studies, The University of Warwick).

Falk, A. (1986) *The Process of Feminist Group Work in Statutory Social Work*, unpublished MA/CQSW dissertion (Department of Applied Social Studies, The University of Warwick).

*Families in the Future* (1983) (London: Department of Health and Social Security).

Feldberg, R. L. and Glenn, E. N. (1982) 'Male and Female: Job Versus Gender Models in the Sociology of Work' in Kahn-Hunt, R., Danield, A. K. and Colvard, R (eds) *Women and Work: Problems and Perspectives* (New York: Oxford University Press).

*Feminist Review* (1986) *Socialist-Feminism out of the Blue: Special Issue on Class*. no. 23, Summer.

Feminism and Non-Violence Study Group (1983) *Piecing It Together: Feminism and Non-Violence* (Buckleigh: Feminism and Non-Violence Group).

Festau, M. F. (1975) *The Male Machine* (New York: Delta Books).

Fillmore, A. (1987) 'Sexual Molestation of Children: Becoming Aware', *Journal of Health Visitors Association*, October.

Finch, J. (1984) 'Community Care: Developing Non-Sexist Alternatives', *Critical Social Policy*, no. 9, pp. 6 – 18.

Finch, J. and Groves, D. (eds) (1983) *A Labour of Love: Women, Work and Caring* (London: Routledge and Kegan Paul).

Finch, J. (1982) 'A Woman's Health Group in Mansfield' in Curno *et al.* (eds) *Women in Collective Action* (London: Routledge and Kegan Paul).

Firestone, S. (1971) *The Dialectics of Sex: The Case for Feminist Revolution* (New York: Cape).

Flannery, K. and Roelop, S. (1984) 'Local Government Women's Committees' in J. Holland (eds), *Feminist Action I* (London: Battle Axe Books).

Fletcher, M. (1987) 'Mail Order Brides: Heartaches or Happiness', *Woman*, 7 November, pp. 22 – 9.

Foner, N. (1979) *Jamaica Farewell: Jamaican Immigrants in London* (London: Routledge and Kegan Paul).

Freeman, N. (1981) 'The Rights of Children When they Do Wrong', *British Journal of Criminology*, vol. 21, no. 3, p. 221.

Freire, P. (1976) *The Pedagogy of the Oppressed* (Harmondsworth: Penguin).

Freud, S. (1977) *On Sexuality*, Pelican Freud Library, vol. 7, (Harmondsworth: Penguin).

Friedan, B. (1974) *The Feminine Mystique* (New York: Dell).

Gavron, H. (1966) *The Captive Wife* (London: Routledge and Kegan Paul).

Gilroy, P. (1987) *There Ain't No Black in the Union Jack* (London: Hutchinson).

GLC (Greater London Council) (1984) *Childcare Programme* (London: GLC).

GLC/IEC (Greater London Council Industry and Employment Committee) (1985) *The London Inclusive Strategy* (London: GLC).

GLC/WEG (Greater London Council) (1986) *London Women in the 1980s* (London: GLC).

Goodison, L. (1983) 'Really Being in Love Means Wanting to Live in a Different World' in Cartledge and Ryan (eds) *Sex and Love: New Thoughts on Old Contradictions* (London: Women's Press).

Gordon, L. (1986) 'Feminism and Social Control: The Case of Child Abuse and Neglect' in Mitchell and Oakley (eds) *What Is Feminism?* (Oxford: Basil Blackwell).

Gordon, P. and Newham, A. (1985) *Passports to Benefits: Racism in Social Security* (London: Child Poverty Action Group and the Runnymede Trust).

Gould, J. (1982) *Women's Organisations in the Labour Party* (London: Labour Party Publication).

Gray, M. and McKenzie, H. (1980) *Take Care of Your Elderly Relative* (London: Allen and Unwin).

Gray, R. (1986) unpublished MA/CQSQ dissertation (Coventry: Department of Applied Social Studies, The University of Warwick).

Green, S. L. (1982) 'Youth Work with Girls' in *Shocking Pink Newsletter*, no. 1.

Greater London Council Women's Unit (1986) *Women in London* (London: GLC).

Greer, G. (1971) *The Female Eunuch* (London: Paladin).

*Guardian, The* (1987) 'The Election Results', 13 June, pp. 12 – 13.

Guru, S. (1987) 'An Asian Women's Refuge' in Ahmed *et al.* (eds) *Social Work With Black Children and Their Families* (London: Batsford).

Hale, J. (1984) 'Feminism and Social Work Practice' in Jordan and Parton (eds) *The Political Dimensions of Social Work* (Oxford: Basil Blackwell).

Hanmer, J. (1977) 'Community Action, Women's Aid and the Women's Liberation Movement' in Mayo (eds) *Women in the Community* (London: Routledge and Kegan Paul).

Hanmer, J. and Saunders, S. (1984) *Well Founded Fear – A Community Study of Violence On Women* (London: Hutchinson).

Hanscombe, G. E. and Forster, J. (1982) *Rocking the Cradle: Lesbian Mothers* (London: Sheba Feminist Publishers).

Harris, C. (1987) *Women and Depression: Working with Groups within a Statutory Agency from a Feminist Perspective*, unpublished MA/CQSW dissertation (Coventry: Department of Applied Social Studies, The University of Warwick).

Harrison, R. (forthcoming) *Women and the Politics of Romantic Love* (Brighton: Harvester Press).

Hartmann, H. (1981) 'The Unhappy Marriage of Marxism and Feminism', *Capital and Class*, no. 8.

Hearn, J. (1983) 'Birth and Afterbirth: A Materialist Account', *Achilles Heel*, no. 5, p. 9.

Heidenson, F. (1985) *Women and Crime* (London: Macmillan).

Hemmings, S. (1982) *Girls Are Powerful* (London: Sheba).

'Hencke Home News' (1985) *Guardian*, 25 February, p. 2.

Hiro, D. (1971) *Black British, White British* (London: Eyre and Spottiswoode).

Holland, J. (1984) *Feminist Action I* (London: Battle Axe Books).

Homans, H. (ed.) (1985) *The Sexual Politics of Reproduction* (London: Gower).

Hooks, B. (1981) *Ain't I A Woman: Black Women and Feminism* (London: Pluto Press).

Hooks, B. (1984) *Feminist Theory: From Margin to Center* (Boston, Mass.: South End Press).

Hopkins, M. (1982) *Homeworking Campaigns: Dilemma and Possibilities in Working with a Fragmented Community*, unpublished MA/CQSW dissertation (Coventry: Department of Applied Social Studies, The University of Warwick).

Howe, D. (1986) 'The Segregation of Women and their Work in the Personal Social Services' in *Critical Social Policy*, no. 15, Spring, pp. 21 – 36.

Howell, E. and Bayes, M. (eds) (1981) *Women and Mental Health* (New York: Basic Books).

Hudson, A. (1983) 'The Welfare State and Adolescent Feminity', *Youth and Policy*, vol. 2, no. 1, Summer, pp. 5 – 13.

Hughes, M., Mayall, B., Moss, P., Perry, J. and Petrie, P. (1980) *Nurseries Now* (Harmondsworth: Penguin).

Humphreys, L. (1975) *Tearoom Trade* (Chicago: Aldine).

Hyde, M. and Deacon, B. (1986) 'Working-Class Opinion and Welfare Strategies: Beyond the State and the Market', *Critical Social Policy*, no. 18, Autumn, pp. 15 – 31.

IASSW (International Association of Schools of Social Work) (1984) 'Taking on Gender in Social Work Education', The Women's Caucus Inaugural Meeting, Montreal Congress.

Jaget, C., (ed.) (1986) *Prostitutes, Our Life* (Bristol: Falling Wall Press).

James, S. (1981) quoted in McLeod (1982) *Women Working: Prostitution Now* (London: Croom Helm) p. 124.

Jayawardna, K. (1986) *Feminism and Nationalism in the Third World* (London: Zed Press).

Jervis, M. (1986) 'Domestic Violence: Why Asian Women Need a Helping Hand', *Social Work Today*, 18 August, pp. 7 – 8.

Jewell, T. (1986) 'Focus – Wendy Savage', *Marxism Today*, February, p. 3.

Johnson, K. A. (1983) *Women, the Family and the Peasant Revolution in China* (Chicago: University of Chicago Press).

Jones, M. (1986) *Strong Kids: Safe Kids*, unpublished MA/CQSW dissertation (Coventry: Department of Applied Social Studies, The University of Warwick).

Jordan, B. and Parton, N. (1984) *The Political Domensions of Social Work* (Oxford: Basil Blackwell).

Key, D. (1983) *Thatcher's Britain: a Guide to the Ruins* (London: Pluto Press).

Kishwar, M. (1986) 'Dowry: To Ensure Her Happiness or To Disinherit Her?', *Manushi*, vol. 6, no. 4, May-June, pp. 2 – 12.

Kitzinger, S. (1985) *Women's Experience of Sex* (Harmondsworth: Penguin).

Kyle, D. (1981) *Women and Medicine* (Manchester: Equal Opportunities Commission).

Labour Abortion Rights Campaign (1978) *Abortion: The Struggle in the Labour Movement* (London: LARC).

Labour Party (1984) *Women in the Labour Party* pamphlet (London: Labour Party).

*Labour Research* (1983) 'Women, the Tory Record', no. 49, May.

*Labour Research* (1987) 'The Parlimentary Privileged', 76(7), May.

Lea, P. and Young, J. (1984) *What Is To Be Done About Law and Order?* (Harmondsworth: Penguin).

*Leeds Other Paper* (1983) 'Ellie Wins Sexual Harassment Case', 16 September, p. 3.

Lederer, Laura (1982) *Take Back the Night: Women on Pornography* (New York: Bantam Books).

Leonard, P. (1984) *Personality and Ideology* (London: Macmillan).

Leonard, P. and McLeod, E. (1980) *Marital Violence: Social Construction and Social Service Response* (Coventry: Department of Applied Social Studies, University of Warwick).

Leventon, S. (1985) 'The National Association of Carers', *Social Work Today*, 16 December.

Livingstone, K. (1987) *If Voting Changed Anything, They'd Abolish It* (London: Collins).

LOC ( Leicester Outworkers Campaign) (1981) *Outworking in Leicester: The Case for a Local City Council Initiative* (Leicester: LOC).

Loney, M. (1983) *Community Against Government: The British Community Development Project 1968-78: A Study of Government Incompetence* (London: Heinemann).

Loney, M. (1986) *The Politics of Greed: The New Right and the Welfare State* (London: Pluto Press).

Longres, J. and McLeod, E. (1980) 'Consciousness-Raising and Social Work Practice' *Social Casework*, vol. 61, no. 5, May, pp. 267 – 77.

Lorde, A. (1984) *Sister Outsider* (New York: The Crossing Press).

LSSC (Leeds Social Security Cuts Campaign) (1986) *The Campaign Against the Fowler Review* (Leeds: LSSC).

LWLC (London Women's Liberation Campaign) (1979) *Demands for Working Women: The Working Women's Charter* (London: LWLC).

Mackie, L. and Pattullo, P. (1977) *Women at Work* (London: Tavistock).

McAndrew, A. (1986) *Bereavement in Maternity: A Role for Hospital Social Work* Unpublished MA/CQSW dissertation (Coventry: Department of Applied Social Studies, The University of Warwick).

McLean, S. (ed.) (1980) *Female Circumcision. Excision and Infibulation: The Facts and Proprosals for Change* (London: Minority Rights Group).

McLeod, E. (1978) 'Prostitutes Organise', *Spare Rib*, vol. 69, April.

McLeod, E. (1979) 'Working with Prostitutes: Probation Officers' Aims and Strategies', *The British Journal of Social Work*, vol. 9. no. 14, Winter.

McLeod, E. (1982) *Women Working: Prostitution Now* (London: Croom Helm).

McLeod, E. (1987a) 'Some Lessons From Teaching Feminist Social Work', *Issues in Social Work Education*, vol. 7, no. 1, Summer, pp. 29 – 37.

McLeod, E. (1987b) 'Women's Experience of Love: The Significance of Feminist Therapy' (research in progress).

McLeod, E. and Dominelli, L. (1982) 'The Personal and the Apolitical: Feminism and Moving Beyond the Integrated Methods Approach' in Bailey, R. and Lee, P. (eds) *Theory and Practice in Social Work* (Oxford: Basil Blackwell).

McLeod, E., Halson, J. and Munro, A. (1986) *An Evaluation of the School Management Development of Women Teachers' Project Training Programme* (Birmingham: City of Birmingham Women's Unit).

McLeod, M. and Sasaga, E. (1987) 'Abuse of Trust' in *Marxism Today*, August, pp. 10 – 13

McRobbie, A. (1978) 'Working Class Girls and the Culture of Femininity' in *Women Take Issue – Aspects of Women's Subordination* (London: Hutchinson and Centre for Contemporary and Cultural Studies).

Magas, B. (1971) 'Sex Politics: Class Politics' in *New Left Review*, No. 66, Mar – Apr, pp. 69 – 91.

Malek, F. (1985) *Asian Women and Mental Health or Mental Ill Heath: the Myth of Mental Illness* (Southwark: Asian Women's Aid).

Mama, A. (1984) 'Black Women, the Economic Crisis and the British State', *Feminist Review*, no. 17, Autumn, pp. 21 – 36.

Mandel, E. (1968) *Marxist Economic Theory* (New York: Monthly Review Press).

Marchant, H. and Wearing, B. (eds) (1986) *Gender Reclaimed* (Sydney: Hale and Iremonger).

Marshall, J. (1984). *Women Managers: Travellers in a Male World.* (London: Wiley).

Mayall, H. (1981) *Working with Women: a Perspective on The Women's Voice Experience*, unpublished MA/CQSW dissertation (Coventry: Department of Applied Social Studies, Warwick University).

Mayall, B. and Petrie, P. (1977) *Minder, Mother, and Child* (London Institute of Education).

Mayo, M. (1977) *Women in the Community* (London: Routledge and Kegan Paul).

Mayo, M. (1980) 'Beyond CDP: Reaction and Community Action' in Bailey and Brake (eds) *Radical Social Work and Practice* (London: Edward Arnold).

Men Against Sexism Group in Birmingham (1983) personal communication to the authors.

Metcalfe, A. and Humphries, M. (1985) *The Sexuality of Men* (London: Pluto Press).

Michelson, W. (1985) *From Sun to Sun: Daily Obligations and Community Structure in the Lives of Employed Women and Their Families* (Toronto: Towman and Allanheld Publishers).

Minford, P. (1984) 'State Expenditure: A Study in Waste', *Economic Affairs*, April-June.

Mitchell, J. (1975) *Psychoanalysis and Feminism* (Harmondsworth: Penguin).

Mitchell, J. and Oakley, A. (1986) *What is Feminism?* (Oxford: Basil Blackwell).

Molyneux, M. (1979) 'Beyond the Domestic Labour Debate', *New Left Review*, July-August, pp. 3 – 27.

Molyneux, M. (1985) 'Family Reform in Socialist States: The Hidden Agenda', *Feminist Review*, no. 21, Winter.

Mooney, B. (1983) 'Beyond the Wasteland' in Thompson (ed.), *Over Our Dead Bodies: Women Against the Bomb* (London: Virago).

Morrison, T. (1986) *The Bluest Eye* (New York: Triad-Grafton Books).

Morrison, P., Holland, G. and Trott, T. (1979) 'Personally Speaking: Three Men Share the Experience of Their Men's Group', *Achilles Heel*, no. 2.

MSC (Manpower Services Commission) (1986) 'Gender Awareness Training', session held at the Management Training Unit in Royal Leamington Spa, December.

Muss, J. and McLeod, E. (1980) *Parents Anonymous Lifeline. Birmingham Second Report* (Birmingham: Parents Anonymous).

NAC (National Abortion Campaign) (1978) *The National Abortion Campaign.*

Nairne, K. and Smith, G. (1984) *Dealing with Depression* (London: The Women's Press).

*National Economic Survey* (1983) (Norwich: HMSO).

NACED (National Association of Carers and Their Elderly Dependents) (1984) 'Caring for Someone at Home', *Newsletter*.

NCC (National Childcare Campaign) (1984) *National Childcare Campaign Annual Report* (London: NCC)

NCC (National Childcare Campaign) (1985) *National Childcare Campaign Policy Statement* (London: NCC).

Nelson, S. (1982) *Incest, Fact and Myth* (Edinburgh: Stramullion).

Nett, E. (1982) *Women as Elders* (Toronto: Resources for Feminist Research).

*News on Sunday*, (1987). 'Looney Left Takeover', 24 May, p.13.

Newson, J. and Newson, E. (1976) 'Day to Day Aggression between Parent and Child' in N. Tutt (ed.) *Violence in London* (London: DHSS/HMSO).

Oakley, A. (1972) *Sex, Gender and Society* (London: Temple Smith).

Oakley, A. (1981) *Subject Women* (London: Martin Robertson).

O'Brien, A. (1987) 'Happy Families', *Socialist Alternative*, Aug-Sept.

Orbach, S. (1982) *Fat is a Feminist Issue* (London: Penguin).

Orbach, S. (1986) 'Guilty Secrets: The Role of Women's Therapy', *Marxism Today* vol, 31, no. 8, August, pp. 24 – 8.

Packwood, M. (1983) 'The Colonel's Lady and Judy O'Grady: Class in the Women's Liberation Movement', *Trouble and Strife*, no. 1, Winter, pp. 7 – 12.

Pahl, J. (1978) *A Refuge for Battered Women: A Study of the Role of a Women's Centre* (London: HMSO).

Pahl, J. (1980) 'Patterns of Money Management Within Marriage', *Journal of Social Policy* vol. 9, p. 326.

Pahl, J. (1985) *Private Violence and Public Policy* (London: Routledge and Kegan Paul).

Parmar, P. (1982) 'Gender, race and class: Asian women in resistance' in Centre for Contemporary and Cultural Studies, *The Empire Strikes Back* (London: Hutchinson).

Parton, N. (1985) *The Politics of Child Abuse* (London: Macmillan).

Pascall, G. (1986) *Social Policy-A Feminist Analysis* (London: Tavistock)

Penn, H. (forthcoming) *Municipalising Mum* (London: Routledge and Kegan Paul).

Phillipson, C. (1982) *Capitalism and the Construction of Old Age* (London: Macmillan).

Pick, E. (1986) 'Open Space', *Guardian*, 2 December, p. 13.

Pizzey, E. (1974) *Scream Quietly or the Neighbours will Hear* (Harmondsworth: Penguin).

Pizzey, E. and Shapiro, J. (1982) *Prone To Violence* (Feltham: Hamlyn).

Plummer, J. (1978) *Divide and Deprive* (London: Joint Council for the Welfare of Immigrants).

Plummer, K. (ed.) (1981) *The Making of the Modern Homosexual* (London: Hutchinson).

Radcliffe Richards, J. (1980) *The Sceptical Feminist: A Political Enquiry* (London: Routledge and Kegan Paul).

Rappoport, R. and Rappoport, R. N., with Bumstead, J. (1978) *Working Couples* (London: Routledge and Kegan Paul).

Raymond, J. (1986) *A Passion for Friends* (London: The Women's Press).

Reitz, R. (1983) *Menopause: A Positive Approach* (London: George Allen and Unwin).

Reynaud, E. (1983) *Holy Virility* (London: Pluto Press).

Riley, M. (1982) 'A Women's Employment Group in Milton Keynes' in Curno *et al.* (eds) *Women in Collective Action* (London: Routledge and Kegan Paul).

Riley, D. (1981) 'Feminist Thought and Reproductive Control: The Stage and the Right to Choose' in Cambridge Women's Studies Group *Women in Society* (London: Virago).

Riley, D. (1983) *War in the Nursery* (London: Virago).

Rimmer, L. and Popay, J. (1983) *Employment Trends and the Family* (London: Study Commission on the Family).

Rowbotham, S., Segal, L. and Wainwright, H. (1979) *Beyond the Fragments: Feminism and the Making of Socialism* (London: Merlin Press).

Rowbotham, S. (1986) 'More Than Just a Memory: Some Political Implications of Women's Involvement in the Miners' Strike, 1984-85', *Feminist Review*, no. 23, Summer, pp. 109 – 25.

Ruzek, S. (1978) *The Women's Health Movement* (New York: Praeger).

Ruzek, S. (1986) 'Feminist Visions of Health: An International Perspective' in Mitchell and Oakley (eds) *What is Feminism?* (Oxford: Basil Blackwell).

Saadawi, N. El (1979) *The Hidden Face of Eve: Women in the Arab World* (London: Zed Press).

Saadawi, N. El (1980). 'Clitoredectomy: Crime Against Women', *Spare Rib*, issue 90, March, pp. 6 – 8.

Sarsby, S. (1983) *Romantic Love and Society: Its Place in the Modern World* (Harmondsworth: Penguin).

Sayers, J. (1986) *Sexual Contradictions: Psychology, Psychoanalysis and Feminism* (London: Tavistock).

Schur, E. (1973) *Radical Non-Intervention: Rethinking the Delinquency Problem* (Englewood Cliffs, New Jersey: Prentice-Hall).

Scott. H. (1976) *Women and Socialism: Experiences from Eastern Europe* (London: Alison and Busby).

Seccombe, W. (1974) 'The Housewife and her Labour Under Capitalism', *New Left Review.*, no. 83, Jan. – Feb. pp. 3 – 24.

Seddon, V. (1986) *The Cutting Edge: Women and the Pit Strike* (London: Lawrence and Wishart).

Segal, L. (1983) *What Is To Be Done About the Family?* (Harmondsworth: Penguin).

Siddel, R. (1987) *Women and Children Last; The Plight of Poor Women In Affluent America* (Harmondsworth: Penquin).

Simpkin, M. (1979) *Trapped Within Welfare* (London: Macmillan).

Skelton, A. (1984) Personal Communication to the authors concerning such a group in Birmingham, visited subsequently by one of the authors.

Skinner, J. and Robinson, C. (Forthcoming). 'Who Cares? Women and the Social Services' in Coyle and Skinner, *Women and Work: Positive Action For Equal Opportunities* (London: Macmillan).

Smart, C. (1976) *Women, Crime and Criminology – A Feminist Critique* (London: Routledge and Kegan Paul).

Smart, C. and Smart, B. (1978) *Women, Sexuality and Social Control* (London: Routledge and Kegan Paul).

Smith, B. (1986) 'The Case of Women's Studies and Social Work Education' in Marchant and Wearing, *Gender Reclaimed* (Sidney: Hale and Iremonger).

Solanas, V. (1971) *The Society For Cutting Up Men Manifesto* (New York: Olympia Press).

*Spare Rib* (1980) 'Decades Talking Across a Century of Women's Lives', no. 160, November, pp. 5 – 12.

*Spare Rib* (1980) 'The Selling of Old Age', no. 154, pp. 6 – 8.

*Spare Rib* (1986) 'Agreeing to Differ: Lesbian Sado-masochism', no, 170, September, pp. 36 – 41.

*Spare Rib* (1987). 'Birmingham's Women's Committee Scrapped', no. 180, July, pp. 12 – 13.

SWAF (Scottish Women's Aid Federation) (1980) *Report From Battered Women and the State Conference*, December.

SWAT (South Wales Association of Tenants) (1982) 'Coming Alive Hurts' in Curno *et al.*, *Women In Collective Action* (London: ACW).

Stacey, M. and Price, M. (1981) *Women, Power and Politics* (London: Tavistock).

Stallard, K., Ehrenreich, B. and Sklar, H. (1983) *Poverty In the American Dream: Women and Children First* (Boston: South End Press).

Stanko, E. (1985) *Intimate Instructions: Women's Experience of Male Violence* (London: Routledge and Kegan Paul).

Stanworth, M. (1983) *Gender and Schooling* (London: Hutchinson).

Statham, Daphne (1979) *Radicals in Social Work* (London: Routledge and Kegan Paul).

Study Commission on the Family (1983) *Families in the Future* (London: SCF).

Symonds, A. (1981) 'Phobias After Marriage: Women's Declaration of Dependence' in Howell and Bayes (eds) *Women and Mental Health* (New York: Bantam Books).

Thompson, D. (ed.) (1983) *Over Our Dead Bodies: Women Against The Bomb* (London: Virago).

Tizard, J. and Hughes, B. (1976) *All Our Children.* (London: Temple Smith).

Tolson, A. (1977) *The Limits of Masculinity* (London: Tavistock).

Torkington, C. (1981) *Women in Action: Preservers of the Status Quo or a Force for Change*, unpublished MA/CQSW dissertation (Coventry: Department of Applied Social Studies, The University of Warwick).

Townsend, P. (1980) *Poverty* (Harmondsworth: Penguin).

Toynbee, P. (1984) 'There is No Hiding Place', in *Guardian* 10 December, p. 10.

TUCRIC (Trades Union Congress Resource and Information Centre) (1980), 'A Woman's Right to Work', *TUCRIC Bulletin., no. 12/13.*, Feb. – May, pp. 2 – 5.

TUCRIC (Trade Union Congress Resource and Information Centre) (1981) 'Alternative Economic Strategies', *TUCRIC Bulletin, no. 22*, Nov. – Dec., pp. 2 – 17.

TUCRIC (Trades Union Congress Resource and Information Centre) (1983) 'Job Share v. Job Split: Who is Interested?', *TUCRIC Bulletin. no. 28*, Spring, pp. 1 – 18.

Tutt, N. (1976) *Violence in London* (London: DHSS/HMSO).

Tyneside Rape Crisis Centre Collective (1982) *'Tyneside Rape Crisis Centre'* in Curno, *et al.*, *Women in Collective Action* (London: Routledge and Kegan Paul).

Valentine, M. (1987) *Developing a Critical Analysis on Child Abuse*, Phd Thesis in Progress (Coventry: Department of Applied Social Studies, The University of Warwick).

Walker, H. (1985) 'Women's Issues in Probation Practice' in Walker and Beaumont *Working With Offenders* (London: Macmillian/BASW).

Walker, H. and Beaumont, B. (1981) *Probation Work – Critical Theory and Socialist Practice* (Oxford: Basil Blackwell).

Walker, H. and Beaumont, B. (1985) *Working With Offenders* (London: Macmillan/BASW).

Walsgrove, R. (1986) *Spare Rib*, p. 25.

Walton, R. (1975) *Women in Social Work* (London: Routledge and Kegan Paul).

Ward, E. (1984) *Father – Daughter Rape* (London: The Women's Press).

Warren, L. (1985) *Older Women and Feminist Social Work Practice in Critical*

*Social Work Monographs* (Coventry: Department of Applied Social Studies, The University of Warwick).

Warwick Feminist Social Work Practice Conference Group (1979) *Feminist Social Work Practice: Notes on the Conference* (Coventry: Department of Applied Social Studies, The University of Warwick).

Webb, S. (1981) *Women's Depression and the Politics of Feminist Therapy*, unpublished MA/CQSW dissertation (Coventry: Department of Applied Social Studies, The University of Warick).

Webster, B. (1984) *Bearing the Burden: Women, Work and Local Government* (Local Government Campaign Unit).

Weeks, J. (1981) 'Discourse, Desire and Sexual Deviance: Some Problems in the History of Homosexuality' in Plummer, *The Making of the Modern Homosexual* (London: Hutchinson) pp. 76 – 111.

Whitehouse, A. (1985) 'A Lot of Catching Up to Do', *Community Care*, 2 May.

Whitlock, M. J. (1987) 'Five more years of Desolation' in *Spare Rib.*, no. 180, July, p.15.

Whittington, B. (1986) '*Sexual Harassment: A Human Rights Issue*', Unpublished paper (Victoria: University of Victoria).

Wickham, J. (1982) 'The Politics of Depression Capitalism: International Capitalism and the Nation State', *The 1978 Conference of Socialist Economist Conference Proceedings* (Bradford: Bradford University).

Wilkes, R. (1981) *Social Work With Undervalued Groups* (London: Tavistock).

Wilkinson, S. (1986) *Feminist Social Psychology: Developing Theory and Practice* (Milton Keynes: Open University Press).

Wilson, E. (1975) 'Feminism and Social Work', in Bailey and Brake, *Radical Social Work* (London: Edward Arnold).

Wilson, E. (1977) *Women and the Welfare State* (London: Tavistock).

Wilson, E. (1980) 'Feminism and Social Work', (Bailey and M. Brake) *Radical Social Work and Practice* (London: Edward Arnold).

Wilson, E. (1980a) *Only Halfway to Paradise: Women in Post-War Britain 1945-68* (London: Tavistock).

Wilson, E. (1983) *What Is To Be Done About Violence Against Women?* (Harmondsworth: Penguin).

Wilson, E. (1987) 'Thatcherism and Women: After Seven Years', *Socialist Register* 1987, pp. 199 – 235.

Wilson, E. with Weir, A. (1986) *Hidden Agendas: Theory, Politics and Experience in the Women's Movement* (London: Tavistock).

Winship, J (1987) 'A Woman's World: Women and Ideology of Feminists' in Women's Studies Group, *Women Take Issue: Aspects of Women's Subordination* (Birmingham: Centre for Contemporary and Cultural Studies).

Winship, J. (1987) 'Reading between the Images: A Look at the Glossies', *Spare Rib.*, no. 180. July.

Wise, S. (1985) *Becoming a Feminist Social Worker Monograph in Studies on Sexual Politics* (Manchester: Manchester University).

Wolffe, J. (1983) *Aesthetics and the Sociology of Art* (London: Allen and Unwin).

Wollstonecraft, M. (1975) *A Vindication of the Rights of Women* (Harmondsworth: Penguin).

*Woman* (1987) 'Where do the Parties Stand on Women?' 13 June, p.21.

Women and Management Discussion Group (1982) 'Women and Management' at the *Feminism and Social Work Conference* held at Goldsmith's College, London, November.

Women in Social Work Network (1986) *Report on the Conference at Ruskin College* (Manchester: Department of Sociology, The University of Manchester).

Women's Caucus of the International Association of Schools of Social Work (1984) *Women's Caucus Newsletter*

Women Working Project (1987) *Women Working in the Eighties: Interim Report* (Bristol: Centre for a Working World).

Wood, E. W. (1976) *The Dynamics of Change: The Association of Community Workers, 1968-76*, ACW Internal Report (London: ACW).

WWAF (Welsh Women's Aid Federation) (1978) *Available for Work* (Cardiff: WWAF).

# Index

abortion 30, 75
Achilles Heel Collective 70, 94
Adamson, O. 6, 134
ageism 4, 39, 152
Akureyri 167
Aldred, C. 25, 131, 134, 136
Allenspach, H. 138
'anglocentric perspective' 77–8
anti-sexism 41, 70, 97–8, 124–5
Arcana, J. 72, 97–8
Ardill, S. 4, 89
Armstrong, J. 143
Armstrong, P. 25, 157
  women and employment 131 134,
    136, 142, 158
Ashurst, F. 163, 164
Association of Women's
    Committees 160
autonomous organisations 5, 168–9
autonomous workplaces 150–2
'availability for work' test 171

Bailey, R. 102
Baker-Miller, J. 78, 82
Bangor Rape Crisis Centre 151
Banks, O. 2, 46
Barker, H. 9–10, 62
Barrett, J. 30, 51–2
Barrett, M. 6, 76, 134
Batley Community Development
    Project 37
battered women  see refuges; violence
Bayes, M. 36, 80, 81
Beaumont, B. 103, 104, 106

Beauvoir, S. de 92–3
Beechey, V. 134
Bell, C. 71
Belotti, E. 97
Benn, M. 37, 133, 135
Bennington, J. 13
Beyond the Fragments
    Conference 168
Bickerton, T. 92
Biggs, S. 111
Binney, V. 38, 76, 81, 151
  refuges 48–9, 55, 72, 114
*Birmingham Daily News* 82
Birmingham Equal Opportunities
    Action Group 61
Birmingham Women's
    Committee 143, 159, 161
Birmingham Women's Counselling and
    Therapy Centre (BWTC) 83–4,
    152, 157
Birmingham Women's Unit
    (BWU) 142, 146, 159–60
Biswas, S. 91
black women 65–6, 172
  feminists 27–8, 29–30
  *see also* racism
Bolger, S. 103, 104, 105
Bonny, S. 47, 109, 131
Bowl, R. 41, 70
Brake, M. 102
Braunstone Anti-Road Campaign 64
Bridges, L. 11
Brittan, A. 80
British Broadcasting Corporation
    (BBC) 54

Brook, E.   15, 22, 24, 46
  statutory social work   36, 107, 113,
    120, 125, 126; education   115;
    support groups   121
Browne,  N. 128, 153
Brownmiller, S.   93
Bruner, J.   108
Bryan, B.   3, 27, 28, 29, 30, 65
business, women in   82

Calder, N.   41
Calvert, J.   135, 148
Camden Council's Women's
    Unit   142, 158, 159, 160, 161, 162
campaigns   see feminist campaigns
Campbell, B.   2, 17, 61, 68, 129
campaigns and networks   47, 50, 72
Campling, J.   4
Canada National Council of Welfare
    (CNCW)   131
Caplan, P.J.   92
Carby, H.   27, 30, 65, 66, 77, 94
caring   47, 81, 107–11, 147
  government and   18–19, 157, 171–2
  jobs in statutory social work   36–7,
    139–40
  working women and   134–5, 138
  see also child care; dual career
Carpenter, V.   52, 66
Cartledge, S.   11, 34, 80, 88, 92
Centre for Contemporary and Cultural
    Studies (CCCS)   96
Chambers-Brown, J.   89
Chapeltown Citizens' Advice Bureau
    (CCAB)   172
Cheetham, J.   42
Cherry, S.   44, 121
child care   38, 110–11, 152–3
  anti-sexist   97–8
  GLC and   128–9
  men and   96–7, 136, 154
  NCC and   74–5
  violence in   72
  working mothers   108, 136, 148–9
Child Poverty Action Group
    (CPAG)   131
Childline   54, 72
children

abuse   72–3, 98–9, 112–13, 126;
    sexual   12, 26, 32, 54, 97, 112
  feminist campaigns and   72–3
  sex-stereotyping   51–2
  welfare   69, 97–100, 153–4
  see also child care
China   35
Chix   65
circumcision, female   66
Claimants' Union   31
Clarke-Stewart, A.   108
class   3, 6–7, 27, 86, 152
  feminist groups   61–4
  statutory social work   103–7
clients
  inferiority   62
  social worker awareness   14, 148–9
  welfare   144–7
Cockburn, C,   36
Cohen, S.   172
Collins, W.   19, 50, 68, 80, 146
  consciousness-raising   34
  cooperation   9, 58
  emotional inferiority   84
  feminists' children   73
Comiso Peace Camp   67
Commission on Racial Equality
    (CRE)   96
Communist Party (CP)   166
community action   10, 38
Community Action   38
Community Care   36
Community Development Projects
    (CDP)   11
Community Programme   172
community work   12–13, 36, 138–9,
    146
  see also feminist campaigns
Confederation of British Industry
    (CBI)   164
consciousness-raising   33–4 41
Conservative Party   170–2
  see also radical right
Cook, A.   69
cooperation   58–9
Coote, A.   2, 33, 37, 61, 68, 133
  feminist campaigns   47, 50, 72
Corrigan, P.   14, 103–4

Coulson, M. 6
counselling 13–14, 38, 40, 99–100, 115–118, 176–7
  *see also* feminist therapy
Coventry's Women's Right to Income Group 48, 63
Cox, O. 133
Coyle, A. 131, 144–5
Crawford, C. 53
Croll, E. 35
Cross, M. 54
Curno, A. 1, 9, 56, 57, 68, 80
  anti-sexism 98
  black women 66
  class 3, 63, 64
  community action/work 13, 36
  waged work 132

Dale, J. 36, 68, 107, 113, 131, 144
Dalla Costa, M. 133
David, M. 68, 76, 81, 111, 138
  child care 38, 72, 98, 108, 128, 153; men and 136, 154
Davis, A. 15, 22, 24, 36, 46
  black feminists 27, 66; interconnecting struggles 175
  international capital 176
  statutory social work 113, 125, 126; support groups 115, 120, 121
Deacon, B. 111
Delmar, R. 19, 49
Delphy, C. 19, 51
Denney, D. 42
Department of Health and Social Security (DHSS) 110, 151, 172
Department of Education and Science (DES) 110
depathologising approach 39–40
dependents 147
depression 81
*Directory of Women* 115
disabilities 4, 54
divorce legislation 26
Dixon, G. 36, 37, 45, 58, 139
Dobash, R. and R.E. 24, 26, 74, 92.93
domestic labour 133
Dominelli, L. 24, 35, 41, 77, 165

community work 13, 36, 46, 58, 59
  feminist politics 156, 168, 174
  health and safety at work 137
  incest 12, 32, 72, 97
  peace movement 67, 69
  racism 94
  statutory social work 107, 112
Donnelly, A. 1, 22, 35, 86, 176
  class 62, 64
  statutory social work 114, 115, 118–20, 125, 126, 127
Doyal, L. 66
Dreifus, C. 2, 32, 33
dried milk 66
dual career 134–5, 138, 148–9

earnings
  loss and caring 108–9
  widening gap 170
economically based oppression 8
Eichenbaum, L. 68, 97
  feminist therapy 38, 47, 78, 79–80, 84–5, 176
Eichler, M. 134
Egerton J. 89
Elliot, M. 72
Ely, P. 42
emotional welfare 1, 44, 76–100
  children's 97–100
  dominance 81–2
  feminist therapy 82–6
  love 89–95; non-possessive 92–4; romance 89–92
  men's 95–7
  racism 87–8
  subordination 78–81
  women's relationships 88–9
Employment Act 170
Engels, F. 7, 133
Equal Opportunities Officers 142, 143, 159
Equal Pay Act 164, 170
equal pay campaign 24–5
equality
  autonomous organisations 152
  feminist campaigns *see* feminist campaigns
  feminist practice 8–10

feminist principles 1–8, 29;
    class 6–7; gender 4–6
feminist therapy 82–4
social relations 32–4
    *see also* oppression
Ernst, S. 77, 78, 88.157, 176
female subordination 38, 47, 80
Eskapa, S. 92
European Court 172
European Parliament Committee on
    Women's Rights 160
Evans, A. 35, 42, 115, 119, 121, 125

Falk, A. 43, 118, 119, 125
Family Credit Scheme 172
female circumcision 66
Feminism and Non-Violence Study
    Group 69, 97
feminist campaigns and
    networks 45–75
    consolidation 73–5
    definition 46
    equality 56–67; class 61–4;
        hierarchies 58–61; Peace
        Movement 67; racism 65–6
    identity 46–51
    impact on society 67–73;
        children 72–3; men 69–71
    objectives and origins 51–6
feminist counselling 99–100, 176–7
    *see also* counselling; feminist therapy
feminist practice 8–10
feminist therapy 38, 76–100, 157,
    176–7
    funding 151–2
    women's emotional welfare 78–88;
        class 86; Freudian
        approach 84–6; projection of
        equality 82–4; racism 87–8
    women's relationships 88–9
Festau, M.F. 5, 70, 95
Finch, J. 59–60, 107, 127
    caring 19, 36, 81, 111, 147
Finer Report 164
Firestone, S. 7, 27
flexitime 136–7, 138
Forster, J. 88
Foster, F. 36, 68, 107, 113, 131, 144

France, P. 128, 153, 154
Freire, P. 70
Freud, S. 79, 84–5, 86
Friedan, B. 2, 81
funding 48, 55, 60, 143, 151–2, 157

Gavron, H. 136
gender
    awareness 137
    equality and 1–2, 4–6
    Marxism and 105–6
    social problems 11–12
    social work theory 34–6
    *see also* oppression
Gill, T. 33
Goodison, L. 38, 47, 80, 94
Gordon, L. 72
Gordon, P. 96
Gray, R. 48
Greater London Council (GLC) 17,
    143, 152
    child care 128–9, 147
    Women's Committee Support
        Unit 142, 158, 159
Green, S.L. 57–8
Green Party 166
Greenham Common Peace Camp 28,
    67, 169
Greer, G. 92, 93
group work 118–20
Groves, D. 81, 127, 147
*Guardian* 109, 111, 174
Guru, S. 152

Hale, J. 22, 77, 115–18, 121, 125, 126
Hanmer, J. 61, 93, 176
Hanscombe, G.E. 88
Harris, C. 39–40
Harrison, R. 91
Hartmann, H. 6
health and safety at work 137
Hearn, J. 5, 26, 71, 96
Heidensohn, F. 112
Hemmings, 91
hierarchy
    feminist groups 58–61
    oppression and 7–8
    women's units 143–4

Hiro, D. 96
Holland, J. 34, 58
Homans, H. 33
Homeworkers' Campaign 56
Hooks, B. 66
Hopkins, M. 13, 56, 139, 147
housing legislation 26
Howe, D. 134, 139–40
Howell, E. 36, 80, 81
Hughes, M. 108, 109, 149, 153
Humphreys, L. 96
Humphries, M. 96
Hunt, M. 108
Hyde, M. 111

Iceland 166–8, 174
Imperial Typewriters 65
incest 12, 26, 32, 54, 97, 112
   child protection 72–3
independent income 26
individual feminist action 169–70
International Association of Schools of
   Social Work (IASSW) 35, 115
International Monetary Fund 165
Invalid Care Allowance 172

Jacques, M. 17, 129
James, S. 55, 133
Japan 67
Jayawardna, K. 2, 66
Jervis, M. 152
Jewell, T. 56
job-sharing 137, 138
Johnson, K.A. 35
Jones, M. 72–3
Jonsdottir, G. 59, 156, 168, 175

Key, D. 134
Kigass 65
Kirk, G. 69
Kishwar, M. 93
Kitzinger, S. 93
Kwenna Frambothid (KF) 167–6
Kwenna Listin (KL) 167–8, 174
Kyle, D. 24

Labour Party 75, 147, 162–5, 174,
   176
Labour Research 170, 171

Lea, P. 126
Lederer, L. 11, 24
Leeds Social Security Cuts Campaign
   (LSSC) 31, 172
legislation 68
   see also Equal Pay Act; Nationality
   Act; Sex Discrimination Act
Leicester Outworkers' Campaign
   (LOC) 146–7
Leonard, P. 14, 35, 41, 103–4, 106
lesbianism 3–4, 57–8, 88–9
Liberal Party 165
Livingstone, K. 129
London Women's Liberation
   Campaign (LWLC) 26, 75, 158
Loney, M. 13, 31
Longres, J. 33
Lorde, A. 77, 87–8, 89, 91, 94, 175
love 89–95
low paid 171

McAndrew, A. 40
McCrindle, J. 49
McIntosh, M. 6, 76, 134
Mackie, L. 133
McLean, S. 66
McLeod, E. 1, 9, 21, 33, 114, 119
   feminist campaigns 48, 53, 54, 57,
   58
   feminist perspective 39
   feminist therapy 83, 169
   gender 34, 36; awareness 137
   male sexuality 71, 96
   prostitution 40, 41, 55, 129
McRobbie, A. 90
Magas, B. 6
Maguire, M. 77, 78, 88, 157, 176
Malek, F. 86
Mama, A. 66
management 36–7, 82, 113–14, 122–5,
   140–1
Manpower Services Commission
   (MSC) 139
Mansfield Hosiery 65
Marchant, H. 22, 35, 36, 106
   statutory social work 115, 118, 120,
   125
marriage 89–91

married women, discrimination against 172
Marshall, J. 76, 82, 127
Marxists 14–15, 103–7, 133, 134
maternity grants 31
maternity leave 170
Mayall, H. 48, 128, 149
Maynard, M. 80
Mayo, M. 9, 56, 57, 58, 63
    community action 13, 36, 38, 48, 59, 146
Members of Parliament, female 163–4
men
    anti-sexism 41, 70
    health and safety at work 137
    non-possessive love 93–4
    oppression 71
    questioning superiority 70–1
    support from 56–7, 71
    welfare 26, 69–70, 154; emotional 95–7
Men Against Sexism groups 70
Metcalfe, A. 96
Michelson, W. 134, 136
miners' strike 52–3
Minford, P. 7, 18, 159
Ministry for Women 163, 164
miscarriage counselling 40
Mitchell, J. 11, 49, 85
Molyneux, M. 6, 133
Mooney, B. 67
Morrison, T. 87
Mungham, A. 90
Muss, J. 53

Nairne, K. 81, 153
National Abortion Campaign (NAC) 46, 136
National Association of Local Government Officers (NALGO) 37
National Association of Probation Officers (NAPO) 37, 122, 129
National Childcare Campaign (NCC) 53, 66, 74, 98, 147
National Economic Survey (NCCED) 47, 134

National Equal Opportunities Committee 122
National Front 65
National Union of Hosiery and Knit Workers 147
National Union of Public Employees (NUPE) 7, 122
National Women's Aid Federation (NWAF) 25, 46–7, 48–9, 74, 150–1, 157
Nationality Act 172
Nelson, S. 12, 24, 26, 32, 97
Nett, E. 135
networks  see feminist campaigns
New, C. 68, 76, 81, 111, 138
    child care 38, 72, 98, 108, 128, 153; men and 136, 154
Newham, A. 96
News on Sunday 161
Newson, E. and J. 72, 98–9
Non-Contributory Invalidity Pension 172
non-possessive love 92–4

Oakley, A. 2, 5, 11, 49, 68, 76
oppression 4–8, 27–30, 71, 105–7
    see also class; gender; racism
Orbach, S. 49, 68, 97, 176
    feminist therapy 38, 47, 77, 78, 79–80; Freud 84–5
Organisation of Women of African and Asian Descent (OWAAD) 65
Organisation of Women in the Labour Market 167
O'Sullivan, S. 4, 89

Packwood, M. 61, 64
Pahl, J. 25, 62–3, 74, 112, 151, 152
paid worker/volunteer friction 60
Parents Anonymous Lifeline 53
Parmar, P. 66, 89, 94
part-time workers 171
Parton, N. 111
Pascall, G. 36
patriarchal social relations 5–7, 11–12, 19, 27, 72–3
    social problems 24–6
Pattullo, P. 133

Penn, H. 110–11
'personal is political' 32–3
Petrie, P. 128, 149
Phillipson, C. 109–10, 147
Pizzey, E. 33
Plummer, K. 96
political presence 17–18, 75, 152–3,
    155–77
    autonomous political party 166–8
    feminist social work 156–8
    future 172–7: alliances 175;
        control of resources 175–6;
        feminist programmes 174–5;
        social work 176–7
    individual action 169–70
    local state 158–62
    political parties: Alliance 165;
        Communist 166;
        Conservative 170–2;
        Green 166; Labour 162–5; left
        minority 165–6; Workers'
        Revolutionary Party 165–6
    sidestepping political
        structures 168–9
    see also state
Popay, J. 108
positive action 114–20, 141
Price, M. 86
principles, feminist 1–8
Programme for the Reform of the Law
    on Soliciting (PROS) 40–1, 48,
    55, 129

racism 3, 87–8, 94, 96, 152
    sexism and 27–8, 29, 65–6, 91,
        124–5
    see also black women
radical feminists 4–5, 27, 28
radical lesbian feminists 169
radical right 31, 127–8, 131
    women as carers 18–19, 31, 111,
        157
    see also Conservative Party
radical social work 14–15, 101–3
Rantzen, E. 54
rape crisis centres 53, 151, 169
Rappoport, R. and R.N. 134
Raymond, J. 82–3

'Reclaim the Night' marches 30
refuges 26 55, 62–3, 150–1, 152
Reitz, R. 24
rejection, feelings of 60–1
Rekjavik 167
relationships
    between women 88–9
    non-possessive 92–4
    romantic 89–92, 94–5
'resuming work programmes' 146
Reynaud, E. 71, 95
Riley, D. 75
Rimmer, L. 108
Robinson, C. 36–7, 113, 123–4, 140,
    141, 173
romance 89–92, 94–5
Rowbotham, S. 27, 49, 166, 168
Russia 35
Ruzek, S. 38, 50
Ryan, J. 11, 34, 80, 88, 92

Saadawi, N. El 66
sado-masochism, lesbian 3–4, 89
safety at work 137
Sarsbv, S. 89, 90
Saunders, S. 93, 176
Savage, W. 56
Sayers, J. 85
Schur, E. 102
Scott, H. 8
Scottish Women's Aid Federation
    (SWAF) 26
Seccombe, W. 133
Seddon, V. 52–3
Seebohm Report 140
Segal, L. 89, 93
self-help initiatives 21
Sex Discrimination Act 164, 170
sexism see anti-sexism; gender;
        oppression
sexual harassment 135
Simpkin, M. 103, 105
Skelton, A. 98
Skinner, J. 36–7, 113, 123–4, 140,
    141, 173
Smart, B. and C. 112
Smith, B. 35, 36
Smith, G. 81, 153

Social Democratic Party (SDP)   165
Social Fund   172
social problems   11–12, 21–44
  gender   22–31; changing
    conditions   30–1; origins of
    oppression   27–30; patriarchal
    social relations   24–6
  promoting equality   32–4
  social work practice   34–44;
    community action   38;
    counselling   38; further
    development   42–4; men   41;
    statutory social work   38–42;
    union activity   37; women as
    carers   36–7
Social Security Act   172
social work theory   34–6
socialist feminists   27, 28–9
Socialist Workers' Party   165–6
Society for Cutting Up Men
    (SCUM)   5
Solanas, V.   5
South Wales Association of Tenants
    (SWAT)   57, 58–9
Spare Rib   152
Stacey, M.   86
Stallard, K.   131, 134, 135
Stanko, E.   135
Stanworth, M,   76
state   10–11, 17–19, 43, 55, 127–30
  local as employer   142–4
  see also political presence
statutory social work   10, 101–30, 157,
    177
  feminist   14–16; anti-sexism and
    anti-racism   124–5;
    carers   107–11;
    counselling   115–18; group
    work   118–20;
    initiatives   114–15; limited
    achievements   125–6;
    managerialism   113–14, 122–5;
    parental failure   111–12;
    politics   127–30; social
    control   112–13; support
    groups   120–2; union
    activity   122
  Marxist critique   103–7

problem redefinition   38–42
  radical social work   101–3
  women workers' welfare   138–44
stillbirth counselling   40
support groups   120–2, 141

Thompson, D.   46
Tizard, J.   109, 149, 153
Tolson, A.   5, 26, 70, 95–6
Torkington, C.   63
Townsend, P.   144
Toynbee, P.   47
Trades Union Congress (TUC)   147
  Resource and Information Centre
    (TUCRIC)   136, 143, 159
tranquillisers   25, 81
Tyneside Rape Crisis Centre
    Collective   58–9, 60

unconscious, the   85
unemployment   144–6, 157–8, 170–1
union activity   37, 75, 122, 141, 146–7

Valentine, M.   113
violence   69
  towards children   72–3, 98–9
  towards women   24, 25–6, 48, 55–6,
    74, 81; consciousness-raising
    groups for men   41
  see also refuges
voluntary sector   10, 138–9, 146
volunteer/paid worker friction   60

Wages Councils   171
Wages for Housework Campaign   133
Walker, H.   103, 104, 106–7
Walsgrove, R.   50
Walton, R.   140
Ward, E.   11, 12, 26, 72, 97
Warren, L.   4, 35, 39
Warwick Feminist Social Work
    Practice Conference Group   22,
    36, 115
Wearing, B.   22, 35, 36, 106
  statutory social work   115, 118, 120,
    125
Webb, S.   103
Webster, B.   68, 109, 142
Weeks, J.   96

welfare
children 69, 97–100, 153–4
clients' 144–7
men 26, 69–70, 95–7, 154
patriarchal social relations and 11
women 21, 22–4, 54–5, 112; social
workers 138–44
*see also* emotional welfare
Welsh Women's Aid Federation
(WWAF) 171
Whitehouse, A. 102, 137
Whitlock, M.J. 143
Whittington, B. 135
Wickham, J. 133
Wilkes, R. 140
Wilkinson, S, 5
Wilson, E. 7, 89, 103, 107, 131
clients' inferiority 62
romance 91
statutory social work 15, 22, 36,
113
Winship, J. 82, 89
Wise, S. 15, 22, 113
statutory social work 42, 43, 115,
117, 125, 126
Wolffe, J. 31
Wollstonecraft, M. 86
Woman 165
Women Against Violence Against
Women 5, 28
Women as Carers groups 47
women-only groups 5, 168–9
Women in Social Work Network 46,
115
Women Working Project 137
Women's Aid *see* National Women's
Aid Federation
Women's Arts Projects 169
Women's Caucus of the International
Association of Schools of Social
Work 115
women's experience 8
Women's Labour League 162

women's movement 2–3, 19–20,
49–51
Women's National Commission 160
Women's Peace Movement 46, 66–7,
69
women's units 142–3, 158–62
women's welfare 21, 22–4, 54–5, 112
social workers 138–44
Wood, E.W. 13
work
health and safety 137
women's rights 31
*see also* working relations
Workers' Revolutionary Party 165–6
working groups 160–1
working relations 17, 131–54
autonomous organisations 150–2;
funding 151–2;
inequalities 152; refuges 150–1
children's welfare 153–4
client/worker awareness 148–9
clients' welfare 144–7;
dependants 147; trade
unions 146–7;
unemployment 144–6
conditions 122, 132–8;
discrimination 133–4; dual
career 134–5; family
commitments 136–7; feminist
initiatives 136–8;
subservience 135–6
feminist political presence 152–3
men's welfare 154
women workers' welfare 138–44;
feminist initiatives 141–2;
managerialism 140–1;
voluntary/community
work 138–9; women as
carers 139–40; women's
units 142–4

Young, J. 126
youth work 52